I HAVE A LADY IN THE BALCONY

I HAVE A LADY IN THE BALCONY

MEMOIRS OF A BROADCASTER IN RADIO AND TELEVISION

by *George Ansbro*

FOREWORD BY LEONARD MALTIN

McFarland & Company, Inc., Publishers
Jefferson, North Carolina, and London

Frontispiece: Brand new on the announcing staff in May 1934.

Library of Congress Cataloguing-in-Publication Data

Ansbro, George, 1915–
    I have a lady in the balcony : memoirs of a broadcaster in radio
and television / by George Ansbro ; foreword by Leonard Maltin.
        p.   cm.
    Includes index.   ∞
    ISBN 0-7864-0425-6 (illustrated case binding : 50# alkaline paper)
    1. Ansbro, George, 1915–   2. Broadcasters—United States—
Biography.   I. Title.
PN1990.72.A58 A3 2000
791.44'028'092—dc21
[B]
                                                    99-045416

British Library Cataloguing-in-Publication data are available

Manufactured in the United States of America

*McFarland & Company, Inc., Publishers
  Box 611, Jefferson, North Carolina 28640
  www.mcfarlandpub.com*

This book is dedicated to my wife,
Jo-Anne, whose devotion, patience, and
humor through the years
deserve my everlasting thanks.

CONTENTS

FOREWORD

Some people are born observers. They take the time to see what's going on around them, along with what's happening to them. And they remember.

When I'm doing research on show business history, I pray to find good observers. Sometimes I'm lucky, and sometimes I'm not. I've met people with great careers behind them who had astonishingly little to say, and others who could talk your ear off and still not tell you anything of value.

When I first spoke to George Ansbro, while researching my book *The Great American Broadcast*, I knew I had found a gem. I wanted to know what had led a young man to become a radio announcer in the 1930s—and what it was like to hold the position during that rarefied time. He had a terrific memory, along with a sense of time and place that put each anecdote he told into a meaningful context.

I called on George again when I was gathering material for a booklet to accompany a CD release called *The Vintage Recordings of Cliff Edwards*. As Cliff's announcer, and friend, during the 1940s, George had an opportunity to observe "Ukulele Ike" both on- and off-stage. His recollections helped to paint a vivid, human picture of this legendary performer.

Now, with this warm and entertaining memoir, George Ansbro has given a gift to all of us who care about the great days of network radio and the early years of television. More than that, he has provided a word picture of life in New York City during the 1930s and '40s, when a young man with a staff announcer's job at NBC might run into Clark Gable at the Stork Club or be called upon to work with anyone from Walter Winchell to Eleanor Roosevelt.

What a storehouse of memories. Radio City in New York was the crossroads of the show business world, and George was there—working with many of the greats, brushing up against others, and making astute observations. The cast of characters in this book reads like a Who's Who of the twentieth century—from Al Jolson to Arturo Toscanini to J. Edgar Hoover.

But this is not a mere collection of anecdotes. It is a kind of diary, and that is perhaps its greatest value for readers like me who weren't around when all of this was going on. Whether describing a knock on the window of Hurley's, the legendary radio artists' hangout, or a chance meeting in the elevator of the RCA Building, George Ansbro enables us to travel back in time with him and experience vicariously the whirlwind of life in the Big Time.

I Have a Lady in the Balcony is a wonderful recap of an extraordinary career in broadcasting.

LEONARD MALTIN • *Spring 1999*

PREFACE

On April 8, 1987, the *New York Times* ran an editorial on the then current rumor about the possibility of NBC's moving from New York City to Secaucus, New Jersey. It contained an error which I apprised them of in this brief letter to the editor published on April 24, 1987:

NBC Radio Days

To the Editor:

In "Live, From Secaucus: It's NBC!" (editorial, April 8), I fear you were off the mark by six years regarding NBC's founding in New York.

The Blue and Red Networks with their New York outlets, WJZ and WEAF, came together as NBC at 711 Fifth Avenue in 1927. A year later I first set foot in that wondrous place as a boy soprano in Milton Cross's "Children's Hour." I was lucky enough to be hired as a page boy in 1931. But the year you mention, 1933, does hold a large place in broadcasting history because that's when NBC, me included, moved into Rockefeller Center.

My current employer is an offshoot (Capital Cities/ABC) of an offshoot (ABC) of an offshoot (Blue Network) of NBC.

GEORGE ANSBRO
New York, April 10, 1987

After seeing my letter in the *Times*, several friends got in touch with me. They all had one point in common: I should gather together interesting memories of my many years as a broadcaster, as well as events leading up to the start of what turned out to be a steady job with essentially the same company for fifty-eight years, three months, and twelve days.

On October 1, 1986, about six months prior to the appearance of my letter in the *New York Times*, I had received the following letter from the undersigned gentleman, a vice president of Capital Cities/ABC, Inc. To say it knocked me out is putting it mildly.

October 1, 1986

Mr. George Ansbro
40-50 East 10th Street
New York, NY 10003

This is a history-making day at ABC and in the world of broadcasting in America. Congratulations on your 55th anniversary with Capital Cities/ABC and all those predecessor companies.

As you know, you've set a couple of records with us. You are our oldest employee in terms of service and you also hold the network staff announcers' record ... and do you realize that if you add CBS and NBC, you are the oldest network employee in terms of service. Period.

The use of words such as "Pioneer," "Unequaled," "Milestone," and all the rest don't do justice to your monumental achievements. We are proud and lucky to have a man like you on our staff, and I, along with many others are fortunate in being able to call you a friend.

Congratulations, and all best wishes for your record-breaking future.

STEVE NENNO

THE TWENTIES

It was my first trip away from home. In the summer of 1922, Mother and Pop took me along in Pop's new Ford touring car. With much excitement, we were off to Long Meadow, a suburb of Springfield, Massachusetts. There we spent two weeks with Aunt Ellen and Uncle Jim Manning. For me, the highlight of the visit was the evening we attended a vaudeville show in Springfield, where I got my very first taste of "showbiz." It was at the B. F. Keith Theater, where the headline act was Singer's Midgets. And they were wonderful. It seemed to me there was nothing these talented little people couldn't do, especially acrobatics and dancing. To me, however, the highlight of the show was a romantic duet performed by a tiny but gorgeous soprano and her handsome little partner. They sang "A Kiss in the Dark," and they just about knocked this seven year old right out of his seat. So much so that when we arrived back at the Manning house and Aunt Ellen asked how I had liked the show, my answer was to open my mouth and sing "A Kiss in the Dark." In those days many households had player pianos, and the piano rolls had the words to the songs so you could sing along as the music played. I guess I was lucky in that Aunt Ellen had one too. Most important to me at least, she also had a piano roll of "A Kiss in the Dark," the Victor Herbert love song which was then extremely popular. By the time we left to go home to Brooklyn, I not only had the words committed to memory, but my dear mother was convinced that her youngest child would become the next John McCormack, the great Irish tenor.

My family was no different from many others I knew in that the parlor, which in later years would be known as the living room, had a prominent piece of furniture called a Victrola. After cranking it up, a record would play on the turntable and remarkably pleasant sounds would come forth. In our parlor, the records played most often were those of the aforementioned John McCormack. This was quite understandable considering that my parents, John and Katie Ansbro, had emigrated from County Mayo, Ireland, before the turn of the century and were extremely proud of the remarkable voice and worldwide fame of their fellow countryman. So now in addition to the many Irish songs I had picked up from listening to McCormack's records, I had "A Kiss in the Dark" to work on as a boy soprano.

There was something else in our parlor that was getting an awful lot of attention and that was our crystal radio. It was amazing. You could hear people talking who were not in the same room with you. Or house. Or for that matter, even in the same city. Besides talk, sometimes singing would come through with accompanying piano music. And this was happening in our parlor which didn't have a piano. To me at that very early age, the baby of seven children, it was most confusing. Incomprehensible. Maybe a miracle. How could it not be a miracle? A miracle was something that happened which was impossible, and that's what was going on here. When you put the earphones on and plugged the wire into this thing they called radio, you could hear sounds "coming through the air," whatever that meant. Even Miss Murtha, my second-grade teacher, who I believed knew everything, tried to explain it to me without much success. But the fact that I couldn't understand what caused those sounds to come through those earphones didn't diminish in the slightest my fascination with what everybody was talking about, the great new invention by an Italian man named Marconi called radio. It was really an odd-looking contraption. It consisted of what they called a "cat's whisker" made out of tungsten, which was placed on a fragment of galena crystal.

One particular day that stands out in my memory was when my brother Jim almost blew a gasket running around yelling at the top of his voice, "I got Pittsburgh—KDKA. I can't believe it—PITTSBURGH! Yowie!" At that time, it was generally understood that anyone who could bring in KDKA was either a genius or had the best crystal set on the block.

In our home, as the technology of radio improved and the crystal set became passé, the next step up the ladder was the acquisition of the Stromberg Carlson. And some years after that, a Majestic, or possibly a Philco. Guglielmo Marconi's invention was becoming the newest facet of "showbiz." To keep up with the demands of its popularity, radio stations were springing up all over the place. Little did I know then what fate held in store for me.

One fond memory of living on President Street in Brooklyn in the years between 1920 and 1925 was when the local Episcopal church ran a charity fair sometime in 1921 when I was six years old. I had heard there would be a magician there. That's all I needed to prompt me to beg my mother for the 10 cents admission. I arrived in time to see him perform a few amazing feats of magic. Inviting his audience to come closer to the platform, he proposed, as advertised, to startle all of us by sawing a lady in half. Being rather short of stature even for that age, I wheedled my way into a viewing position as close to the platform as possible so as not to miss a thing, which is just what happened. I saw more than I should have

for my 10 cents. While leaning on the platform where the magician's table was while the lady was being "sawed in half," I peeked under the long cloth which was draped over the side of the table. Lo and behold, there was the lady's posterior just below the surface, safely out of the way of the terrible saw. That explained to me why she not only didn't look worried or scared, she actually had a smile on her face. Even at the age of six I knew I was being had. And I loudly said so—causing much laughter from the crowd and much anger from the local Houdini. As a result I found myself put back out on the street, gently but firmly. I was really ticked because this fake charity show wasn't even charitable enough to give me my dime back. But, this embarrassing moment aside, I've since become a big fan of magic acts.

During those formative years, I attended St. Francis Xavier school and church. The church boasted a better than average choir consisting of men and us young boys. The men's section included tenors, altos, baritones, and basses. We were the boy soprano section. Every Sunday and on special Holy Days we would assemble in the choir loft, which was elevated in the rear of the church, and sing at the eleven o'clock High Mass.

Another rite to which St. Francis Xavier choir lent its mellifluous sound was the Tenebrae, at which special prayerful songs called matins were intoned. Tenebrae was held at the end of the Lenten season, on the nights of Spy Wednesday, Holy Thursday, and Good Friday before Easter Sunday. Tenebrae required a lot of extra rehearsals because singing matins was a whole different ball game than singing a Mass. Anyway, on the night of Good Friday in 1922, as on the previous two nights, we choir persons were in church doing Tenebrae. But Tenebrae is different from any other rite of the Roman Catholic church in that it is far more solemn. To help make this point, the organ is silent. Instead of being seated in the choir loft, we were on the main altar, joined by the pastor and about a dozen others, including visiting and retired priests as well as the regular parish priests, all of whom were there to add to the solemnity of the occasion. One of the retired reverends, Father Finley, lived nearby with his unmarried sister. In spite of being retired, Father Finley was around a lot, ready and more than willing to perform priestly duties when asked, which I'm sure was not as often as he would have liked. Even at the age of seven, I was aware he was intensely disliked, mostly because, in plain English, he was a grouch who always seemed to be sticking his nose in where it wasn't needed. For instance, if he happened to be the celebrant of the High Mass on Sunday, he could be expected to make some uncalled for remark in his sermon (now called a homily). Like the time he looked straight up at us in the choir loft, shook his head from side to side, and cracked: "Who ever said practice makes perfect? I guess such a person never attended the eleven o'clock Mass at St. Francis Xavier." That was his opening line to the day's sermon on the subject of "If you don't succeed at once, try, try again." If choirs had been unionized back then, we would have walked out in a body.

Here's another example of what a pain in the neck Father Finley was. Frequently he would come over to our school yard and, for want of anything better to do, find fault with the way some kids were dressed, ties crooked, etc. He even went up to the principal and wanted to know why he couldn't "control the children better" during recess. To which, hurray, hurray, the good Franciscan brother was heard to reply: "That, Father Finley is my obligation, not yours. It is also none of your concern."

Back to Tenebrae on Good Friday night. All the participants were seated on the main altar beginning with the men's section of the choir facing the right wall. The next tier of seats was where we, the boy sopranos, sat. In the row in front of us were the visiting and the retired priests and in the first row the regular parish priests and the pastor. As our chanting and singing a cappella progressed, the lights would start going out, gradually, almost unnoticed, beginning in the back of the church. By twenty minutes into the ceremony about half the lights were out, and twenty minutes later every electric light in the entire church was out. Next, the head altar boy put the altar candles out one by one. The only sounds during these otherwise very quiet goings on were coming from the choir. With no music accompanying us, our singing/chanting was deliberately meant to help create a chilling, eerie effect. Now every light was out, every candle was out but one. The church was packed in this holiest of seasons. Our singing/chanting had stopped. The pastor rose from his chair, stepped forward to the only candle which was still lit, raised the extinguisher, and snuffed out that last bit of illumination.

As total darkness enveloped the church, a very loud noise began to erupt on the altar. This noise was meant to signify the moment of Christ's death on the cross when "the earth shook." This has always been the custom at Tenebrae. Standard operating procedure. We created the noise by banging our choir books together and on the sides and backs of the chairs. When you add together the clatter created by forty choir books and about fifteen priests' prayer books, not to mention whatever the altar boys could lay their hands on, you've got some really loud noise! And in a totally dark church yet. The noise then suddenly ended, and simultaneously all the lights returned. This Good Friday Tenebrae was over. But it wasn't, in fact, over. The parishioners, who hopefully had been edified by the ancient ceremony they had just been part of, had risen from their pews and had begun to leave. But not so those in the front pews. They had been distracted by unusual activity on the altar. Everyone up there seemed so agitated that something must have happened. The priests and the choir were all standing kind of in a circle, looking down and bending over something. Or someone. Now the pastor was conferring with Father Williams, the priest in charge of the choir, who then opened the gate of the altar rail and approached a gentleman seated in a front pew, a local doctor. They both returned to the altar to investigate the prostrate form on the marble floor.

The doctor then said that Father Finley, the victim, had been conked on the head. It apparently happened during the brief period when the church was totally dark. We kids were frightened but at the same time thought it was pretty funny. I'm sure countless others besides us had had, at some time or other, the desire to conk Father Finley on the head. But which of us, during such a solemn occasion, albeit a great opportunity, actually had had the gall to do it? In spite of Father Williams' lengthy and intense questioning, the culprit was never discovered. No, I didn't do it.

Father Finley recovered. But he became a changed man, which means he really retired. He and his sister sold their house and moved to Florida.

Sometime in the spring of 1924, when I was nine, Mother and Pop took my next oldest siblings, Kathlyn and Dolores, and me on a one-day excursion to visit our cousin, Tom Costello, who was a young novice preparing to become a member of the teaching order known as the Christian Brothers. The headquarters of the order was in Pocantico Hills, New York, on property which had been donated by John D. Rockefeller. The Christian Brothers' acreage there was a relatively small part of a huge tract of land which comprised the Rockefeller family estate. As Pop was on the property driving us in his open Buick, he could see that we were approaching a fork in the road. He also could see an elderly gentleman walking just ahead, so he decided to stop to ask him if he could direct us to the Christian Brothers' compound.

All of a sudden my eyes began to pop out as I got a good look at the man when

Pop stopped the car. Before he could lean out to speak to him, I quietly told Pop it was Mr. Rockefeller, John D. Rockefeller, the richest man in the world. Poor Pop. I guess I should have held my tongue because with the information I had just imparted to him and with the realization, as he gazed into the stranger's face, that my identification was correct, his tongue got tied in knots. So in a childish way, I suppose, of trying to make an embarrassing moment less embarrassing, I blurted out, "Hello, Mr. Rockefeller." And when he smiled back at us, Pop regained his composure enough to ask which way to our destination, which old John D. graciously told him. Then reaching into his pocket, he took out a coin and, saying, "This is for you, Sonny," handed it to me. Pop then drove the car onto the correct fork in the road as the rest of us waved back at our charming benefactor. Of course I had been able to recognize him because I had seen him several times in the newsreels and in the papers. But I had not known until then that besides his other accomplishments and his great wealth, he was also famous for giving away shiny new dimes.

The Ansbro family moved in 1925 from President Street in the Park Slope section of Brooklyn to 79th Street in the Bay Ridge section. This change of locale was to prove rather fortuitous for me because I had been so smitten that night at the vaudeville show in Springfield. After we moved, my best friends became William Ward and his sister Barbara, who lived across the street. Our friendship was really cemented when I met their father, Will J. Ward, who was a vaudevillian, an actor.

Outside of the live Singer's Midgets show in Springfield, the only other actors I had ever seen were in the movies at the Carlton Theater on Flatbush Avenue, big stars like Douglas Fairbanks, Charlie Chaplin, Mary Pickford, Fatty Arbuckle, Buster Keaton, and Harold Lloyd. I couldn't believe it—Mr. Ward was real flesh and blood, just like anybody else's father. Boy, was I thrilled. He didn't talk down to me, didn't call me "little boy." After all, I was ten. He called me George.

Mr. Ward traveled a lot. I soon learned that the correct way to talk about his being out of town was to simply say, for instance to my mother and father when explaining why Mr. Ward was away so much, "Oh, he's on the road." Of course, I had no idea then that such behavior might today be interpreted as an attempt at childish sophistication.

But when Mr. Ward was not "on the road," he would appear at "local" theaters, which meant any vaudeville theater in Manhattan, Brooklyn, the Bronx, Staten Island, etc., of which there were many. And frequently, especially when he was playing in Brooklyn or Manhattan, he would have Barbara and William and their newest best friend, yours truly, tag along with him. Of course, Mrs. Ward was usually along too, keeping a watchful eye on us.

When other friends of mine would inquire what his act was, I would answer, "He does a single." Next question—"What's that?" Answer—"He's all by himself onstage, just him and a concert grand piano." Question—"What does he do?" Answer— "He plays the piano, of course, and he also sings and tells jokes. The audiences just love him, and they keep bringing him back onstage for encores and more jokes." The word "encore" had just found its way into my vocabulary. Needless to say, the Ward family's "newest best friend" was in heaven whenever I was invited along. Just entering the stage door of a theater instead of having to pay at the box office gave me gooseflesh. I guess that's what made me a celebrity nut at a very young age. When approaching a theater where Mr. Ward was playing (later I considered myself very "in" when I said "working"), I would swell with pride seeing his name "Will J. Ward" up in lights on the marquee.

As time went on, I found myself meeting other far more famous personalities through Mr. Ward, and being invited by them to watch their acts from backstage. Such people as George Jessel, Eddie Cantor, Bert Lahr, Jack Benny, Sophie Tucker, and Burns and Allen. And boy, did I love watching the acrobats limbering up before they went on. But once when Mr. Ward was "on the road," I found myself aching to meet Gertrude Ederle, the great swimmer who had recently in August of 1926 conquered the English Channel, breaking all records. When she returned to New York, she was glorified by Mayor Jimmy Walker in a gigantic ticker-tape parade on Broadway which I had seen in the Pathé newsreels at the movies. Miss Ederle was doing a vaudeville tour, and she was appearing at Loew's Bay Ridge Theater a few blocks away from my house. On a very cold day in January, I stood outside the stage door, my teeth chattering, for an hour or more until she finally came out. When I asked for her autograph, she couldn't have been nicer. She put her arm around me and patted me on the head. She then asked me my name and wrote in the autograph book which I had provided, "To George Ansbro, Swimmingly yours, Gertrude Ederle." That done, she advised me to go right home before I froze to death, which advice I took, pronto.

Even though we had moved from downtown Brooklyn out to Bay Ridge, my parents thought it best I continue at the same grammar school. So now at the ripe old age of ten, I became a subway commuter. The trip was about thirty minutes each way, not counting the wait for trains.

After graduation in January of 1927, I was enrolled into St. Michael's High School. It was a very difficult first term in which I failed both Latin and algebra. My parents, teachers, and I attributed my failure to my immaturity at the age of twelve instead of the usual fourteen or so. This occurred because I had skipped two grades in grammar school. At any rate it was decided I should repeat the first half of my freshman year in a different school. I did so at Xavier High in Manhattan, a military school, which required the purchase of

The author at age 12 in Bay Ridge, Brooklyn.

expensive uniforms. By June of 1930 I had completed three happy scholastic years at Xavier, but we had a major problem facing us for the fall term. My uniform, worn for the past three years, no longer fit. The Great Depression, which had started in October 1929, created the need for a great decision—buy a new uniform or change schools. Without too much agonizing, the decision was made. Change schools. In September of 1930, I switched to De La Salle Institute on West 74th Street, also in Manhattan, and I graduated from there in June 1931.

Another change of address was forced upon us by a fire which totaled our 79th Street house in March of 1927. I heard about it on my way home from school. I had turned the corner from Fourth Avenue onto 79th Street when a couple of kids greeted me with "Hey, Ansbro, your house burned down." Then I saw two fire engines just leaving. Frantically I screamed at the kids, "Where's my mother?" and one of them answered, "I dunno." Next I saw the house itself, or what was left of it, still

smoking. Some neighbors, including my closest friends, the Wards, did their best to comfort and console me and assured me my mother got out safely and was now in my uncle's house, which was not far away. Some kind neighbor drove me there. Pop was there too, and understandably, he was terribly broken up. It was then that I learned my mother had been alone in her bedroom on the second floor when she smelled smoke. Rushing to the front stairs, she had found it was impossible even to attempt going down because the living room below was a ball of fire which was rapidly engulfing the stairway. Fortunately, the house had a back stairs which the flames had not yet reached, and she was able to escape into the back yard.

Being in the real estate business locally, my father was able to find an interim apartment without too much trouble until he could purchase another home for us, which he did not too long after. In July 1927, we moved into the house on 85th Street where the family was to reside for many years.

MAYOR JIMMY WALKER

It wasn't just actors and big swimmers and little midgets I was gaga about. In 1926, an ex-vaudevillian, James J. Walker, had succeeded in becoming the mayor of the city of New York, and he began to enter my consciousness. Here's how it came about. His picture was on the front pages all the time. On Saturday afternoon at the movies, you could count on seeing him in the Pathé newsreels for one reason or another, and everybody just seemed to love him.

I once shook hands with Mayor Walker, and it was all because of the Woolworth Building, which was the tallest building in the world, 52 stories high. One of the things to do when sightseeing in New York was to visit its observation tower, which I had wanted to do but couldn't because I didn't have the fifty-cents admission. But some kid I knew told me a secret about how he would go up there for nothing. He would get off the elevator at the next highest floor, the 51st, and have a ball looking out the windows at the breathtaking spectacle of New York there before him. The great view from the 52d floor tower couldn't have been that much better than from the 51st, and on floor 51, it was 100 percent cheaper. All I would need to do to emulate my friend was to ask my mother for the subway fare, which was only a dime, a nickel each way. When I told her my plan, she was pretty amused by it and threw in a penny for a Tootsie Roll to eat on the subway ride back home to Brooklyn.

The plan worked perfectly. I was a little worried, however, that the elevator operator might ask me why I was getting off at the 51st floor. This was long before the advent of the self-service elevator. So as my friend had instructed me, I made sure to always carry an official-looking package with me so that in case he did ask, I could tell him I was delivering it to "such and such" an office on that floor. Of course "such and such" was actually a legitimate company on the 51st floor whose name I took from the listings on the wall in the lobby. Fortunately, the operator didn't ask. Not that first time nor the several other times I found myself drawn as if by a magnet to that beautiful building.

But it was not just my love affair with the great view from the 51st floor that kept me coming back. Looking directly down from my high perch I could see that City Hall was only a block away. And who spent most of his time there? Why, Mayor Jimmy Walker, of course. So I decided to walk over and check things out. It was late afternoon one day in the summer of 1927, and the steps of City Hall were quite familiar to me because I had seen them many times in pictures, usually when the mayor was greeting somebody famous and giving them the "key to the city." I had trouble with not being able to understand how one little key could open up everything in the city. Anyway, here I was in front of City Hall, and right near the bottom of the steps was a beautiful car, the most luxurious car I had ever seen.

Sitting behind the wheel was a man in a fancy uniform. Later in life when I had acquired a touch more sophistication, I was to learn that such a person was a "liveried chauffeur" and the car was called a limousine. Anyway, I got up enough nerve to approach him to ask what make of car it was. Very pleasantly, almost proudly, he said, "This is a Dusenberg."

It began to dawn on me that it was after 5 o'clock, so he must be waiting for the mayor in order to drive him home. Or somewhere. I had read that Mayor Walker went to a lot of parties and nightclubs and made a lot of speeches. He made people laugh a lot. He was known to be a regular fellow and also very charming. By now, I guess because the driver was so nice to me and didn't tell me to scram, I had come as near to the car as I dared, my heart beating a mile a minute in anticipation of seeing the famous mayor of New York—in person, close enough to touch.

All of a sudden, there he was coming out of the main door of City Hall. He sauntered to the steps, leisurely walked down and over to the car, where by now the driver was holding the back door open for him. As he was about to step in, he happened to notice me staring up at him. Very gently, with a seemingly understanding smile, he said, "Hello, young man" and extended his hand to me which, with my eyes popping out, I grasped eagerly. He then got in, as did the driver, and off went the Dusenberg into the evening. At that moment, I made a determination never to wash my right hand as long as I lived. But before too long, I found that this was impossible for obvious reasons. And sadly, I had to break this promise to myself.

Buoyed by my mayoral experience in front of City Hall and the good reaction I got when I told my family about it, I decided to check out Mr. Walker's home, which I had learned was on St. Mark's Place in Greenwich Village. Once I found St. Mark's Place, it was easy to pick out his house because even though it was one of a long row of look-alike brownstones, it was the only house with a police booth on the sidewalk in front of it with a cop on guard duty around the clock. So from time to time on these outings to the Woolworth Building, City Hall, and St. Mark's Place,

especially the latter two, I found I had made some new friends—the mayor's liveried chauffeur, who, I must say, was a very nice man, and some of the cops on duty in the police booth in front of his house. Although a few of them didn't encourage my attempts at being inquisitive about the man whose house they were guarding, others, probably because they were lonely, didn't seem to mind at all and seemed to enjoy discussing Mr. Walker with me. Once I happened to be on hand during the changing of the guard and two cops were there— two that I had felt were friendly to me and hopefully would take in stride what I had decided to tell them and not arrest me or at least report me. So with my fingers crossed, I told them about my by now frequent visits to the top of the Woolworth Building, less one floor, thus saving half a dollar. I even told them about the phony package I would carry "just in case." My daring to openly tell real policemen about my breaking the law, not once but several times, really paid off because they both had a good laugh over it. And it sure acted as a catharsis for me. Nevertheless, even after that delightful session of camaraderie with the cops, I thought it best not to push my luck too far. So, reluctantly, I decided no more fun escapades in the Woolworth Building for me.

Jimmy Walker presided over several ticker-tape parades through the canyons of lower Broadway honoring heroes who had performed daring exploits. The most spectacular parade was that given for the youthful Col. Charles A. Lindbergh after his amazing nonstop solo flight from New York to Paris. Lindbergh's flight was the impetus for the growth of transoceanic flying.

Mayor Walker seemed to become more popular with each parade. As for me and where I stood on the subject of Jimmy Walker, I guess it was pretty obvious I wore my heart on my sleeve. I thought he was terrific!

That brings up one more tale of my mayoral adulation. In the spring of 1928, it

had been announced that a great new road-
way was to be built on the west side of
Manhattan alongside the Hudson River. It
was to be named, appropriately, the West
Side Highway. Mayor Walker, of course,
was to officiate at the gala groundbreaking
ceremonies. The culmination of the affair
was when the mayor of the city of New
York, with a silver-plated shovel, dug into
the earth and extracted a pretty generous-
sized shovelful of soil. This exercise was
the official signal that construction of the
West Side Highway could now begin.
Among the many spectators was yours
truly. However, I was not there just because
of my individual interest in the doings of
the mayor. I was there as a student of
Xavier High School, which Mayor Walker
had attended when he was a boy. As I mentioned earlier, Xavier was a military academy which was run by the Jesuit order of
priests, and it enjoyed an enviable reputation both scholastically and its military discipline. We were required to wear what we
liked to think was a distinctive-looking uniform, the better to make the cadet himself
appear distinctive.

Well, the entire school body was there,
the school band providing the music, and
every last man of us standing stiffly at attention. When "At ease, men" was called,
that was the colonel's signal that our duties
at the affair were over and we were on our
own. Most of the students began breaking
up immediately and wandering off in
different directions, mostly to the subway
or trolley cars (no buses then) to go home.
But I delayed going to the subway for a few
minutes and walked directly to the spot
where the mayor had dug the first shovelful
of soil and, of course, the soil he had dug
up was still there. Looking around me so
nobody would think I was crazy, I furtively
grabbed some handfuls of what was, to my
mind at least, hallowed ground and stuffed
it into the pockets of my spanking clean
uniform. This coup accomplished, I then
made for the BMT (Brooklyn Manhattan
Transit) subway, gloating over my brilliant

accomplishment all the way home. I just
knew I had something. The very first
shovelful of dirt from the West Side Highway to be. And some day what I had in my
two pockets would be very valuable. If not
monetarily, certainly sentimentally. After
all, who was the person who had dug up
this wonderful soil I now owned and would
keep, probably forever? The world-famous,
kind, and understanding mayor of New
York, Jimmy Walker. Wasn't it he who had
put his hand out to me to shake that day at
City Hall?

When I got home, I found myself going
on about the big day I had just been
through and how much I had enjoyed it
even though I had had to stand at attention
for the best part of an hour. I was perhaps
even more tired than when I had recently
marched up Fifth Avenue with the other
Xavier cadets in the St. Patrick's Day parade, but I didn't mind because I had seen a
lot of famous politicians again, most especially Jimmy Walker. My mother was listening to all this, seemingly with rapt
attention. When I paused for breath, she
looked straight at me, but now with her
stern look, and wanted to know how those
filthy smudges got all over my recently dry-
cleaned uniform. I had not wanted anyone
to know of my good fortune in being able
to obtain dirt from the first shovelful until
the new highway would be completed,
probably in a couple of years. I had
planned to hide it high on a shelf in my
closet and not take it out until then, which I
figured would be the propitious time to
show everybody what I had. I must say I
hadn't given any thought at all as to just
who might be interested in going out of his
way to view a pound of dirt. Mother was
still staring sternly at me, and as she did I
became quite flustered, could hardly hold
back the tears, and blubbered out the whole
story of how I was the only one at the ceremonies lucky enough to even think of the
great significance, as well as value, of
something actually as authentic as the con-
tents of my pockets. And then, as a citizen,

going ahead and taking it with my bare hands. After all, wasn't it the American way to preserve something as interesting as this historical bit of soil?

Slowly her stern look began to soften into a smile. Then she came over, gave me a squeeze, and kissed me on the top of the head. This sudden change in my mother's attitude pleased me very much but also confused me. Then she allowed as how she agreed with some of what I had to say. She said that at first she was pretty mad when she saw the dirt on my uniform but when she listened to me and understood how much what I had done meant to me, and also how much she loved me, she just had to relent. But no way was she going to let me keep all of Jimmy Walker's dirt. She would compromise. She would allow me to keep some of it, a cupful. And not upstairs in my closet either, but "right here behind the glass door in the kitchen closet where everybody can see it." Which is where it stayed for quite a few years. On many occasions during that period, our kitchen was the scene of much merriment as the story of George's West Side Highway dirt was repeated to visiting guests by the other members of my family. Before too long, even I couldn't help but see the humor in it. By the time I was sixteen, I would laugh out loud when the subject of my precious dirt came up.

There's no doubt that during those early years I had a penchant for shaking hands with the famous or getting autographs from them, be it Gertrude Ederle, Mayor Walker, or Governor Al Smith. Someone else I sought out was the Prince of Wales, who one day would become king of England. His title after he gave up the throne was duke of Windsor. Suffice it to say, I was with my parents on a trip to Montreal. We were in a public square, and all of a sudden, people started pointing and running in a certain direction. I couldn't bear not finding out what was happening, so I ran too. Of course my mother and father didn't follow but yelled that they would wait right there for me and to please be careful. In short order, word had spread that the "young Prince of Wales" was being photographed for a spread in a British magazine. I was only six or seven, but I recognized him from his many photos I had seen in the newspapers and in the newsreels at the movie theaters. Squirming my short stature through to the front of the crowd, I found that he was right in front of me. "He's the Prince of Wales, the next king of England" kept going over and over in my head until I suddenly darted forward toward him, stuck out my right hand, which he, seemingly amused, took hold of and shook heartily to some cheering from the onlookers. End of story. Except yes, I did get back to my folks, and they were highly amused at the shenanigans of their youngest.

I guess I liked to think that such handshakes meant I was touching greatness. I was too young then to know or understand, for instance, the inner sadness of Jimmy Walker's life, his open love affair with a Broadway dancer, Betty Compton, which caused the breakdown of his marriage.

In later years, Bob Hope, in probably his only departure from comedy roles, was excellent in portraying the heart-rending drama that was the life of James J. Walker, mayor of New York City, 1926–1932. I still enjoy sitting down in my living room to sort of reacquaint myself with old Jimmy in *Beau James* when it's shown on the American Movie Channel. Many years after he had been banished from his exalted position at City Hall (a humiliation which was brought about by his erstwhile friend who was then the governor in Albany, Franklin Delano Roosevelt), I occasionally saw him dining in the early 1940s, sometimes alone, sometimes with another gentleman, in Toots Shor's, a well-known restaurant which catered to the sports crowd, movie people, and theater and radio personalities. In short, showbiz folks and their aficionados. This was before TV became a major part of the world's culture. Of course, whenever I saw Mr. Walker up close again, it brought back the pleasant memories I've just reviewed. At the same time my heart would go out to him across the room, and I could feel nothing but fondness and warmth for this person who now seemed so sad sitting over there, this wonderful person who, without ever knowing it, had brightened my childhood so much.

In November 1946 at the age of 75, Jimmy Walker passed away. I had been married five months earlier and my bride, Jo-Anne, really didn't know anything much about him because when she was born in 1927, he had recently become mayor. All she knew was what she had heard—and that mostly from me. So she suggested it might be better if I were to go alone to Campbell's Funeral Parlor to pay my respects, which I did. And I was pleased to see many, many others there doing likewise, which I'm sure pleased Jimmy Walker, wherever he was.

MY FIRST RADIO APPEARANCE

My mother, I guess in pursuit of her dreams of making a great singing star out of the youngest of her offspring, engaged a singing teacher for me. The only thing I can remember about "the Great" Thomas Barry Hannom, for that's how my siblings referred to him, was that he scared me. He was a huge man, both in height and avoirdupois, and when he opened his mouth to speak, you could hear him across the street. But that sound was nothing compared to what happened when his vocal efforts turned into song. Simply put, the rafters shook. Or so it seemed. At least to this not quite yet teenager. I suppose the truth is that I was intimidated by his presence. But I will go so far as to say that maybe, just maybe, he did help to improve my singing efforts if even just a little bit.

I can't recall what caused my singing lessons to stop. But Mr. Hannom did leave me a legacy I will always be grateful for. He had a connection with someone at WNYC, the radio station owned by the city of New York, which at the time of this writing is still in operation. One afternoon the station was going to open its microphones to newcomers to display their singing abilities. Then, hopefully, they would become stars. It wasn't touted as an amateur program but in reality, I would say that's what it was. Anyway, "the Great" Thomas Barry Hannom and I took the subway over to City Hall station and walked to the Municipal Building right behind City Hall and then up to a high floor where WNYC was located. It turned out that the connection Mr. Hannom had at the radio station was Tommy

Cowan. The name was familiar to me because I had heard him on the air and had read about him in radio columns which said that he was the very first radio announcer ever. He had started working at WJZ in 1920, and a year later he was instrumental in hiring Milton J. Cross, about whom I will tell you more later.

Mr. Hannom introduced me to Tommy Cowan, who then brought me into the studio and introduced me to the pianist, who wanted to know what song I was going to sing. I had brought along the sheet music for "Mother Machree," a big Irish favorite at the time, which along with "My Wild Irish Rose" and "Little Town in the Ould County Down" was high on the list of requests I received at family gatherings of uncles, aunts, and cousins. Such sentimental Irish ballads were popular because some of those relatives had, like my parents, emigrated from Ireland and the others who were present were their children, my cousins.

Before I realized what was happening, I found myself being positioned by Mr. Cowan in front of the microphone into which he was already speaking as the pianist began to play from the sheet music I had given him. Tommy Cowan had by now uttered my name into the mike followed by the words "Mother Machree." Next he pointed his finger in my direction which I took to mean I should start singing, which I did. "There's a spot in me heart which no colleen may own…" When I finished, Mr. Cowan thanked me very pleasantly on the air, and Mr. Hannom and I left together. He had an appointment somewhere else so I went back home to Bay Ridge alone on the subway, which in those days was no cause for worry. After I had left the subway and was walking home, some friends who lived nearby, the McGuinn kids—Eddie, Francie, and their sister Anne—came running toward me all excited that they had just heard me on the radio and they couldn't get over it. It was still hard for people to understand how sound, human or otherwise, could travel through the air. The McGuinns knew to tune in when they did because my mother had called their mother. I never did find out how many others Mom called. Looking back I don't think the McGuinns could have cared less about how I sang the song; as a matter of fact they didn't mention whether or not they particularly liked my rendition. It was just that they heard me on the radio, and that was enough to get their juices flowing. As for me, the whole incident was a very big thrill. Little did I realize that my radio appearance that day was the forerunner of thousands more. But not as a singer, which my mother would have liked. As we shall see, something else was in store for me.

GOVERNOR AL SMITH

One sunny day in the summer of 1928, as on many other such days, I was enjoying myself at Coney Island at Ocean Tide Baths. With friends from my neighborhood I alternated between the pool and the ocean and in between spent some time on the beach. I happened to be in the pool when word spread like wildfire that New York's Governor Al Smith was on the beach in front of the bathhouses, shaking hands all over the place and being photographed. He had very recently been nominated for the presidency by the Democratic party. Listening to his acceptance speech at the convention, which was broadcast, I was fascinated by the way he pronounced the name of the great new invention which I was becoming so taken with, radio. Al called it radd-ee-o, like in radish. Nevertheless, I found it terribly exciting that a man as important as he, most likely our next president, would come to the exact same beach that my friends and I hung out on. When I started talking with the pool lifeguard about Smith's appearance, he told me the governor was actually in front of McMahon's, the bathhouse next to Ocean Tide, probably because the governor's sister had a house on the beach in Sea Gate. Sea Gate was really an extension of Coney Island, with only a long fence jutting out into the water separating it from McMahon's beach. The difference was that it was a community of private homes, while Coney Island was world renowned for its amusement parks and vast expanse of beaches. At any rate, I wasted no time skedaddling from the Ocean Tide pool to McMahon's beach to see, hopefully up close, yet another public figure I held in very high esteem. When I got there, it wasn't

hard to find him because he was already surrounded by a huge crowd, almost being swamped by them in their frenzy. I immediately put on my squirrel act, which had worked pretty well in the past. So squirreling through the mob, I eventually was near enough to see Governor Smith. He was all smiles, in a bathing suit of course, and waving in response to his worshippers. Standing with him was a man I recognized from his pictures I had seen in the papers, John H. McCooey, the head of the Democratic party in Brooklyn. Mr. McCooey was easy to spot because he wore a Gene Shalit type mustache. At some point either an aide to the governor or a lifeguard must have decided the crowd was getting out of hand because the governor abruptly stopped waving and conferred with Mr. McCooey and one or two other men. Suddenly a lifeguard was escorting Mr. Smith, Mr. McCooey, and another man into a large lifeboat. Safely seated in the boat, which by now was bobbing in the breaking surf, the governor renewed his waving to his admirers as the lifeguard shoved the boat into the oncoming waves, then hopped aboard, grabbed the oars, and began to row.

While this was going on I had waded into the water, the better to see everything happening. It was then I noticed a strand of rope about two feet long attached to the rear end of the boat. Yes, it really did catch my attention because the next thing I knew I had grabbed hold of it and found myself being towed by a rowboat containing the real live governor of New York, Alfred E. Smith, and I just knew he was going to be the next president of the United States. At that moment I was in heaven. I was also in water over my head. Very much over my head and, accordingly, hanging on for dear life. At the same time I was scared to death.

Adding to my discombobulation, the lifeguard, busy as the proverbial one-armed paper hanger, was rowing the boat using every ounce of strength he could summon forth as it scaled the waves with its precious cargo. I soon realized the precious cargo, Governor Smith and Mr. McCooey, both occupying the rear seat, had become aware of my presence and had conveyed this interesting bit of information to the lifeguard and the other passenger in the front seat. The lifeguard stopped rowing long enough to yell to this urchin hanger-on to let go of the rope and go back. At the same moment the governor and John H. McCooey were leaning over the rear indicating to me that they were pretty much in agreement with the skipper. I don't know why, but it hadn't occurred to me that I might be asked to leave, which indeed I had just been, and with the concurrence of Al Smith, the beloved "Happy Warrior." After all, I thought, I wouldn't have grabbed the rope in the first place if the governor hadn't been in the boat. But these foolish excuses aside, what I really was, was mortified. Didn't think I had ever been more embarrassed in my life. But I had to tell them something, and quick, before the lifeguard might produce a penknife and have Mr. McCooey or Governor Smith cut me loose. Because even if they were such big shots, the law of the sea said they would have to obey the skipper's orders and do as he said. With this awful scenario going through my head, I yelled at the boat as loud as I could the very important information that I wasn't a good swimmer, had never been in water over my head before, and please, oh please, don't cut my lifeline. By now the lifeboat had reached the end of the long fence separating McMahon's beach from Sea Gate beach and the lifeguard/skipper had begun his turn, with me still hanging onto the rope, which, thank God, was still attached. The turn completed,

the two distinguished passengers in the rear seat (aft, I later learned it was called) looked back, pleasantly smiling at me. Not until that moment was I sure that everything was going to be all right, that these two "all powerful" men were not going to have me sent to a home for wayward children. Just to see them smiling at me was all I needed to know they were nice. As the boat came closer to the shore, I could touch my feet on the sand under me and I knew the water was no longer over my head so I let go of the rope and ran up onto the Sea Gate beach, which by now had its own crowd, applauding and greeting "the next president" as he got out of the boat. The first person to approach him, I later learned, was his sister. As she escorted him and Mr. McCooey up to her house nearby, the governor was "working the crowd," as we say today, shaking hands with one and all as he went, kids included. I had positioned myself near the stairs to the house he was approaching and like the others, stuck my hand out as he got to me. He was by now pretty much doing his hand shaking by rote, mine included. But he paused while shaking my hand and must have suddenly recognized me from the episode just concluded. He tightened his grip and gave me a real hearty, honest-to-God handshake followed by a pat on the head and "Take good care of yourself, kiddo." Thrilled, I rushed back to my bathhouse at Ocean Tide Baths, changed clothes, and rushed to the 86th St. trolley car for the ride back home, hardly able to contain myself, waiting to tell the folks about my extraordinary day at the beach.

Easter reminds me of another incident regarding Governor Al Smith. It was after he had been defeated in the 1928 election by Herbert Hoover and, of course, he was no longer governor. I had a job on Saturdays delivering flowers for a well-known florist on Fifth Avenue at 58th St. whose name escapes me. On Easter Saturday I was given an order of flowers to be delivered to "Governor Alfred E. Smith" at his penthouse in a lower Fifth Avenue apartment building. I was also given twenty cents to cover my round trip on the Fifth Avenue bus. The subway fare was a nickel, but the Fifth Avenue bus cost a dime, twice as much I guess because it was considered more high class, especially if you chose to ride on the open top, which I did. I enjoyed sightseeing from the open top of a Fifth Avenue bus a lot. But this particular ride was much more exciting than I would normally have experienced. From the moment I settled in a front seat, my heart began to beat faster with the expectation of again seeing one of my idols, probably even having some conversation with him because this time it would be in his own home, no crowds around, nobody except maybe Mrs. Smith. And I just knew she would be nice. I had been very sorry when Hoover beat him, but Governor Smith sure took it like a man judging by that smile on his face in the papers. I guess he smiled a lot because he figured if he had become president, they would be beating him over the head instead of Herbert Hoover and blaming him for the stock market crash. Maybe, I hoped, when he came to the door and took the flowers from me, he would let me step in for a few minutes. Then I would remind him I was the kid hanging on behind the lifeguard boat last year in Coney Island and thank him for being so warm to me when he shook my hand that day instead of turning me over to the cops for what I had done. I thought he would like to hear that. And

when he did, and remembered me, he would probably double the tip he would normally give. Of course, I wouldn't stay more than a minute or two. It wouldn't be polite to stay any longer. Never wear out your welcome, as my mother would say. After all, I was just a delivery boy.

When the bus reached Fourteenth Street, I realized I had to come back down out of the clouds quickly so that, with Al Smith's flowers, I could climb down the narrow spiral stairs before I missed my stop at Twelfth Street. As I left the bus and crossed Fifth Avenue, my excitement was at fever pitch with visions of what was just ahead. The doorman let me into the lobby, sent me to the service elevator, and in no time at all there I was in front of the penthouse door. I rang the bell, my heart by now beating a mile a minute, and in a little while the door opened. A lady in a maid's uniform reached out and took the flowers from me. The only thing she said was, "I'll see that Governor Smith gets them." Then she closed the door and was gone, leaving yours truly standing there alone and more dejected than I had ever been before in my whole life. Wow, what a letdown.

Fifteen years later I did get to visit, if only for a very brief moment, with Governor Al Smith. It was October of 1944. He was being honored in death as few laymen are. I was one of many thousands who came to view his remains lying in an open coffin in the center aisle of St. Patrick's Cathedral.

5

"HELLOOOOO KATHLYN, HELLOOOOO JIM"

One Labor Day, I'm not sure exactly what year but it must have been after my radio "debut" on WNYC, I had read in the radio section of the *Brooklyn Daily Eagle* that station WMCA would carry ceremonies celebrating "the Great American Labor Movement" from Fort Hamilton, the large military installation dating back to the Revolutionary War which faced New York Harbor from the southern tip of Brooklyn. Thinking I might see Mayor Walker or Governor Smith there, I decided to attend, not that I knew anything about the labor situation in America at that age, nor in all honesty could I have cared less. It was just that, being as taken with radio from afar as I was and at that point in my life having never actually seen anyone other than Tommy Cowan speaking into a live microphone, I thought this would be a good opportunity to see radio on the "sending" end instead of always being only on the "receiving" end at home. I might even have thought of it as "getting involved" because as I was leaving the house I mentioned to my brother Jim and my sister Kathlyn that I was going to Fort Hamilton to watch a patriotic radio program about Labor Day. On the spur of the moment, I told them that if they would tune in to WMCA, there might be a surprise for them. The walk to the polo field at Fort Hamilton took about fifteen minutes. Then it was just a matter of following the stream of people who were also attending. And because I had made sure to get there early enough, I plunked down into a seat right in the front row, as close to the platform as it was

possible to get. Even though I had a good seat, I was disappointed the only politicians there were people I wasn't interested in, like aldermen and borough presidents whose names meant nothing to me. No Jimmy Walker. No Al Smith. But my interest sure picked up when I spotted a man on the platform whose face I had seen in the paper. He was A. L. Alexander, and there he was sitting in front of a microphone with the letters WMCA on it. The microphone was directly above and in front of my seat, and I knew he was the chief announcer at WMCA because that's what the paper said. While I was taking this in, the program must have started because I could see that Mr. Alexander was leaning close to the "mike," which I was to find out later was what those in the business—those in the know—called it. His lips were moving, but I really couldn't hear what he was saying and I felt sure nobody else sitting there could either. But I was fascinated to think he was only a few feet from me and I could hardly hear him and yet others who were far away could hear him through their radios. I just couldn't figure it out. When his lips stopped moving, he leaned back from the mike and pointed his finger at the musicians, about seven or eight of them, who then began to play the "Star-Spangled Banner." From the far side of the platform came a lady I hadn't noticed before. She stood in front of a different mike. I don't know how I could have missed her. She was fat. Boy was she fat. Then we all heard Francis Scott Key's familiar lyrics "Oh, say can you see by the dawn's early light." No problem hearing her. I began to put "two and two" together. A. L. Alexander had been speaking in a normal, conventional voice while the fat lady was projecting. I thought maybe that was the way all fat ladies sang because they had so much to project with. While thinking these deep thoughts, I suddenly remembered about the surprise I had told Jim and Kathlyn to listen for. So when the music ended and the fat lady was sitting down and before the local politicians started their speeches, I decided it was my turn. Still in my seat I opened my mouth and as loud as I could yelled, "Hellooooo Kathlyn, Hellooooo Jim." Then seeing the look of horror mixed with fury on A. L. Alexander's face, I ran as fast as I could from the polo field, out of Fort Hamilton and halfway home before I slowed down.

As I went in the front door my brother and sister, Jim and Kathlyn, were almost as excited as I had been yelling greetings to them from Fort Hamilton. After all, their names had gone out over the radio and were heard by who knows how many people all over the city. But to me the most exciting thing about it was that they actually heard me. Then my mother came downstairs and put the icing on the cake when she said that she had heard me too.

Many years later when I had been in the business quite a while, I had occasion to meet A. L. Alexander on the eighth floor of NBC. He had become the star of his own prime-time hour coast-to-coast on Sunday nights at eight sponsored by Chase and Sanborn Coffee. His program, broadcast out of NBC's largest studio, 8H, was *The Court of Human Relations*, an early version, you might say a forerunner, of Oprah, Donahue, and Geraldo on TV. Even after such a span of years, I was a little hesitant about bringing up the subject of that long ago Labor Day in Fort Hamilton. But I threw caution to the wind because I had to know if he remembered, and if he did, how he would react now. When I broached the subject, his face was blank. But when I threw in the fat lady singing and the fresh kid screaming something and then running off and that the fresh kid was me, that did it. It was such fun to see him laugh, because I just knew he had been really mad that day. It must have been embarrassing for him. But here he was, a big radio star now, having a great laugh over one of my childhood peccadillos which, when it took place, displeased him very, very much. As for me, I've got to say that was one of the most pleasant conversations I ever had on the eighth floor of NBC. And I've had plenty of them.

6

DREAMING AND WONDERING

It was shortly after we moved into the house on 85th Street that we acquired our Stromberg Carlson, a floor piece containing a radio and a phonograph, with a loud-speaker serving both. Marconi's invention had come a long way in the six years since everyone went gaga over his crystal set. The old Victrola had now become the phonograph, considerably reduced in size and very much improved in performance.

New radio stations were coming onto the scene, augmenting on the dial those already established, like WJZ. It was WJZ I found myself drawn to a lot, especially on Sunday mornings at nine o'clock. What attracted me was the *Children's Hour*, a program featuring, what else, children. Boys and girls of diversified talents—musicians, actors, singers. The genial host was Milton Cross, who always seemed to be genuinely enjoying himself in the role. And so was I in my role of listener. Sunday after Sunday I would find myself glued to the Stromberg Carlson between nine and ten in the morning. I had become a real fan of these kids—Jean Carroll, soprano; Dorothy Somerville, contralto; Walter Scott, violinist. Mr. Cross used to have fun teasing Walter, calling him Sir Walter Scott. Other participants on the show included a girl named Winifred Twomey and Billy Halop and his sister, Florence, all of whom were actors.

The person whose performances I really enjoyed the most though was a boy soprano whose singing knocked me out he was so good. His name was Michael Favata. He was equally at home, it seemed to me, singing an aria, a sacred hymn, an Irish

ballad, or a good, full-blooded American love song. One Sunday he sang Victor Herbert's "A Kiss in the Dark" and brought me back in memory to the time, five years earlier in Springfield, when the two Singer's Midgets had impressed me so with their romantic rendition of that song. After listening to him week after week, I began to realize that no matter how good my folks and my relatives told me I was as a boy soprano, I had a long way to go to approach being in his league. No Michael Favata was I. Why even Milton Cross himself, who would later become the official announcing voice of the Metropolitan Opera for forty-five years on the air every Saturday afternoon from the Metropolitan Opera House, dubbed him the "Lily Pons of boy sopranos." There's no doubt, looking back now, that listening to the *Children's Hour* was a harmless exercise in dreaming. In dreaming and wondering about what course my life would eventually take. And when?

One day I was telling the kids who lived next door, Kewpie and Buddy Fusco, about the *Children's Hour* and how much I liked it and what a good singer Michael Favata was. At first I was a little let down when they said they had never listened to it, but then I figured they weren't into singing or showbiz in general the way I liked to think I was.

However, a day or two later the Fusco kids met me coming down the street and were all excited because they had found out somehow that my idol, Michael Favata of the *Children's Hour*, lived a block and a half away on 84th Street and Third Avenue.

We were on 85th, halfway down the block from Third. Wow, I thought. This had to be more than a coincidence, if true. How to find out? Well, I said to myself, start walking the block and a half. When I got there in no more than sixty seconds flat, I saw it was an apartment building so I looked at the names on the doorbells and sure enough there it was—Favata—on the second floor. My finger pushing that doorbell would turn out to be the most momentous, the most far-reaching exercise of my entire life. Michael answered the bell, and when I told him who I was and that I was a fan of the *Children's Hour* and lived around the block, he invited me to come up and say hello. I must say that I didn't need an engraved invitation. When he opened the door and invited me in, now that I was there and not knowing exactly what to say, I blurted out that he didn't look at all like Lily Pons. That did it. Without intending to, just nervous I guess, it turned out I had broken the ice because he thought that was pretty funny and I liked the way he laughed over it, like a real good sport.

That's the way our friendship began. Soon after, when I told him I had sung as a boy soprano in the choir at St. Francis Xavier, he invited me to go downtown with him to choir rehearsal at St. James Pro-Cathedral on Jay Street. Up until then I had not been aware of the existence of a diocesan choir. When we arrived there, before the rehearsal was to start, he introduced me to Father Lawrence Bracken, the choirmaster. It then dawned on me that Michael must have called Father Bracken and already spoken about me and my past choir experience at St. Francis Xavier because Father suggested I audition for him, which with my knees knocking, I did. I think I was more nervous singing in front of Michael than Father Bracken because I just knew there was no comparison between Michael's boy soprano voice and mine. But I did manage to get through the "Panis Angelicus" without falling apart, and I felt much better when Father Bracken said:

"Thank you very much, George, and I'll see you in the choir loft at the 11 o'clock Mass on Sunday. Of course, you're staying with the other boys for today's rehearsal," which I was more than happy to do, to put it mildly.

It was during that rehearsal I learned that Michael was the soloist of the choir—and boy could he solo. Of all the sacred solos I had heard him sing during that early period of our lives, my favorite was his rendition of Gounod's "Ave Maria." In a way it seemed like old times for this twelve year old. But instead of the choir at St. Francis Xavier Church of a few years earlier where some kid had conked old Father Finley on the noggin, here I was a member of the choir at the most prestigious Catholic church in Brooklyn, St. James Pro-Cathedral. So, even if it wasn't St. Patrick's Cathedral in Manhattan, I still felt pretty good about it.

What I was really hoping for after my first few weeks in the choir with Michael was that he would ask me to go with him one day to a *Children's Hour* rehearsal at station WJZ. He had told me the show rehearsed two afternoons a week, and I was chomping at the bit to be invited, if even just once, to go with him and meet the other kids I had heard so often. One of the things my mother used to say was "patience is its own reward."

As it turned out, I was awfully glad I had paid attention to some of her little "golden nuggets." One afternoon at choir rehearsal Michael suggested I go with him the next day to the *Children's Hour* rehearsal to meet Madge Tucker, who was in charge of putting the show together, the producer. He told me he had spoken to her about me and she had said to bring me in and she would listen to me. She needed to fill a spot in the small choral group used occasionally as backup for a soloist. A boy in the group was moving to another city, and she had to replace him. So, through Michael, she was willing to audition me.

To repeat a phrase from my letter to the editor of the *New York Times* reprinted in the preface to this book, I first set foot in that wondrous place in 1928. The exact date escapes me, but I've never forgotten the significance of that first visit to the National Broadcasting Company with my newest friend, Michael Favata. Madge Tucker, a lovely, charming lady, listened patiently as I did my best with "Mother Machree." Before I finished I could almost tell from the expression on her face that I was in. When Ethel Hart played the final note of her piano accompaniment, Miss Tucker allowed as how she didn't have to look any further. "Welcome to the *Children's Hour* gang," she said to me as Michael beamed his approval followed by "Welcome to the club." Madge Tucker herself would become familiar to young radio listeners sometime later as the star of *The Lady Next Door*, which ran on NBC five days a week for several years through the thirties and into the forties.

7

MUCH SOUL SEARCHING

All of a sudden my life had changed. Busy, busy, busy, but no complaints. Xavier High until 3 o'clock every day, with one afternoon for military drill when the whole student body marched in full uniform the two and a half blocks down Seventh Avenue to an armory on West 14th Street and drilled for an hour and a half. One afternoon a week in choir rehearsal at the Pro-Cathedral in Brooklyn. But best of all, two afternoons a week in heaven, or to me what was its equivalent, the time I spent at NBC attending rehearsals for the *Children's Hour*.

On Sunday mornings, being a part of the program itself was like a continuation of the bliss I enjoyed during the midweek rehearsals. Meeting Milton Cross in person. Mr. Cross saying my name over the air, as part of the choral group. Then, when the program ended at 10:00, Michael and I wasted no time crossing 55th Street from Fifth over to Seventh Avenue to catch the BMT back to Brooklyn just in time to sing the 11 o'clock Mass at the Pro-Cathedral, which in itself was a wonderful experience.

About a year after all this action began, I got a job on Saturdays at Abraham & Straus in downtown Brooklyn. Position held—marking and checking boxes of merchandise in the receiving department. Salary—30 cents per hour. I'm not sure how long my Saturday association continued with A & S, but it was a good "interim position" until my next step up, which was delivering flowers, also at 30 cents an hour, but plus tips, sometimes. All in all, I can honestly say it was a pretty full week.

Oh, one more thing. There was no

compensation for the *Children's Hour*, but I knew about that from Michael before they even accepted me and it didn't take away one bit from my happiness in being part of the program. Like the old saying, I liked it so much that if I had to, I would have paid them for the job.

During the period I was part of Milton Cross's *Children's Hour*, I couldn't help observing a lot of other things going on at NBC. First of all, as you approached the building, 711 Fifth Avenue, you could spot George Malcolm, the doorman, from a few blocks away because he actually stood seven feet tall. He was a huge man and as pleasant as he was large, with lots of funny stories made funnier by his British accent. He was a good friend of a particular policeman whose name I can't remember. His beat included several hours a day up in the police booth which stood aloft on stanchions, I called them stilts, in the center of Fifth Avenue at 55th Street. It was his duty to direct traffic from on high, so to speak, about fifteen feet above the avenue. Such elevated traffic booths stood at every block up and down Fifth Avenue, which at the time was a two-way street.

On rehearsal days I couldn't wait to get uptown from Xavier to NBC. "Who might I see today?" was on my mind while riding the subway. I took the subway instead of the Fifth Avenue bus because it cost half as much, a nickel. Also it was a lot quicker. Anyway, the reason I was engaging in the "who might I see today?" game was because I had stepped into an elevator one day and almost flipped because who was standing there big as life, but Babe Ruth. Another time, Al Jolson, people like that.

27

With that kind of thing happening, it's easy to see how exciting it was just to go there. Added to that was the fact that I was on a radio program myself. Pretty heady stuff.

During the period of almost three years that I was having such a wonderful time on those two afternoons a week plus Sunday mornings on the air, other things did not go unnoticed. Two in particular. First, musicians carrying their instruments were always around. They were mostly on staff, meaning they were employed by NBC to do whatever programs they were assigned to. But others known as freelancers were there a lot too, augmenting the house musicians when needed, which from what I could observe, was often. One big reason was the three full hours a week on the air at 10 P.M. on Tuesdays, Thursdays, and Saturdays sponsored by Lucky Strike cigarettes and featuring B. A. Rolfe and his orchestra. Popular music, dance music, jazz, waltz, and what-have-you kind of music. Thirty-five or forty men shaking the walls of Studio B on the thirteenth floor arrived at what I'm sure B. A. Rolfe expected to be nothing less than musical perfection during those three "on the air" hours requiring many hours of rehearsal. The musicians for the Lucky Strike shows were around so much you would think they lived there. The theme song for the show was "Lucky Days Are Here Again" to the melody of "Happy Days Are Here Again." It was sung at the open and close by an unidentified male vocalist.

The other thing that made its mark on me was the page staff. It consisted of about sixteen or eighteen boys in uniform who primarily were gofers and helper-outers. The requests for their services went through the receptionist on each floor (we called them hostesses then), who would inform the page standing beside her desk what his particular mission was and for whom. Pages assigned to the thirteenth and fourteenth floors, where most of the broadcast studios were located, had as their major concern the wants and needs of the

people connected with programs or rehearsals going on in those studios. When a studio was on the air, a page would be on duty outside with a sign declaring it was "on the air." Of course, his presence and the sign meant "stay out." Sometimes another page would be assigned to stand inside to dissuade anyone from leaving early, thus preventing any possible noises—footsteps, door slams, etc.—from going out over the air. These rules were strictly adhered to and heaven help the poor page boy if someone got into the studio when his back was turned. If old Mike Farley found out about it, he would loudly read the riot act to him. Mike Farley was a grandfatherly type who, I was told by some of the pages I had gotten to know, was strict, but fair. Other page boys ran errands for the office staffs of the top executives like Merlin H. Aylesworth, NBC's first president, who was known to his peers as Deak.

Earlier I mentioned the big decision made at home for me to change high schools because I had outgrown my Xavier uniform. The decision had been made at the end of my third year at Xavier. That's the point I've reached now in my story.

It was the end of June of 1930. Xavier was behind me as I looked forward to spending my last year of high school at De La Salle Institute beginning in September. But something else was happening, had been happening increasingly to me and also to my friend, Michael Favata. Change of voice. Mother Nature decreed zillions of years ago at the beginning of time that when boys reach a certain age their vocal apparatus undergoes a gradual change, from a high register to a lower register. And, as the old saying goes, "there just ain't nothin' you can do about it." That ancient decree of Ma Nature's also meant bye-bye soprano voice, bye-bye NBC, and of course, bye-bye Brooklyn Diocesan Choir. No more *Children's Hour* and all it had meant to both of us. We knew it would happen sooner or later, and with us fortunately it was later, but when it did happen,

PER.'S 7-41

File __Employe__

NATIONAL BROADCASTING COMPANY, INC.
APPLICATION FOR EMPLOYMENT
Atlantic

Date __May 4, 1931__

NAME __Ansbro__ __George__ __Andrew__ PHONE __5-3159__
     (LAST) (FIRST) (MIDDLE)

KINDS OF WORK FOR WHICH QUALIFIED __Page boy – 10-3__

PRESENT ADDRESS __254-85th Street, Brooklyn,__ CITY AND STATE __N Y__

PERMANENT ADDRESS _____ CITY AND STATE _____

IN CASE OF ACCIDENT NOTIFY _____

ADDRESS _____ PHONE NO. _____

WHEN CAN YOU BEGIN WORK? _____

SALARY DESIRED __$15.__ MIN. YOU WILL CONSIDER _____

HEIGHT __5'10½"__ WEIGHT __135__ ANCESTRY __American__ AGE __18__ SEX __Male__
                    (FRENCH, GERMAN, SWEDISH, ETC.)

FOR WHAT PERIOD DO YOU WANT EMPLOYMENT? _____

DATE OF BIRTH __1/14/13__ PLACE OF BIRTH __Brooklyn, N Y__
            (MONTH) (DAY) (YEAR)

WHAT FOREIGN LANGUAGES DO YOU READ? _____

SINGLE __X__ MARRIED ____ WIDOWED ____ DIVORCED ____ SEPARATED ____ NUMBER OF CHILDREN ____

SPEAK? _____ WRITE? _____

FATHER'S BIRTHPLACE _____ MOTHER'S BIRTHPLACE _____

ARE YOU A BOOKKEEPER? _____

NAME OF FATHER _____ OCCUPATION _____

STENOGRAPHER? _____ SYSTEM _____ SPEED _____

NAME OF MOTHER _____ OCCUPATION _____

ARE YOU A TOUCH TYPIST? _____ SPEED _____

NAME OF HUSBAND OR WIFE _____ OCCUPATION _____

HAVE YOU HAD EXPERIENCE IN FILING? _____

DO YOU RENT, OWN YOUR OWN HOME, LIVE WITH PARENTS, OR BOARD? __Live with parents__

WHAT OFFICE APPLIANCES CAN YOU OPERATE? _____

EDUCATION

GIVE NAMES AND ADDRESSES — DATES

HIGH SCHOOL OR PRIVATE SCHOOL __Xavier High School__ FROM __3 yrs__ TO _____ GRADUATED? __No__ MAJOR SUBJECTS __Academic__

ADDRESS __30 West 16th Street__

High school __De La Salle Institute__ FROM __1 yr__ TO _____ DEGREE __No__ MAJOR _____ Academic

ADDRESS __74th Street & Amsterdam__

PROFESSIONAL OR TECHNICAL TRAINING _____ FROM _____ TO _____ DEGREE _____ SUBJECTS _____

ADDRESS _____

EXPERIENCE (LIST MOST RECENT FIRST)

FIRM	KIND OF BUSINESS	POSITION HELD	DATES FROM	TO	SALARY (MO.) MIN.	MAX.	PERSON TO WHOM YOU WERE RESPONSIBLE	REASON FOR LEAVING
NAME __Abraham and Straus__ ADDRESS __Brooklyn, N Y__		Marking & checking boxes of merchandise in receiving dept			$.30 per hr weekend job		Miss Funnell	Better position
NAME _____ ADDRESS _____								
NAME _____ ADDRESS _____								
NAME _____ ADDRESS _____								
NAME _____ ADDRESS _____								

MAY WE REFER TO SCHOOLS AND EMPLOYERS LISTED ABOVE? _____

SHOW HERE YOUR NAME AND ACCOUNT NUMBER AS REGISTERED UNDER THE SOCIAL SECURITY ACT.

REFERRED TO NBC BY WHOM? _____

NAME _____

My application for a page boy's job at NBC. Being only 16, but knowing 18 was the minimum age requirement, I fibbed on my date of birth. I put down January 14, 1913 instead of January 14, 1915, thus opening the door to what turned out to be 59 years of continuous employment with essentially the same company.

it was understandably hard to take. Not just ending the friendships made during those years, but no longer being able to enjoy the wonderful atmosphere of NBC.

Getting back for a moment to my telling about the page staff. I neglected to mention that with one of them it was a renewal of an earlier friendship when I had lived on President Street. Harvey Gannon was somewhat older than I but even so had been part of the same bunch. Just his being a friend at NBC seemed to make it easier for me when I first joined the *Children's Hour.* After I had been there a while I had men-

tioned to Harvey what a swell job I thought he had and that when I got older I would give anything to wind up there too as a page boy. I had written down the name of the personnel director he had been happy to give me, Ruth Keeler. But knowing I was only fifteen, he told me to forget about it for a while, at least three years until I was eighteen because that was the NBC minimum age for hiring page boys.

September came and with it right after Labor Day, De La Salle, new friends, new teachers, and like old Mike Farley at NBC, the Christian Brothers were strict, but fair.

It didn't take me long to understand that, and when I did, the path ahead for me was immeasurably smoothed because of the respect I felt for these kind and dedicated men.

In January of 1931 my final semester began—on or about the same day as my sixteenth birthday, January 14. It had been agreed to at home by Mother, Pop, and me that come June, only five months away, I would graduate, get a summer job, and enter Manhattan College, a school with an excellent reputation which was also run by the Christian Brothers. I'm sure my folks were more than a wee bit prejudiced in favor of Manhattan because my oldest brother, Ray, had gone through there several years earlier, leaving everybody, Ray included of course, quite happy with the experience. So it's understandable that I was genuinely looking forward to my freshman days in the fall. But, as some sage once observed, "There's many a slip twixt the cup and the lip."

In May, a month before graduation, against Harvey Gannon's advice, I made a big decision to go see Ruth Keeler at the NBC personnel office and fill out an application for a page boy's job for the summer. I had it all figured out. Simple. Where it said "date of birth" I put down January 14, 1913, instead of 1915. Voilà! I became eighteen instantly, with no harm done to anybody. If they found out, they couldn't put me in jail. But they wouldn't find out, unless they made me bring a birth certificate, and I had already checked out that possibility in conversations with other kids on the page staff. I've got to confess though that I went through some strong misgivings before reaching the big decision, mostly about what I had always been taught you just don't do. Trifle with the truth, lie, fib, prevaricate, etc. My other self offered what I considered a very good argument in favor of doing all of the above, but, of course, just in this particular case. Simply stated— NBC had more to gain by hiring me, even if only for the summer, regardless of my age, because they would be getting someone who for three years had been a close observer of page boys performing their regular duties. I thought I knew their job as well as they did themselves so the company wouldn't have to waste time training me. To top off my other self's argument, I not only wanted the job, I needed it. What with the Great Depression rapidly making inroads everywhere, the regular paycheck I would receive would cover my expenses handily and help relieve Pop's other financial burdens caused by the falling real estate market. I found myself, as the saying goes, "on the horns of a dilemma," with much soul searching going on.

The winner? My other self. On May 4, 1931, I completed an application, a copy of which I've kept all these years, for the exalted position of page boy. But I was greatly let down by the information I had received from Miss Keeler when I called her for the appointment. NBC had a policy against hiring part-time employees she said. And that included summer jobs. But she alleviated the situation slightly by very pleasantly suggesting I come in and fill out the application anyway because one never knew what the future might bring, which is what I did. Parenthetically, I might add, I've never been sorry.

A ROTTEN SUMMER

June came. With it graduation ceremonies on the stage of Town Hall Manhattan's auditorium where I received my diploma from De La Salle Institute. The next thing was to find a summer job. With the unemployment rate sky high, it wasn't going to be easy for a guy whose only experience was marking and checking merchandise at A & S and delivering flowers.

After I applied at several places with no luck, my father happened to remember he knew a man who was manager of a resort complex on the ocean near Coney Island called Oriental Beach. His name was John McGuire. Pop said he didn't know him well, but he would at least call him. Mr. McGuire told Pop he could use a busboy in his cafeteria and for me to be there to punch in the time clock no later than eight o'clock the following morning. Salary: $3.00 per day. Pleased that my job search was ended, I was up before dawn to be sure of getting there in plenty of time to learn about my duties. But, not knowing the trip took about an hour and a half, including a long walk from the BMT to Oriental Beach, I was lucky to arrive at the time clock with only a few minutes to spare.

After I had punched in, somebody told me to go see Mr. McGuire in his office, which I did. He was a fat, puffy person, rather unpleasant looking. He didn't have much to say other than laying out what a busboy's duties were. Only once during this recitation did John McGuire appear to lose his dour manner and that was when he got to telling me about his cafeteria. His face actually seemed to brighten, almost smile, albeit very briefly. He was extremely proud that "his" cafeteria, which I hadn't seen

yet, was the largest in the world. Which, to the unhappiness of my feet, I discovered all too soon.

There were other unhappy things I was to discover also, but first things first. The cafeteria—take all the synonyms for huge, put them together, and that says it all about Mr. McGuire's cafeteria. Up until then the largest eating place I had ever been in was Horn & Hardart's Automat on Broadway near Times Square. To my young eyes, this place was ten times bigger than the Automat. Next, Mr. McGuire let me know that I would be allowed to serve myself, right after punching in, a cup of coffee and two slices of buttered toast. I wasn't sure if this was out of the goodness of his heart or because I was the son of a fellow Irishman he had known only slightly named John Ansbro. As far as my duties were concerned, I was to start bussing as soon as the coffee and toast was over. My job definition of busboy at Oriental Beach Cafeteria, summer of 1931: fill tray with dirty dishes and silverware you've removed from a table and unload in kitchen for washing. Return to same table to remove accumulated trash and empty it in one of the many garbage receptacles located throughout cafeteria. Return again to table with damp rag and clean off thoroughly. Continue this procedure at any other soiled table you spot where the customers have already left. Do this until you are notified by Mr. Grogan to go to lunch. Eat lunch in the help section of kitchen where you had coffee and toast. You may have a bowl of soup and three slices of bread or toast, rice pudding for dessert, and coffee again. This sumptuous lunch was, wonder of wonders, on the house. Lunch over, repeat above procedure until cafeteria closes, average time, 6 o'clock. If the call of nature beckons, locate Mr. Grogan for permission to seek relief.

My summer in that cavernous place was really something. The tables were large rectangular ones seating ten. Without exaggeration, there must have been at least a hundred of them, and I was one of only ten busboys trying to keep them all clean and presentable. The human traffic to get a table didn't begin to slow down until late afternoon. All in beach attire. All kinds of beach attire. Some real beauties. I had begun to notice an interesting pattern, however, going on with many of the "customers." I put the word in quotes because I had come to realize some people were using the tables without purchasing anything from the many food counters, but instead were members of the BYOL Club. Translation: bring your own lunch. (A decade later I found myself invited to a couple of BYOB parties—bring your own bottle.) And as might be expected from such cheapskates, they were the worst slobs of all. Regardless, we had to clean up after the freeloaders the same as the paying guests.

Around my third day, in the middle of my toast and coffee, the first drops of rain started and in no time at all, it was really coming down. As I was entering the cafeteria, freeloader's heaven, ready for work with my damp rag in hand, I was tapped on the shoulder from behind. It was Mr. Grogan. The decision had been made, he said, not to open the cafeteria for business because of the rain and I was free to go home. "But what about my punching in, punching the time clock?" He then told me that didn't make any difference because it was the policy of management, Mr. McGuire's policy, that when it rained they didn't open. But the help still had to punch the time clock and stay a while in case it suddenly stopped raining and cleared up. In that event, it would be a normal working day. Then I asked him "what happens if it's still raining when I wake up tomorrow morning?" He said everybody had to punch in as usual to be sure they would be there in case it cleared up. Next my big question, "What about pay, do we get paid when the cafeteria closes because of rain?" "Of course not," he said. "Why should you get paid when you're not doing any work?" Considerably dejected, I spent the ride home on the subway trying to figure out Mr. Grogan's logic. I couldn't, so needless to say, it was a rotten summer. I spent three hours a day commuting seven days a week to a job that all too frequently was canceled for the day. Reason being, it was an unusually rainy summer. Not only were my earnings practically nil, but I wound up at summer's end with fallen metatarsals that have plagued me ever since.

9

711 FIFTH

Right after Labor Day I became a member of the incoming freshman class at Manhattan College, beautifully located in the northernmost section of the city known as Spuyten Duyvil where the Harlem River meets the Hudson. It was a ten-minute walk up a hill from the subway station at 242d Street and Broadway, the end of the line. My hours every day were 9 to 3. To be there on time for my first class meant leaving home at 6:45, but I had had plenty of practice riding the subway the previous summer.

Three weeks into the semester I received a call from Ruth Keeler, head of personnel at NBC. A page boy's job had just opened up on the night shift, 5 to midnight, six nights a week, and would I be interested? If so, please let her know as soon as possible, like tomorrow, because she would like me to start on October 1, that Thursday. Wow! That was late Monday afternoon. I can't recall if I ate any dinner my heart was pounding so, but I do remember there was plenty of discussion among Mother, Pop, and me. The others pretty much kept out of it.

My parents knew how much I had loved the three years I had spent in and around NBC while on the *Children's Hour* and the friends I had made. To say nothing of the excitement of just being there. Their main concern was that it would be too much for me—not enough time for sleep and no time to study, a very strong argument. I told them five hours of sleep should be enough, meaning I would be in bed by one o'clock and up at six. As for studying, I said what with all those hours on the subway every day, that's when I would study. I think they knew how heartbroken I would be if they

didn't allow me to at least give it a try, to take what I unoriginally called "a once in a lifetime opportunity." Looking back, I also think they felt sorry that I had to make this big decision at such an early age when I was hardly even out of short pants. And so they weakened and said, "Okay, take the job."

The time between Monday night's decision and the end of my last class on Thursday seemed interminable. Of course, Tuesday I had called Miss Keeler to say I would be happy to accept her offer. She had suggested I arrive a little early, at 4:15, and come directly to her office, which I did after the ride down from Manhattan College. After a few nervous minutes, her pleasant manner relaxed me considerably. Then old Mike Farley walked in and welcomed me to the page staff, recited some of the duties of a page, and before he left said he would see me at a quarter to five, lineup time for the night shift, in the hallway outside of Studio E on the thirteenth floor. I thanked Ruth Keeler, and with a few minutes to kill before lineup, I went down to talk to George Malcolm, the giant doorman, and tell him that in ten minutes he and I would be working for the same boss, Deak Aylesworth. He remembered me from the *Children's Hour* and wished me well.

Back upstairs at the pages' lineup, Mr. Farley introduced me to my fellow workers, some of whom I had gotten to know in those earlier days. And guess whose eyes were popping out when he warmly greeted me. My old friend, Harvey Gannon, who had tipped me off about NBC not hiring anyone under eighteen. I had not seen him since I had left the *Children's Hour* at the time my voice changed, so he was probably dying to know how I got the job. The first chance I got later that evening I told him about faking my year of birth on the job application from 1915 to 1913, thus instantly adding two years to my age. He was genuinely pleased it worked and assured me "mum's the word."

Since Mike Farley knew that Harvey and I were old friends, he assigned him the pleasant task that night of breaking me in. I use the word *pleasant* because it wasn't really a task at all. It consisted of introducing me all around the place. To Georgia Price, the chief hostess, whose bailiwick was the thirteenth floor, where the action never seemed to slow down, especially on Tuesdays, Thursdays, and Saturdays. That's when the many musicians from the Lucky Strike show, members of B. A. Rolfe's orchestra, were in and out of Studio B, the second largest studio. Miss Price was a charming lady and welcomed me to my new job. About fifteen feet away from her desk was the coat room, also called the hatcheck room, with its open counter facing the elevators. It was manned by Alvin Simmons, a middle-aged black man who must have been born with a smile on his face and a heart to match. I would later find out you could never pass his coat room without his telling you a joke, then slapping his leg and laughing uproariously. And sometimes, even when you might not get the point, you just couldn't help but laugh and join in the fun anyway. Harvey then took me to the fourteenth floor to meet Martha Trueblood, the pretty hostess on duty there. Up one more flight to the top floor, the fifteenth, to meet Helen Evans, who was almost too busy to say hello because Studio H would be going on the air in a little while and her phones were ringing furiously with mostly messages for musicians. The program was the *Pond's Program* with Leo Reisman and his orchestra featuring the voice of Lee Wiley, whose elegant looks balanced her sultry singing style. That first night I don't think I actually did any errands at all because Harvey was so busy explaining and introducing me as he led me around. One spot I had heard about during my *Children's Hour* days but had never seen was the master control room. I will not attempt to explain it to you here, but outside of Leo Reisman and Lee Wiley, it was the high spot of my first day on the job.

Mike Farley had made an appointment for me before work the next day with a nearby tailor to be measured for my page's uniform. When I came back the next week for a fitting, he and I agreed it couldn't fit any better, so, carrying my own clothes in a box which the tailor provided, I preened down the avenue in my handsome new threads, my brand new NBC page's uniform, proud as the proverbial peacock. George Malcolm saluted me as I approached 711. Without missing a beat, what with my Xavier training, I grinningly returned same as I swung into the main hall and took the elevator to the seventh floor, where the pages' locker room was. Mr. Farley had assigned me a locker, but until now I had never had occasion to use it. As I entered, four or five other pages applauded at the sight of the new boy on the block finally sporting a uniform. Later I was pleased to notice, I guess because of the uniform, that I was finally not being treated any different from the others. Happily, I had the feeling I had been on the job much more than a week, although I was a long way from being considered part of the furniture.

After dinner that night, old Mike told me to go up on the roof and pick up a bucket of steam which, he told me, was to have been dropped there about twenty minutes earlier by a new special airmail night delivery system. I was then to bring it down to master control. If it had been anyone else but Mr. Farley I might have said, "You've got to be kidding," but old Mike was not one to fool around. He always seemed so serious. So up I went and for the best part of a half hour I searched in the dark for the bucket of steam, getting more frantic every minute, scared to death old Farley might fire me, even on my first day in uniform, if I returned downstairs empty-handed. Heart pounding, down I went. When they spotted me the screams of laughter could be heard all over the thirteenth floor. Mike Farley must have busted a gut, and Alvin Simmons in the coat room was nearly rolling on the floor while Georgia Price, the hostess, was trying her lady-like best to control herself. Such was my baptism at NBC.

At Christmas time that year, 1931, the Radio City Music Hall opened its doors for the first time with, it was reported, a magnificent show featuring all the stars it was possible to assemble on its huge stage. Our page staff was called into service to help out, but I was one of the skeleton staff who stayed behind, working a normal evening at NBC, because I was low man on the seniority pole. Same thing happened when the new Waldorf Astoria Hotel opened on Park Avenue around that time. The old Waldorf, which had stood at Fifth Avenue and 34th Street for many years, had been torn down. It was being replaced by what would become the tallest edifice in the world, the Empire State Building, with over one hundred stories, a far cry from the time the Woolworth Building of my boyhood held that honor.

January of 1932 arrived and with it the end of my first semester at Manhattan College. Even though my intentions were the best when I took the page boy's job, as the weeks turned into months I had pretty much come to realize it just wasn't working. The onerous schedule I had accepted for myself was proving more than I could handle. Much more. My very poor grades told the story. Although I had insisted to my parents and to myself that I could get my required studying done while commuting on the subway, that had not happened. What with all the hustle and bustle that goes on in the subway, I found it very difficult to concentrate on the new and serious subjects I was supposed to be learning.

But the toughest thing was to dismiss from my head what had gone on the previous night while on the job at NBC—who I had seen and what I had done. And hopefully, could tonight possibly top last night? As to the other part of my earlier discussion which persuaded my mother and father that five hours sleep would be sufficient, well, I never really found out because I seldom got five hours for one reason or another. So during my classes at school I was never as wide awake as I was in the locker room donning my uniform just before Mike Farley's lineup at 4:45. Not just wide awake, but filled with excitement as to what the evening ahead might bring.

My bad grades called for another big decision—whether to quit NBC or to drop out of Manhattan College. My father thought the least he should do was to join me in a meeting with the headmaster of the college. On the appointed day Pop and I sat with him and seriously talked over the pros and cons of both options. What with the Depression getting worse, the hunger lines getting longer, and unemployment at an all-time high and growing every day, our meeting ended with an agreement, unofficial of course, that I would continue working another year, maybe two, then quit my job and start over at Manhattan College. Leaving the headmaster's office, Pop seemed genuinely pleased with the meeting and the decision.

With my scholastic situation settled for the next year or two, my attention became completely focused on my job. My constant worry of oversleeping in the morning disappeared and the luxury of going to bed without setting the alarm clock paid off handsomely. I enjoyed the assignments I was given and the people I met. Because the decision about delaying my college studies occurred in January of 1932, that date brings to my mind one of those people. His name was Russ Columbo, a young man in his mid twenties whose popularity as a romantic baritone was rising very rapidly. He was featured every night at

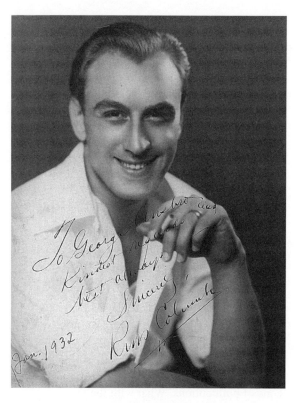

Russ Columbo was half of what the press in 1932 called "the battle of the baritones." The other half was Bing Crosby.

11:00 accompanied by an NBC house orchestra directed by Hugo Mariani. Both he and his manager, Con Conrad, had befriended me and on occasion would use me as a gofer. My reward was that they asked old Mike Farley to let me guard Russ's studio from the inside while his program was on the air. After a few weeks of such guarding I began to feel like one of the family. It was one of the smaller studios with nobody inside during the broadcast but me. Here I was only in my fourth month as a page boy, and I had become quite close to this up-and-coming radio personality. At the same time that his star was rising, so was that of another young singer by the name of Bing Crosby who was heard on CBS every night. The press, mostly the radio columnists of the day, had a field day reporting on what they called "the battle of the baritones." I still sentimentalize when, on occasion, I

open my album of ancient radio trivia and am reminded of these thoughts when I come across Columbo's photo, with his handwritten inscription—"To George Ansbro: Kindest regards and best always. Sincerely, Russ Columbo, January 1932." Not too many years later his career came to an abrupt end. He had been visiting at the home of an old friend in California who had a remarkable collection of antique guns. As he was examining one of them, it slipped and when it hit the floor, it discharged, causing the bullet to ricochet off the wall. In rebounding it pierced the skull of my friend Russ Columbo, killing him instantly.

Around the same time as the so-called "battle of the baritones," the press (this was way before the word *media* came into common usage) concocted another alleged battle. Because the two participants were tenors, their encounter was labeled, what else, "the battle of the tenors." Morton Downey, who had already gained quite a reputation as a tenor, was paired on the same program with another tenor who had become big on the West Coast, Donald Novis. They would alternate singing solos, but for whatever reason, the producer never had them mix it up in a duet. To my way of thinking, it was strange programming.

Other prominent names heard regularly on NBC in the early thirties included Jessica Dragonette on the *Cities Service Concert Customer Hour* with a large orchestra conducted by Rosario Bourdon and Ray Knight's *Koo Koo Hour*, which was an early forerunner on radio of the kind of comedy shows such as *Saturday Night Live* that would later appear on TV. A gentleman by the name of Cesare Sodero was conductor of the orchestra at the Metropolitan Opera House. He also directed the *Slumber Hour*, which ended at midnight, the same time I finished work. Old Cesare lived a block away from me in Bay Ridge, Brooklyn, so several nights a week we would ride home together on the subway. Another musical name of the day was

Harold Sanford, whose forte was directing light opera. They used to say Harold actually wrote a lot of the music Victor Herbert was credited with.

Billy Jones and Ernie Hare, the "Happiness Boys," had an enviable run on the air sponsored by Happiness Candy, and when their price got too sweet for the Happiness Company they were promptly picked up by the Interwoven Company, which renamed them the Interwoven Pair. With the same old act of songs and patter, they continued to enjoy many more years of popularity peddling their sponsor's socks.

10

ON THE CHEAP TO ALBANY

In those early days it seemed everybody knew everybody else. The executives and their secretaries, general employees, musicians, and performers were friendly toward us page boys and frequently addressed us by name. We, in turn, knew their names—it was part of our job. Among the employees was a group that caught my attention from the start, the announcing staff. More than anything else it was probably because one of its members was Milton Cross, whom I had first known on the *Children's Hour*. He had greeted me warmly when I appeared as a new page and wished me well. If he happened to be in the company of other announcers and I would pass by, he would stop and introduce me to them with a few pleasant words about my having been one of the "kids" on his show, which by now had been renamed *Coast to Coast on a Bus*. Mr. Cross was truly a gentle person, a gentle man whose affection for children was one of his many endearing qualities. Years later I was to learn of the sorrow he and his wife Lillian endured, losing their only child when she was a little girl.

Some of the other announcers, like Mr. Cross, were familiar names to the public because of the popularity of the shows they appeared on. James "Jimmy" Wallington was a good example. In 1932, when he was 25 years old, he was the announcer for the comedian Eddie Cantor for an hour every Sunday night. But besides announcing the show and doing all the Chase and Sanborn coffee commercials, he played stooge to Mr. Cantor and was the foil for many of Cantor's pranks. Another program he did was the *Fleischmann Hour*, featuring Rudy Vallee, his orchestra, and celebrated guests.

These two shows alone made Jimmy Wallington a household name.

It was pretty much acknowledged that Graham McNamee was America's best known announcer. He first achieved fame in 1924 when the Democratic National Convention in Madison Square Garden seemed to never end. It went on for weeks. It was the first political convention ever broadcast, and the sheer novelty of being able to listen, uninterruptedly, to such an important event practically guaranteed an enormous audience. During those weeks it was Graham McNamee alone at the microphone who kept the radio audience informed of the goings on. The job he did during that convention, it was said at the time, caused sales of radio sets to skyrocket, as well as his reputation as an announcer. His devoted fans became legion and kept him on top of the heap for many, many years. It was he who announced all of the other great events of the twenties—the Democratic and Republican conventions of 1928, the inauguration of President Herbert Hoover in 1929, and several great tickertape parades through the canyons of lower Broadway led by beloved Mayor Jimmy Walker. Besides these giant public events, he took on sports, and before long he was equally renowned as a sports announcer, wearing that crown all through the thirties. He didn't begin to get serious competition as a sportscaster until the early forties, when Clem McCarthy was used to call most horse races and a young fellow named Ted Husing began to cut into Mr. McNamee's popularity by broadcasting many of the same events on CBS, thereby cutting somewhat into his audience. Nevertheless,

Mr. McNamee's overall prominence as a broadcaster was to continue in yet another role—straight man. He was cast as the foil, or stooge, for a very funny fellow named Ed Wynn who was billed as the Perfect Fool. McNamee would feed Wynn the lines, and Wynn's replies, together with his physical foolishness, would bring gales of laughter from the studio audience. The Perfect Fool's son, Keenan Wynn, enjoyed many years as a major personality in motion pictures.

Besides Milton Cross, Jimmy Wallington, and Graham McNamee, NBC boasted fourteen other announcers, each with his own distinctive sound. One of these was John S. Young. An NBC press release circa 1932 described him thusly: "One of the best-dressed men in America. Smart too. Studied at Yale, Cornell and Columbia, has lectured at Oxford and N.Y.U., holds honorary LL.D. Has different suit for every day in month, plus miscellaneous pieces, 300 neckties. Knows exactly what he will be doing 24 hours, 32 minutes, and 15 seconds hence, barring accidents. Likes music and drama most. Russian pajamas his only weakness. Born in Springfield, Massachusetts in 1902, single. Height 5'10½". Weight 168 lbs." I would add that John Young was a good-looking man, affable, outgoing, and an excellent announcer. He did many programs in the studios as well as "remotes." Any program from outside 711 was called a "remote," including pickups of dance orchestras from hotels or restaurants. I can recall two of his studio programs in particular. One was the *Catholic Hour* on the air every Sunday evening featuring a choir singing sacred songs. Its big attraction was a young priest, Father Fulton J. Sheen, whose radio sermons attracted increasingly wider audiences. Father's clerical status rose, in proportion to his fame, to monsignor and, while he was still a young man, to bishop. As Father Sheen's fame increased on the *Catholic Hour*, so too did the recognition of the name John S. Young. Of course, as with all religious programs,

there was no commercial sponsorship of the *Catholic Hour*. This rule has held fast right up until now.

John S. Young announced another program that enjoyed high ratings. It starred John McCormack, the Irish tenor of the Metropolitan Opera, the man whose voice I had so admired in my boy soprano days. The only others in the studio with Mr. McCormack during the broadcast were his exclusive piano accompanist, Teddy something, John Young, and, as often as I could wangle the assignment from Mike Farley, me. After Mr. Young opened with a commercial for Vince Mouthwash, John McCormack would take over. After greeting his listeners, he would talk about his first song. Next he would say "Play, Teddy," and Teddy would vamp a bit while John would help himself to a wee sip of gin into a paper cup he had just poured from a flask on the piano. This finished, he would open his mouth and pour forth his golden voice. Wow! Did I ever feel privileged to be right there, within touching distance, while this great man was singing to millions. He would never do the gin bit more than three times during the half hour program. The only movie he ever made, *Song of My Heart*, was making the rounds then. Maureen O'Sullivan made her debut in the picture, which was produced in Ireland.

One of the dance remotes that John Young did was Vincent Lopez and his orchestra from the very fashionable St. Regis Roof three or four nights a week. He was fortunate in that he had fans in three important segments of the radio audience— the religious from the *Catholic Hour*, the classical music audience of John McCormack, and the young at heart of all ages who tuned in to Vincent Lopez's popular dance music at the St. Regis.

In the fall of 1932, Mr. Young approached another page boy, Al Binney, and me to ask if we would like to drive to Albany with him and return in time for work the next day. He had decided to go, he said, on the spur of the moment while on the phone with a lady he was keeping company with, an actress who was playing in the road company of *Mourning Becomes Electra*, which had been a big hit on Broadway. Thrilled beyond words to be invited in a car with such a celebrity, we both said yes immediately. But this thought must have hit us at the same time—wouldn't it be pretty late to be starting out for Albany at midnight? Not to worry, he assured us. Shouldn't be any problem once he had spoken to Mike Farley, asking him to let us off two hours early so we could leave at 10 o'clock. Meantime, he suggested we each call home to get permission. Al Binney and I were really excited. We had both seen John Young's car parked on Fifth Avenue outside 711 many times, as had probably a lot of other NBC people, as well as total strangers. The reason it attracted all those envious stares was that it was a gorgeous 16-cylinder Cadillac roadster. Later on roadsters were called convertibles. The difference was that roadsters had rumble seats which could be opened and used for two passengers or kept closed, giving the appearance of a car trunk. Back then, any Cadillac might attract a car lover's eye. But this one, especially being parked in front of the prestigious studios of the National Broadcasting Company, with its top down, this simply demanded close inspection. Maybe, a stranger might think, just maybe if you stood here long enough you would see some big star like Rudy Vallee or Al Jolson drive it away.

When I called home, my mother was thrilled that such an important announcer as John S. Young would think enough of me to invite me to be a traveling companion. To her way of thinking, he must be a wonderful man because he was the announcer for the *Catholic Hour*. Why of course I could go. Did I have enough money? I told her not to worry because Al and I were his invited guests, and, he would probably put us up wherever he was staying and, of course, take care of our meals. Then she asked: "How about clothes? Overcoat?

After all if it's an open roadster, it could get mighty cold without an overcoat." I told Mom not to worry because I had worn my topcoat that day and it was only November, not January. I said that my topcoat would be just fine and I was sure if it got really cold, Mr. Young would put the top up and turn on the heat, making us nice and cozy, just like all the comforts of home. I thanked her for letting me go and said I would be home after work the next night.

Al and I ate dinner at the counter in Miller's Drugstore, both of us dying for ten o'clock to come so we could get in that fancy Cadillac and be off. When the time came, we quickly changed from our uniforms and were out on the sidewalk a few minutes after ten. Mr. Young was already sitting at the wheel of his knock-em-dead car waiting for us. Neither Al nor I had ever ridden in a rumble seat, so we asked him if we could sit in it for a while. He replied, "Sure, be my guests, help yourselves," which we promptly did. It was surprisingly comfortable. When he turned the ignition key, we could hear all sixteen cylinders respond and, in a jiffy, off we went, up Fifth Avenue, into the transverse at 79th Street across Central Park, and over to the new West Side Highway. Through Riverdale we went, into Westchester and then continued north. Of course, in 1932 there was no New York State Thruway. The roads, with few exceptions, were two-laners. As we progressed onward in this sensational sports car with our driver, a very well-known person in the world of radio, we didn't have to be hit over the head with a hammer to know that our celebrated chauffeur was not only exceeding the speed limit, but by a very wide margin. Before too long, it was not only our safety we were concerned about. We were freezing. Riding in a rumble seat might be fine on a beautiful July afternoon but not in the middle of the night in November, with no covering on us other than our topcoats and fedora hats. No gloves. No blanket. No nothing. To add to our distress, there was no way we could communicate with Mr. Young because at the speed he was driving it was impossible for him to hear us yelling our heads off to please stop so that we could join him in the front which was at least protected by the windshield from the freezing cold wind. Unhappily, but resigned to the fact that we would have to stay in the back, we crouched down on the floor, hoping to find it a bit warmer. It was not only terribly cramped and uncomfortable but not a whole lot warmer either. I prayed that a cop would stop us for speeding, reckless driving, whatever. Anything to make him stop. An hour or so later part of my prayer was answered. No cop stopped us, but he did stop at an all-night diner. Uncoiling our stiff, cold bodies, we looked up to see Mr. Young in his raccoon coat, hat, and gloves. We had mixed feelings, envy for his warm clothes, and relief that he had stopped. He was beckoning us to follow him in. We all three had coffee but nothing else. We ordered nothing more because he didn't. Nor did he invite us to. Over the coffee we explained how cold and windy it was in the back, so could we please sit up front with him? And because of our lack of warm clothes maybe he would even put the top up and the heater on. He said it was okay to move in with him, but about putting the top up, he was "afraid not." It would take too much time (that was before push-button mechanical tops came into use) which he didn't want to waste, and without the top up it would make no sense turning the heater on. Hearing this was quite a letdown, but we tried not to show our disappointment. Getting up from the counter, he asked what he owed. The man told him coffee was a nickel. The celebrated John S. Young put his hand in his pocket, took out a handful of change, selected a nickel, put it on the counter, and started out the door. You know, there are some moments in life you can never forget. Well, in my life that's one I've never forgotten. Al and I just stared at each other. We couldn't believe this was actually happening. With that,

John Young stuck his head back in the door, slightly impatient, to ask that we "move it" because he didn't want to lose any more time. Standing in the open doorway, he watched as Al Binney put a dime on the counter, saying very audibly, "George, it's my treat." To which of course I replied, "Thanks, Al."

Back in the car, having put the rumble seat down, Mr. Young was true to his word and allowed us to sit with him. But he didn't change his mind about putting the top up and the heater on. Having been fortified by a lousy cup of coffee halfway to Albany, we were now off on the second leg of our, to say the least, unusual trip. The only difference between the second part and the first was that Al and I were not freezing on the floor of the rumble seat but were freezing in the front seat. The fact that the windshield was there didn't make much difference because, at the speed we were traveling, the wind kept pounding us from the side.

Arriving in Albany, Mr. Young found a gas station that was open and while filling up asked where the nearest YMCA was. Before taking off again, Al and I, while using the bathroom, couldn't figure out why a man of his importance would even think of staying at the YMCA. It puzzled us. But not for long, however. Some minutes later, in a rather shabby section of town, he drove up to a dilapidated-looking building with an ancient sign hanging over the door, "YMCA." We were now relieved of our puzzlement. He was not staying there, we were. He told us to have a good sleep, and he would pick us up at eleven-thirty for the ride back. Oh, and be sure to eat first because he would prefer, if possible, not to stop and waste time. And with a wave, off he went. I don't remember exactly what the "Y" cost, but it was probably about a dollar and a quarter, Depression prices. As late as it was, Al and I had plenty to talk about before falling asleep. Next morning, after we paid for a sparse breakfast, Mr. Young picked us up right on schedule. And off we headed back to New York. In our favor, it was a bright, sunshiny day the entire trip.

When we went back to work the following night, it was hard not to share the pertinent details of our enviable trip with our eager and curious coworkers. However, Al and I had decided not to do so, at least for a while. Many years later our story evoked some good laughs from those who were older and wiser and who considered John S. Young and the word *cheap* to be synonymous.

11

TALES OF 711

This is as good a time as any for some random recollections of "711" as they occur to me in no particular order.

When B. A. Rolfe and his huge orchestra were dropped by Lucky Strike, the new Lucky format featured Walter Winchell in New York introducing name bands in different cities all around the country. He would blow a whistle and shout into the microphone, "Okay, America," at which point the just-introduced band leader in Chicago, San Francisco, Oshkosh, or wherever would take over until it was time for Winchell to introduce another band in another city. One night Mr. Winchell walked in with Jean Harlow, who was then at the height of her movie fame. Just being in the presence of the world-famous sex symbol was one thing, but when she asked me to go down to the drugstore for cigarettes—wow!

Buddy Ebsen was then a hoofer on Broadway, but he would later star on TV in the *Beverly Hillbillies* and even later as *Barnaby Jones*. One evening as I happened to glance down the hall where Studio E was located, there he stood, all six foot three of him, in a smooching embrace with Walter Winchell's secretary, his "Gal Friday," Rose Bigman.

A certain trumpet player, I forget his name, was afflicted with acrophobia, the fear of high places. He had once tried to jump out of a window on the thirteenth floor but was stopped just in time. Ever since then his poor wife had to come to work with him to make sure he didn't try it again. No, I don't think his name was Gabriel.

Freeman Gosden and Charles Correll, of the *Amos 'n' Andy* show, occasionally would visit from Chicago where they normally did their program. By now they were well on their way to being the biggest stars NBC had. On a couple of their visits, I was fortunate enough to be stationed on the fourteenth floor, where they broadcast from Studio L, an intimate, living-room-type studio, and I could watch them from the control room. It was common knowledge that they never performed before a studio audience. But Deak Aylesworth, the genial president of NBC, always dropped down from his office on the fifteenth floor to greet them cordially and then watch and listen to their hilarious performance from the control room. The only others there besides Mr. Aylesworth on those infrequent occasions were the audio engineer, the production man, and me. An experience like this is what made getting a check every week icing on the cake. Speaking of paychecks, I well remember that on payday we would go from our lobby through Miller's Drugstore, across 55th Street into the beautiful lobby of the St. Regis Hotel, where the cashier would obligingly cash our checks which, as pages, amounted to exactly $15. In those days nothing was taken out.

Moe Gale, who owned the Savoy Ballroom in Harlem where such later stars as Ella Fitzgerald had their start, sold NBC on the programming idea that the Pickens Sisters could be NBC's answer to the Boswell Sisters, who were on CBS. In reality, however, they never achieved the heights of the Boswells. I remember when the Pickens trio first started; only two of them were really sisters, Jane and Helen. Little Patti was only about thirteen or fourteen, and she would drop around occasionally with her schoolbooks. When she reached sixteen or so, they fired the ringer and Patti took her place. And in a couple of years when she quit to marry a tenor, Robert Simmons, the trio broke up. It probably would have anyway because Helen "drank a little." Incidentally, Patti's husband must have strained something reaching for a high note because he dropped dead not too many years later. Jane kept on soloing but never caused Connie Boswell, by now also soloing, to lose any sleep. When Jane stepped out of the singing limelight, she scored very high on the New York society circuit. She became the wife of Walter Hoving, the chairman of Tiffany's.

Among the NBC house musicians, I can still see old Miff Mole, the trombone player, and Ross Gorman, the saxophonist. Later, when the Dorsey brothers became big, Tommy graciously admitted it was Miff who really taught him the wonderful finesse he had mastered on the trombone. And, likewise, Jimmy Dorsey credited Ross Gorman with much of his success in becoming a virtuoso of the sax.

A man who remained with NBC for many years as a news executive did occasional on-the-air news reports at that time. His name was William Burke (Skeets) Miller. He became famous because of interviews he had done in 1925 with Floyd Collins, a poor unfortunate who was trapped in a mine cave-in somewhere in Kentucky. Skeets was 21 and the only radio reporter small enough to crawl into where Collins was trapped. His interviews, with millions listening, and his bravery were largely credited with comforting Floyd Collins while he was still alive. Skeets Miller became a celebrity overnight. Deservedly so.

I can remember being part of the page boys' guard of honor when the king of Siam came to inspect the studios at 711. His host in New York was Clarence Mackey, who was with the king on this occasion. Mr. Mackey was chairman of the board of Postal Telegraph which, at the time, was Western Union's biggest competitor. Not too long after he visited NBC with the king, Mackey's daughter Ellen married Irving Berlin, who at the time was just making a name for himself as a song writer. Rumor had it there were fireworks in the Mackey household because Irving was Jewish. Despite such a rocky beginning, as most everyone knows, Mr. and Mrs. Irving Berlin enjoyed the happiness of marital bliss far longer than most other mortals.

In 1932, Florenz Ziegfeld, perhaps the greatest theatrical producer of his time, passed away. He had been instrumental in having another theatre, much smaller, constructed atop the New Amsterdam Theatre on West 42d Street. He had used this smaller theatre for intimate review-type shows other than his world-famous *Ziegfeld Follies*. The National Broadcasting Company, even then, was bursting at the seams for additional studio space. Accordingly, after Ziegfeld's death NBC leased the small theatre and converted it into a broadcasting studio, the first of its kind anywhere. The seating arrangement for an audience was left intact. The stage also remained pretty much the way it had been except for one thing. Instead of a typical theatre curtain, NBC installed an all-glass curtain to keep out any sounds that might disturb the program in progress onstage. The thinking then was to accommodate an audience's curiosity in wanting to view a program but not allow that audience to be heard on the air as part of the action. Today the very thought of such a thing is hard to imagine. Well, this experiment didn't last very long. One afternoon the curtain got stuck in an "up" position. Nobody could get it down before air time, so the program that night was the very first audience participation show ever with lots of applause and laughter and all of it heard on the air. This accident clearly indicates that audience participation shows were inevitable. Their huge success has proved that over these many years.

The New Amsterdam Theatre was

literally the house of hits. It was the home of many highly successful, long-running Broadway shows of the twenties and thirties. As a page boy I was assigned with others to usher at NBC's theatre upstairs over the New Amsterdam on broadcast nights— Rudy Vallee's *Fleischmann Hour* on Thursdays, Eddie Cantor's *Chase and Sanborn Hour* on Sundays, etc. The thing I liked best about being assigned there was a stairway. This particular stairway led from a room off the stage down to the top balcony of the New Amsterdam. During the run of any smash hit, most of the house was sold out in that big theatre except for a few seats in the last rows of the top balcony. While seated high up near the ceiling, I saw my first Broadway show, *Fifty Million Frenchmen*, a musical starring William Gaxton, Victor Moore, and Vivienne Segal. Another biggie I remember seeing from my elevated perch was George White's *Murder at the Vanities*, a highly successful musical mystery. Back then, curtain time at all Broadway shows was 8:45 P.M., and the New Amsterdam was no exception. The NBC programs originating upstairs were mostly on the air from 8 to 9 P.M., which meant that we ushers couldn't leave until the studio audience had cleared out. Therefore, we could never get downstairs until 9:15. And in my case, if I had to be back at 711 for Russ Columbo's program at 11, I would have to leave at 10:30. As a result we never really got to see these wonderful shows in their entirety. But we loved the fun of it anyway. One thing was for certain, I sure looked forward to ushering at the New Amsterdam roof, especially when a new show was booked into the theatre downstairs.

Another tidbit pops into my mind that happened in 1932. It concerns a chap whose name was Harry Cohn. Mr. Cohn was a young gossip columnist on the *New York Graphic*, a tabloid which specialized in sleaze. It was generally acknowledged that the *Graphic* was at the low end of the totem pole as far as newspapers were concerned, and the Cohn column was proof enough of that assertion. Like many other newspaper people, he often hung around 711 to get stuff for his column. One night one of the pages, Bob Lamkie, refused to let him in to a particular broadcast because the show was already on the air. Bob was only doing his job. Absolutely livid, Cohn carried on so with Lamkie that he actually threatened to go to John F. Royal, the vice president in charge of programs, and get Bob fired. But Bob, knowing that Cohn was pretty much disliked around NBC, stood his ground. The incident was finally settled when Mike Farley told him to shut up and leave. I guess the reason this less than earth-shattering incident has stayed with me all this time is that years later the same Harry Cohn went on to Hollywood and wound up as the all-powerful head of Universal Pictures where, it was said, he toyed with the lives and careers of even the biggest stars with ruthless abandon. I'm very glad Mr. C. never had anything to do with my life.

A couple of other executives come to mind. One was a lady. Not just any female, but a real lady. Bertha Brainard by name, was a vice president of the program department, and this was eons before the feminist movement started. As I remember, she had charm, good looks, and brains. She also had the respect of those who came in contact with her as well as those who worked under her. In the late thirties, I recall, she married the head of her production department, Bill Rainey. Then there was that great little guy, John de Jara Almonte, the very personable official NBC greeter. We would kiddingly refer to him as the vice president in charge of handshakes. He was just as smooth with Mrs. Cornelius Vanderbilt when she would occasionally drop by as he was with Al Smith, Babe Ruth, or Giulio Gatti-Casazza—the boss of the Metropolitan Opera.

When we pages would assemble every day at quarter to five for lineup, among other things, we would be given our various assignments, including what floor we would be on that night. Seldom did a page work the same floor two nights in a row, which was great. Boredom never set in. Up until now I've only talked about the floors where the broadcasting studios were located, the thirteenth, fourteenth, and fifteenth. On the twelfth floor were the offices of the production staff and several rehearsal studios. The eleventh floor was the headquarters of the NBC Artists' Service. Those who performed on NBC's airwaves, for payment, had ten percent deducted from their checks by the Artists' Service. This was discontinued in 1938 when AFRA came into existence. AFRA began as the American Federation of Radio Artists. Some years later, when television became recognized as something that might very well catch on, might even be here to stay, the letter "T" was added. Thus AFTRA became the new name of the performers' union.

Sometimes the craziest things stick in one's memory. Like the eleventh floor. After five o'clock, when most of the regular employees had left, the page boy on duty sat there in almost total solitude at the reception desk. It was great if you had a good book. Of course, inevitably, some members of the Artists' Service would find themselves with their desks piled high and working overtime a few hours. Two such come to mind. One was Ernest Chappel, who in later years would become a very busy freelance announcer. One of the many products he sold on radio for a long time was Pall Mall cigarettes. His fellow announcer on those commercials was Cy Harrice. Ernie would do hard sell for 55 seconds pushing Pall Malls at you. Then Cy's mellifluous tones would be heard in the remaining 5 seconds seducing the radio audience with the line, "And they are mild." I've been told that Ernie Chappel was less than happy because Cy Harrice received exactly the same remuneration for his 5 seconds of work as Ernie received for 55 seconds.

The other artists' representative I can still visualize was Richard Himber. This was several years before he went on to become a highly successful band leader, one of the real biggies in the "Big Band" Era. What sticks out in my mind about Richard Himber? Well, I'll tell you. To get to the men's room from his office, he had to walk across the eleventh-floor lobby past three elevators and my reception desk. The return trip, of course, was exactly the same in reverse, except that he would never stay in the men's room long enough to button his fly. The process of fly buttoning didn't begin until he left the john. This was a few years before zippers came into vogue; they probably hadn't even been invented. He would continue what appeared to be a monumental task of buttoning his fly as he walked back all the way across the lobby and, still fly fidgeting, would enter his office. On nights when I would be assigned there and was perhaps into a good book it was time out from the book so as not to miss Richard Himber's performance. Guaranteed. At least once an evening. I would sit there just fascinated. After some checking around with pages and hostesses who worked on the eleventh floor in the daytime, when the sofas and chairs were pretty well occupied with folks waiting to keep appointments with the Artists' Service, I learned that the same thing happened in the daytime. It made no difference—day or night—Mr. Himber's bizarre behavior never varied. His wasn't just a "fly-by-night" situation.

NBC occupied only two other floors below the eleventh—the seventh and the third. On the seventh floor, aside from the pages' locker room, were offices of the staff members involved in company funds—comptroller, cashier, etc. Their immediate boss was NBC's treasurer, Mark Woods, but he as the exalted money person of the company was on the fifteenth floor with the top brass beginning with Deak Aylesworth, the president, and George McClelland, the executive vice president. Mr. McClelland was credited with being the father of commercial broadcasting. It was generally understood that Marconi's invention became so commercially successful in a relatively short time because Mr. McClelland pursued his vision of selling broadcast time to advertisers. Sadly, in spite of his business success, his personal problems became so overwhelming that one day he shot himself at his desk. His replacement as NBC's number two executive was Richard C. Patterson, who, after not too many years with NBC, took over as the official greeter of the city of New York when Grover Whalen quit that job to become the boss of the New York World's Fair of 1939.

Last, but not least, floorwise, was the third. I should say last, but definitely not least. Because the third floor at 711 was where old man fate had a trump card up his sleeve with my name on it. The main business on that floor was the NBC Press Department, occupying a considerable amount of space. The boss man was a gentleman named Johnny Johnstone, and under his aegis the literati of newspapers and magazines dropped by regularly for whatever morsels concerning NBC talent they might pick up worthy of printing. Such people as Jimmy Cannon, who had a radio column in the *New York World-Telegram* some years before he became celebrated as one of the top sports writers in the country. Nick Kenny, who was famous for his radio column in the *New York Daily Mirror*. Jo Ranson who wrote a daily radio column in the *Brooklyn Daily Eagle*, and many such others appeared there quite often, always in search of something of interest to write about.

After a while I developed cordial relationships with a lot of these people of the press when I was on duty on the third floor. One in particular became an influence in helping things work out for me the way they did. Let me explain. The gentleman I speak of was C. J. Ingram, the radio editor of the *Jersey Journal*, a daily newspaper circulated in northern New Jersey. As editor, he also wrote a regular column under the pseudonym "One Dialer" in which he kept his readers informed of happenings in the world of radio. He also hosted a half-hour program on Sunday afternoons on WAAT, Jersey City, which had close ties to his paper. Even though the station had no network connection, it enjoyed a large audience in North Jersey as well as the entire New York metropolitan area. Largely because of this extensive coverage, together with the fact that he was held in high regard by the people in the radio community, any invitations to guest on his program were seldom turned down. The biggest stars made the trek to Journal Square on any given Sunday to chat with "C. J.," as they called him, and also to throw in a few songs, a few jokes, or whatever. The fact that these appearances were gratis was an indication of the way the stars felt about C. J. If he had had to pay the guests their usual high fees, his program would have collapsed in no time.

Sometime in December of 1932, Mr. Ingram stopped by my reception desk and engaged me in a friendly chat, mostly about how I liked my job and where did I think I might like to go from there. I told him I loved being a page and hoped one day to be a performer, preferably an announcer. I said I was fortunate that right under my nose here at 711 were several fine NBC announcers I had already been observing and I had high hopes some of their expertise might wear off on me if I were to continue to study their individual techniques. I told him that no two sounded alike, yet all were excellent. I admitted I also listened to the CBS staff announcers, and in all honesty, they were every bit as good and as professional as our friends here at NBC. He then inquired if any of my fellow pages had aspirations similar to mine. My answer was that probably all of them did in one way or another. Then came the biggie, though it wasn't a question. C. J. Ingram suggested I keep my eyes and ears open for potential talent among my cohorts and select three other pages and put together an outline for a half-hour program of fun, frolic, and lightheartedness. This done, I was to show him the script and if he approved, he would let us take over his time on the air one Sunday afternoon. And he would see to it that WAAT threw in the house orchestra. Wow! I was overwhelmed. I also wasted no time.

Within a few days, I came up with three other pages who seemed just as excited as I was about the prospect of doing our own show. Bruce Wallace would write the script and direct. Harvey Gannon, Bob Lamkie, and I would perform. It would be called "A Radio Nightmare" and would consist of satires and burlesques of popular radio features and lampoon popular personalities of the day. In short order, Mr. Ingram was shown the script and approved it, met the boys and approved. He arranged to have us rehearse with Tommy Gordon and the house orchestra at WAAT and booked "A Radio Nightmare" on the air the following Sunday in place of his regular *Stardust* program. The following Sunday happened to be Christmas, and our show proceeded with nary a hitch. The enthusiastic reception our efforts received from people at the station made the day all the more festive. Best of all was the rave review the "One Dialer," C. J. Ingram, gave us in his column the next day. He ended it with this zinger—"It wouldn't surprise us to learn that John F. Royal is to have the boys put a similar show on for NBC network listeners."

Shortly after "A Radio Nightmare" aired, Jay Stanley contacted me. Jay was chief announcer at WAAT, and he said he was wondering if I would be interested in coming over to the station from time to time at my convenience to relieve the announcer on duty for a spell. He had been impressed, he said, by my work on our show. Even though he couldn't offer any payment, he wanted me to know that besides being helpful to him it would look

great on my résumé. Who in his right mind in my position could say no to a proposition like that? Experience was being handed to me on a silver platter, adorned with goodwill. The goodwill of the radio station and its people, and the goodwill of C. J. Ingram and the *Jersey Journal*. My instincts told me Jay Stanley didn't just do this on his own but had the approval of others before extending the invitation. "Yes, Mr. Stanley," I replied. "I would be very happy to. When would you like me to start?" He responded: "Anytime. It's up to you. I know you work nights on the page staff so how does noonish, for a few hours, sound? Of course I won't expect you to come every day, only when you can. And stay as long as you like. On your day off for instance. Oh, and by the way, please call me Jay. In Jersey City we're less formal than on Fifth Avenue." When I asked, "Will tomorrow be all right?" he replied, "Great."

Thus it was that on that long ago "tomorrow" during Christmas week in 1932, three weeks before my eighteenth birthday, I did my first stint as an announcer. Jay Stanley introduced me to Rawls Hampton, the announcer I was to spell. Rawls, a man my father's age, showed me the copy book containing the commercials to be aired and the program sheet with the records to be spun. This was before announcers did the actual spinning. That chore was performed by the engineer on the other side of the glass in the control room. With the approach of 12 o'clock, Rawls Hampton signed off, signature music was played, a time beeper went out over the air, Rawls left the booth, and I was on my own for the next two hours. And, as it turned out, not only for those two hours, but for well over a hundred thousand more hours before my retirement from announcing in 1990.

12

CALL FOR PHILIP MAWRREESS

So there I was, first time ever, in an announce booth. Understandably, I don't recall what records were played. But I do remember, will never forget, the first commercial I read. Schainuck's was the name of the men's clothing store I went on about, and on and on, for a full page and a half. A couple of more records, each with ad-lib intros (another newie to my vocabulary) followed by a different, but just as long, Schainuck's plug. So it continued until two o'clock when Rawls Hampton returned, thanked me, and took over again. Jay Stanley called me from home to say he had listened while he was having lunch. He had some nice things to say as well as a couple of pointers. On the whole he was very encouraging and hoped I would be back soon again. Which indeed I was, again and again and again.

Station WAAT didn't only offer recorded music to its listeners. It also included in its schedule occasional live entertainment. Which is why they employed a house orchestra of seven or eight pieces. One such program featured a young singer named Jimmy Brierly whose specialty was romantic ballads. He was billed as the "Troubadour of the Moon," and indeed, he had a very pleasant and romantic sound. One day when I was doing my thing in the announce booth, he came in while a record was playing and introduced himself. He wanted to know if I would mind also announcing his program, as long as I was coming to the station so often. My answer was pretty straightforward. "How could I mind? Why would I mind?" I went on to explain I was

flattered to be asked and very pleased because it would be a whole new broadcasting experience for me. His invitation was a further source of encouragement because my instincts told me he had surely consulted with the station management before approaching me. It was an indirect, but pleasant, way of showing their confidence in me.

Announcing Jimmy Brierly's program, doing the record show with commercials for Schainuck's et al., and my nightly stint at 711 added up to a pretty busy, yet highly enjoyable schedule. Indeed, to use the old cliché, I loved every minute of it.

The "Troubadour of the Moon" and I hit it off just fine, both on and off the air. One day when his show had been canceled for one reason or another he called me at the station to invite me to his house for lunch. He told me he lived in Newark with his parents, and he gave me the street and number. Even though I had never been in Newark before, I followed his instructions for trolley cars, etc., and eventually found myself at his house, a turn-of-the-century, four-story brownstone with a high stoop at the main entrance leading into what was then called the parlor floor. As brownstones generally do, his looked just like all the others on the block with no distinguishing marks. If you didn't have the exact address, you would never know one from the other. As I climbed up the stoop, I became aware of the sound of music, good popular music—jazz, as a matter of fact. As I neared the top I realized it was coming from inside and was easily heard because, being summer time, it was coming through the screen door. After I rang the doorbell, the volume decreased slightly, and Jimmy Brierly's voice greeted me from atop the stairs to the third floor, saying to come right in and make myself at home, he would be down in a jiffy.

Happy to know that he also liked jazz as I did, instead of only the sentimental ballads which he usually sang on his program, I pushed open the screen door, stepped into the front hall, and automatically turned into the large room on my right, the parlor. If I had been the fainting type, that's when it would have happened. There at the far end of the room lay a well-dressed elderly gentleman in a casket. What an incongruous situation—the corpse in front of me and loud jazz filling the room from upstairs. Just about then, thank God, my host came into the room from upstairs. One look at my face and he knew he had blown it. Quickly he ushered me out of there and up the stairs to the third floor living quarters, gave me a cold glass of water and sat me down to explain. First, and most important, that he was mortified. He continued, saying that it had become a part of his life and he gave it very little thought, but his father was an undertaker. And then, as if he had read my mind, he answered the question on the tip of my tongue. No, there was no funeral home sign on the outside of the house because the old one had gotten into such bad condition his father was having a new one made. We did finally settle down to a tasty lunch which the "Troubadour of the Moon" had prepared himself. But, try as I may, it took a little while to get over the unexpected situation I had walked into downstairs in the parlor on my way to lunch.

Ray Diaz was a page who didn't have to attend the 4:45 lineup every day because he worked exclusively at night in the announcers' office. Ray told me about a new announcer who had been hired and fired on the same day. His sin? Well, first I must explain that when an announcer was scheduled

to do a program involving music, classical music mostly, his program sheet contained the pertinent information such as the name of the program's musical conductor at the top of the page. Then, listed on the left side in numerical order were the titles of the selections to be played. On the right was the composer's name and to the right of that the name of the arranger. But more often than not the arranger's name just didn't merit mentioning. It was entirely up to an announcer in his ad-lib introduction to each selection. For instance, he might say, "The next selection was composed by Johannes Brahms and arranged by So-and-So." But usually So-and-So's name didn't mean a thing to the listening audience. That's where an announcer's judgment came in. The unfortunate announcer who fell from grace on his first day was assigned such a classical program. Somewhere into the show his boss, Pat Kelly, who was listening in his office, was horrified to hear him say "The next selection was composed by Rimsky and arranged by Korsakov." End of story. End of job.

I never did know if John F. Royal, NBC's all-powerful vice president of programming, heard our program "A Radio Nightmare" on WAAT. But if he didn't, then someone mighty close to him must have whispered something good about us in his ear. One evening after our lineup, Mike Farley told me Mr. MacFayden, a producer and director, would like to see me in his office. I knew he was on the twelfth floor, so off I went down the fire stairs having absolutely no idea what Mr. MacFayden, a man I hardly knew, could want of me. He greeted me pleasantly, with a big smile, and invited me to sit down. With that kind of a reception, I knew that what was coming couldn't be anything bad. He then bowled me over by saying he had been commissioned to put together a one-time program, a special featuring nothing but page boy talent. It had already been put on the schedule for broadcast on Friday, March 31, at 11:30 P.M. over WJZ and the

Blue Network. He had heard, he said, about what I had done on the WAAT program and just assumed I could handle the job of master of ceremonies for this show and was that all right with me? I'm sure that from the look on my face he knew I would give him no argument. He then went on to say he had already done some investigating about other talent the page staff might have to offer. He said he was happy to see that I was pleased about the idea and he would be in touch with me when he had the rest of the package put together. He would arrange a time for the first rehearsal. My head spinning, I thanked him profusely and went to my assigned floor for that night.

By the end of the second week in March, Mr. MacFayden had completed casting the other pages to be on the show in addition to me as emcee. Jack Treacy, a page who worked in Bertha Brainard's office, was to write the script, and Milton Cross had agreed to do the announcing at the open and close. The program was to be called the "Brass Button Revue." Some of its features would be an orchestra organized and directed by a page, comedy and impersonations, songs, a hot guitar, a ukulele quintette, studio gossip by a Walter Winchell impersonator, and a jazz harmonicist. And if the excitement of the whole thing didn't get the best of us, I was to be the emcee.

The night of our big broadcast I happened to notice Jimmy Cannon standing just inside the studio door a few minutes before air time. Well, I thought, the well-known radio columnist of the *New York World-Telegram* didn't come to our studio just to get in out of the rain. His column in the paper the next day told his readers what he had observed in our studio and pretty much what he thought about our overall performance.

If Mr. Royal and his program chieftains had had any qualms as to how the show was received, I'm sure Jimmy Cannon's kind words laid such misgivings to rest. The quantity and the quality of mail we re-

Pages Come Into Their Own

Couriers for the Broadcast Kings Present Performance Themselves from WJZ Studio.

By JAMES CANNON,
World-Telegram Radio Editor.

THE studio page boys walk with the great. Stars tease them, and tip them. They guide captains through the crooked confusion of station corridors, and click their heels to broadcasting kings. But no one ever seems to know their names. They are quick, polite young men, who live in happy obscurity in the reflected radiance of those whose errands they do.

But the NBC pages eluded their anonymity for a half hour last night, and stepped through the looking glass into the land which goes on in your living room and mine on the other side of the microphone. They performed on WJZ in a jubilee of solemn enthusiasm, a jamboree of nervousness and rainbow chasing called "The Brass Button Revue." They loafed in whispering knots as the clock crept toward 11:30. They had doffed their gray, glittery-buttoned uniforms.

All seemed to have collars starched uncomfortably stiff. Their faces looked red and sore as if they had shaved too carefully. Their hair was polished until it gleamed in the glare of the studio lights.

Ansbro and Murphy Steal the Show.

GEORGE ANSBRO and Johnny Murphy were full of theatrical larceny. They snatched the show with an easy charm. Ansbro, a slight, handsomely dark chap with an oily voice, was the master of ceremonies. He seemed as capable as a lot of network announcers I have heard.

Murphy is a laughing lad who tries to be solemn. He directed his own orchestra, which plays the flashy, muffled rhythm of the Lombardos as most young orchestras do. Murphy tried hard to frown, and brandished his baton as if it were a king's sceptre, which performed a miracle with each gaudy flourish. But every time Murphy looked at his musicians he laughed.

Johnny seems destined to be a lady killer. The girl in blue with the black hair swirling over her shoulders kept giggling to her escort in the spectators' rows that Johnny was "too cute for words."

Exit Magnolia.

THERE was once a sprightly ragtime sonnet which hymned the yellow charms of a Southern belle and concluded:—"And what do you get—Magnolia!" Well, it seems that after you get Magnolia it turns out to be Mandy Lou. At least that is what happened to Artie Bell McGinty, the smiling Negress who impersonated Magnolia, a giddy servant, on Fred Waring's WABC jubilee.

After establishing the character of Magnolia the sponsors have been compelled to call their character Mandy Lou. Georgia Simmons, who is not a Negress, arrived in town several days ago and proved that she had used the aerial alias of Magnolia on West Coast and Middle West networks as far back as seven years ago. The character was the same type silly servant girl, and drawled her hokum, too. So from now on Magnolia is Mandy Lou.

Boston Marathon To Be Broadcast by NBC.

THE Boston marathon, a carnival of fatigue which April 19 straggles through the streets of the Massachusetts capital, will be broadcast either by WEAF or WJZ. The NBC will try a new trick. They will have a mobile transmitter on a truck following the runners and will break into the programs of the selected network to tell the tale during the day.

Lady with a Problem.

SHE is a luminous lady, a polished planet in the galaxy of the stars. There is a regal air when she stalks across a stage, and she can preach a sermon with an arched eyebrow. But the lady is very nearsighted and always wears glasses offstage.

The other night she came to NBC studios as a guest star. They gave her a script in an anteroom and she scanned it through her spectacles. There was an audience gathered to watch the program, and when she realized that the lady was upset. She was so sorry, but she didn't see how she could read the part without her glasses. And she would never permit her adoring admirers to see her with them on.

The sponsors pleaded. But the lady declined affably. She would go on, but would not use her glasses. She read her part all right, pressing it close to her pretty face. But once or twice she stammered as she overlooked a word and she didn't give the fiery performance the sponsors had desired as she strained to see the words. But the lady was satisfied. The public still had its illusion of her—a golden goddess untouched by any worldly troubles.

New York World-Telegram *columnist Jimmy Cannon reviews our "Brass Button Review" as he saw it in the studio.*

ceived also attested to that. Almost everyone who wrote liked what we had done and wished us well. In truth, it left us all on top of the world.

Those of us who appeared on the "Brass Button Revue" spent the next couple of days around the hallways of 711 happily accepting congratulations and taking bows. One day during this period of euphoria a young woman who was one of Bertha Brainard's secretaries asked me if I had heard the news about Philip Morris. My blank look was my answer so she continued, but now in a much lower tone of voice. She told me she didn't want to be overheard letting the cat out of the bag because the Philip Morris gossip concerned me. And now that she had opened the door on the subject she knew it wouldn't be fair to keep me in the dark. In a nutshell, what she let slip was the news that some top executives of the Philip Morris Company had heard and liked our show. They were seriously considering approaching me to work for their company in a huge new advertising concept aimed at increasing the sales of their cigarettes. Their thinking was to use a photograph of me in a snappy page's uniform offering an open pack of cigarettes to the viewer. Such a photo, with variations, would be used everywhere—billboards, newspapers, magazines, store windows, trolley cars, subways, etc. They were also going ahead with plans for two radio programs on NBC. What the content of the programs would be had not been decided yet, but one thing was for sure. The idea of a youthful page offering their cigarettes would be on both programs, and having liked my sound and been shown a group picture of the page staff by Bertha Brainard, they knew what I looked like and approved.

I was thrilled by the information my friend had just passed on to me, even though it had to remain hush-hush. At least until Miss Brainard or someone from Philip Morris or their advertising agency contacted me. And, boy oh boy, was that ever a hard secret to keep. When it reached the point where a couple of columnists printed the rumor, mentioning me by name, it got real tough denying it, which I had to do because I just didn't have anything to say about it.

I was pretty much beside myself when my informant asked to meet with me at the counter in Miller's Drugstore. I could tell by her voice it wasn't good news. She felt terrible, she said, for ever having told me in the first place without verification. But, she went on, at the time she had first told me, she knew that her boss, Bertha Brainard, had thought it was a done deal. With a few tears running down her cheeks, haltingly and rightfully embarrassed, she then told me that as far as I was concerned the bubble had burst. The Philip Morris people had dropped their plan to use me. They had become enchanted with, and were now definitely employing, someone else.

What happened was that two top executives of the company were in Chicago staying at the Palmer House. One of the bellhop staff attracted their attention. The reason he stood out so was because of his diminutive size. He was a midget. And no way could he possibly carry heavy luggage. Instead, his only function was to page people. "Call for John Jones," "Call for Sally Smith," etc. When Mr. Jones or Miss Smith responded, this handsome little guy would give them an envelope containing their message. Instead of him going around calling for So-and-So, the two executives envisioned him substituting the name Philip Morris for Jones or Smith. That's how their trademark line "Call for Philip Morris" was born. Almost on the spot they signed him up.

But I must confess—it was quite a letdown. Before too long their campaign was in full swing. Pictures of Johnny Roventini, that was his name, were everywhere. And each of their radio shows would open with the voice of Charles O'Connor announcing over the musical signature "Here he comes, stepping out of thousands of store windows, Johnny." Next Johnny would be heard with his "Call for Philip Mawrreess." Yes, that's how he kind of sang the sponsor's name. It proved to be one of the most successful advertising campaigns of that era and it went on for many, many years.

Because Lady Luck waved her magic wand over him one day in the lobby of the Palmer House in Chicago, young Johnny Roventini became the best-known and probably the most prosperous midget in the country. But in hindsight, looking back through all those decades, Lady Luck also did me a big favor by anointing little Johnny for that job instead of me. For countless, wonderful reasons.

13

SO LONG 711,
HELLO RADIO CITY

The main topic of conversation around 711 during the summer and early fall of 1933 was the gigantic move about to take place. Soon it would be "So long 711, hello Radio City." Or Rockefeller Center, take your pick. The Radio City Music Hall had opened around Christmas of 1931, and it occupied the northeast corner of Sixth Avenue and 50th Street, in what was then known as the RKO Building. Another theatre, every bit as beautiful but not quite as large, opened around the same time. It was the Center Theatre, and it housed first-run Broadway shows, musicals, and revues. The Center was on the southeast corner of Sixth Avenue and 49th Street, a part of what was then the U.S. Rubber Building. The new home of the National Broadcasting Company was to be the RCA Building on the Sixth Avenue block bounded by 49th and 50th streets.

During the period prior to the move when I would find myself with some spare time, I would stroll down Fifth Avenue, five blocks from 711 to the construction site. Somewhere inside this magnificent edifice was where I would "hang my hat" come November. And sometimes during those periods of personal inspection, I found myself attempting to peek into my future. There was no way at that crossroad in my life that I would be able to answer questions like: "After I'm ensconced there and I do know exactly where I'll hang my hat every day, how long will I continue wearing the uniform of a page? If I do get a job change at NBC, what might it be? How long before such a change might come about? If and

when it does come, will I be happy? If not, why?"

November came and with it the changeover. But we pages were not required to be there until the formal opening when broadcasting would actually begin. When that day arrived, we were all decked out in snappy new uniforms and proud as peacocks just to be there, to be in at the beginning of an entirely new era of the entertainment industry. This was the icing on the wedding cake officially proclaiming the marriage of radio broadcasting to "showbiz." Being part of such an auspicious occasion was indeed thrilling. So thrilling that the troubling questions which kept popping up in my mind gradually took a backseat.

An early article promoting Radio City read "Radio City, U.S.A.—Capital of Radio World—Home of RCA and NBC—Loftiest sign in U.S. identifies RCA Building in giant blazing neon letters. Soaring 850 feet above Fifth Avenue, Radio City houses 22 of NBC's soundproof studios." The loftiest sign the promo referred to was also probably the largest, as well as the simplest, just the three corporate letters of identification, RCA, each letter stretching three stories high, enabling the sign to be seen many miles away.

The night NBC's new headquarters officially opened was a gala occasion with a program in the prime-time hours which featured just about every NBC star as well as available super stars of stage and screen. The broadcast was in Studio 8H, which was four or five times the size of NBC's old Studio H, and the largest one in 711. My assignment that night was to wait under the NBC marquee on the 49th Street side of the building for a limousine which would drop off the chairman of the Columbia Broadcasting System, William S. Paley, and Mrs. Paley. With much inner excitement, I did. They arrived about 7:30, as did many other VIPs. Recognizing the youthfully handsome Mr. Paley from pictures I'd seen of him in the papers, I made myself known to him and his wife and escorted them into an elevator and out onto the eighth floor, where they were greeted by David Sarnoff, the chairman of RCA, Deak Aylesworth, NBC's president, and their wives. The Sarnoffs and the Aylesworths took over then and escorted Mr. and Mrs. Number One Competitor into Studio 8H and to their front-row seats.

While walking from the elevator to 8H, Deak Aylesworth lagged behind his guests for a moment and with a "Psst, young man" approach asked if I would be good enough to stay with the Paleys when the inaugural program was over and take them on a tour of the new studios. I replied with, "Why, of course Mr. Aylesworth." But, to comply with his request, I knew I would have to forfeit the pleasure of viewing the very first broadcast from Radio City with its galaxy of stars. It seems the other part of my evening's assignment was to wait inside 8H until the program ended and then escort Mr. and Mrs. Paley out of the building and to their waiting limousine. But now Mr. Aylesworth's request caused a slight change of plans on my part. I couldn't stay in the back of 8H and watch the show because in order to do his bidding I first had to find out a few things about the place myself, this being my first day actually on duty in Radio City.

I remembered I had seen all kinds of informative pamphlets piled high on the receptionist's desk outside 8H, so after I had made sure the Paleys were comfortable and happy with their hosts, the Sarnoffs and the Aylesworths, I made a

discreet beeline out of the studio and armed myself with some pamphlets containing the kind of information I should know before escorting anyone, much less Mr. and Mrs. William S. Paley, through this new broadcasting heaven on earth called Radio City. Next I went into Studio 8G. Finding it empty, as I expected, because all the action was in 8H, I plunked myself down and attempted to learn all I could about the new studios in the relatively short space of time I had.

When the big broadcast ended, I returned to 8H and, during the enthusiastic applause, approached Mr. and Mrs. Paley to indicate that I was at their disposal and would be happy to conduct them on a tour of the studios. Mr. Paley said that would be just fine if I could cut it down to a short version as they were expected at a reception within the hour. With a great feeling of relief, I replied, "No problem, Sir." And so for the next half hour, we visited as many studios as time would allow with me babbling on about things I had learned less than an hour before. As they were getting into their limousine, they both thanked me and allowed as how I had helped to make their evening more pleasant. As the car pulled away, I was reminded of an old saying, "Sometimes the bigger they are, the nicer they are."

The worldwide publicity which the new studios received had the desired effect. There were strong indications that people from all over were eager to tour this marvel of the age, which is just what the public relations people at NBC had hoped would happen. So, very quickly, a decision was made to accommodate them. In order to facilitate that decision, a staff of young men would be needed to conduct tours through the new studios. An NBC guide staff would be created. And for starters, some of the pages would be promoted to the new guide staff immediately.

Accordingly, a few days after the opening festivities several of us were sent across the street to the Radio City Music Hall's backstage area, where we were to gather outside the office of Mr. S. L. Rothafel. Mr. Rothafel was a celebrated figure in the entertainment industry who was known everywhere as Roxy. He had recently become the impresario of the Music Hall after several years as managing director of a theatrical palace just one block west, on Seventh Avenue, which in his honor was named the "Roxy." Now, as head of the Music Hall, he became the chief competitor of his former house of glory. When he was the boss at the Roxy, his chorus line was known as the Roxyettes. At the Music Hall, he called his new chorus line the same thing except for a slight twist. For the letters "x" and "y" he substituted "c" and "k." No longer the Roxyettes, the great chorus line became internationally famous as the Rockettes.

Roxy stepped out of his office and greeted us pleasantly. He asked us to please form a line from left to right so he could get a good look at us. After quietly looking us over for two or three minutes, he went over to the left end of our line and, continuing to study us, walked slowly toward the other end. As he moved along, he pointed to different ones and said "You," "You," "You." When he had finished, he stepped back and asked all of us he had selected to stay and said the others could leave.

That's how the NBC guide staff came into being, and that's how I got my first promotion at NBC, from pageboy to tour guide. The job, I was shortly to learn, would require the know-how and responsibility of conducting a tour of fifty people, five times a day, through the new NBC studios while supplying a running commentary and answering the tourists' questions. Admission to the tour was to be 50 cents. We guides were to receive $20 per week for the usual six-day week, an increase of $5. At the time, happy as I was to be selected, I found it hard to understand why we were

entrusted with such a vocal job without Roxy ever finding out if we could even speak.

Fortunately, I didn't allow that to bother me long. I settled into the job that I was thrilled to be doing very quickly. Conducting tours of up to fifty people for an hour and a half as many as five times a day was very challenging. Before too long I found I was becoming increasingly at ease with each new tour. The tourists, who were a cross-section of the world, generally listened with rapt attention to what I was telling them. Sometimes their questions were tough, but answering such questions was all part of the learning process.

A few of my fellow guides who had been hired after Radio City opened went on to become quite famous. When the early morning *Today* show first started, it was hosted by Dave Garroway. Gordon MacRae was to achieve stardom in motion pictures, mostly musicals, as a romantic baritone. Earl Wrightson, also a baritone, became known to the public in early television. During the fifties he was featured every Sunday on the Goodyear Show with Paul Whiteman and his orchestra. He continued for three more decades entertaining audiences in traveling Broadway musicals like *Kismet* as well as on the concert stage. There was another chap who conducted tours and reached the pinnacle of success in Hollywood. He was not one of us at NBC but was employed by RCA as a guide. The RCA guided tour included a visit to the observation tower as well as a peek inside the Radio City Music Hall. Our paths would frequently cross as I was ending a tour in the main hall of the building and he was leading his people toward the 50th Street exit to cross the street to the Music Hall. He was quite tall and hard to miss. He and I developed a "Hello, how are you? Nice to see you" relationship. His name was Gregory Peck.

14

MAY 19, 1934

A perfect example of why I enjoyed guiding so much and why I found it so rewarding is contained in a letter to Gordon Mills, an executive in the NBC Service Department which operated the guide staff. The writer, L. Earl Wilson, expressed his appreciation for my handling of his group, the Lehigh Alumni. He also asked if I would address a luncheon meeting of the Lions Club of New York, of which he was chairman of the program committee. A copy of his letter follows along with my reply and a "thank you" note from a prominent merchant who attended the luncheon at the Hotel Astor.

Between Mr. L. Earl Wilson's invitation to speak, written on April 30, and my appearance at the Lions Club luncheon on June 21, a lot was happening in my life. Sometime during April a rumor spread that there was a possibility our company would soon expand its announcing staff by one. But, and this was what interested some of us guides as well as pages and mailroom boys, NBC was not going to pick the new announcer from one of its affiliated stations, its usual method. Instead, according to the rumor, because of the Great Depression which had grown far worse since the Wall Street Crash of 1929 and was showing no signs of abating, NBC would pick the new announcer from among its own New York employees. And because such a person would not have had previous professional experience, he would not merit the status of the other staff announcers. Therefore, the new man would be called a junior announcer and would receive less money than the regulars. Of course it didn't take a genius to figure out that what was behind

this change in policy was the saving of a few dollars to show that NBC, like so many other companies, large and small, was willing to tighten its corporate belt to achieve corporate savings.

I mentioned earlier that when I was hired on the page staff at 711, a few pages did not work the floors. Instead they were "male assistants," the equivalent of a cross between a private secretary and an office boy. Tommy Velotta was one. He worked in the office of Richard C. Patterson, who replaced George McClelland as executive vice president after his death. Tommy's father was also at NBC. The senior Mr. Velotta was beloved by one and all as the official shoe shiner. Every day he would shine all the executives' shoes in their offices, starting with Deak Aylesworth, going down through the ranks, including many secretarial shoes along the way. He even came by the pages and guides' locker rooms once a week. Another page/male assistant was Ray Diaz. When I started on the page staff in 1931, Ray worked in the announcers' office as night assistant to Marley R. Sherris, the supervisor of announcers. Somewhere along the line Mr. Sherris was replaced by Patrick J. Kelly. In his job, Ray was privy to most of what went on concerning that office. He was very well liked by all of the announcers and by his boss, Pat Kelly. Because of his rather short stature, the announcers' term of endearment for him was "Chiefie." Soon after hearing the rumor that NBC would be hiring a junior announcer, I thought I would chance going to the horse's mouth, so to speak, for verification. But rather than approach Ray while he was in his office

THE HOST CLUB
<u>to All Lions</u>
HOTEL ASTOR
TIMES SQUARE.

April 30, 1934

Mr Gordon H Mills,
National Broadcasting Co.,
New York City

Dear Mr Mills:

While we were waiting for the various tours to be
organized last Friday night, following the Cities
Service broadcast at which a number of Lehigh Alumni
and friends were present, Mr Porter, brought in one
of your guides to keep the crowd pacified while they
were waiting. I understand this young man's name is
Ansbro.

He so impressed me with his ready wit and knowledge of
the events which had taken place since Radio City had
been opened, I asked Mr Porter, if it would not be possible to bring the chap over sometime in June, to give
us some rapid-fire comments on the various news events
and happenings that had taken place withing and without
the studios.

We have two open dates in June, the 14th and the 21st.
Would it be convenient to Mr Ansbro, to talk to us on
either of these dates? If it is, we should be very happy
to have you, or Mr Porter, bring him over with you.

As you may know, we meet at the Hotel Astor every Thursday at 12: 0 PM. The time for the talk would be about
thirty minutes, beginning at 1:15 and ending probably at
1:45 PM. If you can arrange this, we will appreciate it
very much.

A word or two about the arrangements last Thursday -- everyone
was delighted with the broadcasts and I am sure all enjoyed
the tours.

                        Sincerely yours,
(signed)   L Earl Wilson

                        Chairman of the Program
                        Committee

L Earl Wilson
IMD
1440 Broadway

A request to my boss that I address the Lions Club of New York.

June 15, 1934

Mr. Earl Wilson
Retail Research Assn.
New York City

My dear Mr. Wilson:

You requested from me an outline of some of the topics on which I
am going to speak at the Lions Club Meeting on the 21st. I had
originally intended to base my entire talk on the N.B.C., its programs, artists, studios, etc. When you asked me to tell something
about myself also, I was "stumped". Although I can't see where the
subject of "I" would prove any too interesting at such a meeting,
nevertheless, since you asked for it, it shall be there. (To be
truthful, the supply of material on that particular subject, I think,
is none too good.)

I am listing here several points to be spoken about:

    (1) How it came about that I should speak at this meeting.
    (2) Various happenings which took place, and outstanding things
         which I remember during my two years at 711 Fifth Avenue
         (NBC's old headquarters)
    (3) Tracing N.B.C. back to its formation.
    (4) N.B.C. headquarters in Radio City.
    (5) My first week, working as a page boy in the new headquarters.
    (6) N.B.C. Guide Tours and what they cover.
    (7) Unusual happenings and people on the tours.
    (8) The first tour I conducted through the new headquarters.
    (9) Various people whom I have met since I have been with N.B.C.
    (10) N.B.C. Announcers.
    (11) How it came about that I am now one of them.
    (12) Invitation of questions from members of the club.

Hoping that this will be satisfactory, I am

                              Sincerely yours,

                              George A. Ansbro

My acceptance letter.

LUNCHEON
AT THE LIONS CLUB

BEHIND THE SCENES
JUNE 21, 1934

in the
N.B.C.
STUDIOS

Mr. GEORGE ANSBRO
Broadcaster

Mr. Ansbro formerly acted as one of the guides for N. B. C. at Radio City.
Besides being an excellent talker, he will give us some interesting comments
regarding various news events and happenings that have taken place within
and without the studio. He will answer such questions as - How far does
Ed Wynn run? And why? What celebrities broadcast in costume? Etc., etc.
We are sure that you will find this half hour with Mr. Ansbro very interesting and worthwhile. So be sure to be on hand on the 21st.

THE LIONS CLUB *of* NEW YORK

LUNCHEON
MEETING
Every
THURSDAY

The
NATIONS
HOST
from
COAST
to
COAST

HOTEL
ASTOR
12:30

JUNE 21, 1934

A promotional piece sent to the Lions Club Members.

Paul Shotland, Inc.

ESTABLISHED 1896

Merchant Tailor-Importer

425 FIFTH AVENUE
NEW YORK
TELEPHONE CALEDONIA 5-7472

June 26, 1934

Mr. George Ansbro
    National Broadcasting Studio
      Radio City

Dear Mr. Ansbro:

    I wish to express my gratitude for having had
the pleasure of listening to your excellent and
instructive talk at the Lions Club, on Thursday,
June 21.

    Not only was your speech interesting, but it
was exceedingly instructive to a layman who is not
familiar with the inner circles of broadcasting
studio life. It was indeed, a great revelation to
me and I am sure that speaks for others as well.
Again, I thank you for this privilege and opportunity of listening to you.

        Very truly yours,

        Paul Shotland

My first fan letter.

working and possibly get in his way, I called and asked him if he would join me for dinner downstairs in the Kaufman-Bedrick Drugstore, which was the Radio City replacement for the Miller's Drugstore of 711.

When I brought up my question at dinner, Ray said he knew of the rumor and was surprised that no one had approached him about it before now. The answer was yes, it was true. In his position, up until now he shouldn't, therefore wouldn't, have talked about it. But, he said, "by tomorrow or the next day" a memo would go out from Pat Kelly to the heads of the mailroom, the pages, and the guides, confirming that what we all had heard as a rumor was now a fact. The memo would state that the position of junior announcer was being created and those interested in auditioning for the job should get in touch with Pat Kelly's office on the fifth floor. Before we left Kaufman-Bedrick, I left no doubt with Ray Diaz that, indeed, I was very interested in auditioning for the job. Ray laughed and said that under the circumstances I was the first to apply.

Two days later the arrival of Pat Kelly's memo was official confirmation of what Ray had told me. It also included the date of the audition, Thursday, May 17, about two weeks away. During that period I did a lot of "boning up" for the big day. Of course I was still going over to Jersey City on days off and whatever other spare time I could find. The announcers at WAAT, Jay Stanley and Rawls Hampton, were still pleased when I would arrive to spell them for a while, so when I told them about the audition they wished me well and volunteered to help me prepare for it in any way they could. I told them the one thing I thought I could use some coaching on was pronunciation of foreign names. In high school I had had three years of Latin and two years of Greek. And at Manhattan College I had struggled through one semester of Spanish before dropping out, and that was one of the subjects "el flunko" or however the Castillians might admit to not

getting a passing grade. Jay Stanley immediately went into his office and came out with a long list of foreign composers, operas, etc., each with the correct phonetic pronunciation, and it was mine to borrow for as long as I would need it.

During the next two weeks, I found myself going over and over, aloud, the pronunciation of these names until I came to feel pretty much at home with them. I also listened, with much greater concentration than ever before, to several of our NBC announcers, most especially to Howard Claney, whose sound and style I had come to admire very much.

On May 17, fourteen of us very nervous young men (no women in those days) were on hand to compete in the all-important audition which would reward just one of us with the much sought-after position of NBC network announcer.

The aspirants were from the mailroom, the page staff, and the guide staff. I thought the main competition for all of us was a fellow guide whose name was Hugh James because he had a fabulously distinctive voice. So the next day when I was told I had won, I could hardly believe it. Promoting someone from the uniformed ranks to join the celebrated members of the announcing staff had never been done before. It was indeed exhilarating. Not only because of the promotion itself but because I was getting publicity. The radio columns of the New York newspapers and the trade papers stated that Bert Parks of CBS would be "relinquishing his status as N.Y.'s youngest (22) Network Staff Announcer to the newly appointed George Ansbro (21) on the NBC Announcing Staff." Of course I was really only 19 because I had fibbed on my original application for the page boy's job.

Saturday, May 19, 1934, the day after I got the good news, was my first day as the first junior staff announcer at the National Broadcasting Company. On that happy day someone said I should get down on my knees and give thanks for the Great Depression because without it NBC would

Ladies and Gentlemen:

I am speaking to you for the purpose of trying
to become associated with the announcing staff of the NBC.

I understand there are four major steps in this
audition. The first is to test my diction. The second is
to determine my adaptability to the smooth-running commercial
continuity. The third is to test my selling force over the
air. And the fourth in order that you may judge my powers
of extemporaneous speech.

My language requirements may be judged by my pronunciation of the following names:-

> Cesar Cui
>
> Modeste Moussorgsky
>
> Josef Haydn
>
> Ottorino Respighi
>
> Ruggiero Leoncavallo
>
> Giovanni Sgambati
>
> Charles Gounod
>
> Leo Delibes

Among the works best known to the radio audience
we include the following:-

> Die Fledermaus by Johann Strauss
>
> Lucia di Lammermoor by Gaetano Donizetti

One portion of the NBC announcer's audition.

never have created the job of junior announcer in order to save a few bucks. The daily routines for the existing senior announcers and the newly created job of junior announcer were essentially the same. Only the weekly salary was different—$45 for them, $25 for me.

When I doffed my uniform for the last time in the guides' locker room the day before starting my new job, the fellows made a fun ceremony out of it, threatening to take the uniform out on the street and auction it off to the highest bidder, bringing both laughs and a fond and sentimental farewell to the joys I had shared with my peers in that locker room. But now, in my new job, the world I had known at NBC was to change quite a bit for me. While conducting a guided tour, among many other things I would find myself telling my people about a particular responsibility an announcer had in addition to announcing his program. It was known as the announcer's delight, so-called because when first trying to learn how to operate it an announcer found it anything but a delight. It was very difficult for all new announcers to grasp the significance of the array of buttons, with corresponding white lights and red lights, each one having to do with a particular segment of the Red Network or the Blue Network. It was understood that pushing a wrong button would invite network chaos, to say nothing of possible announcerial heart failure. There was an announcer's delight in every studio. It was sort of a desk top, two feet wide and almost chest high extending from the wall. It was always located near the control room window to make any facial or hand communication easier. Several years would pass before the company agreed to do away with the announcer's delight and transfer the technical responsibility it represented into the control room where, in my opinion, it belonged in the first place.

Newcomers like me received instruction and guidance from the experienced staff announcers to whom things like the announcer's delight had become second nature. During my first couple of days, Pat Kelly had me tag along with different staff members as each followed his assigned schedule.

Of course, I was to observe closely everything the announcer did. Especially when he operated those all-important buttons on the announcer's delight. The men I followed around those first days were both affable and good instructors. Having already known, pretty much, about those scary buttons from explaining them as a guide to the people on my tours, I guess I was several steps ahead of any apprentice announcer who had never seen one before. That made it much easier for my instructor/announcer. On the third day of my indoctrination, I was scheduled to be with announcer Clyde Kittell while he did a 15-minute program with the two-piano team of Muriel Pollack and Vee Lawnhurst in Studio 8C at 7:45 A.M. Pollack and Lawnhurst, like many other daytime performers, were on the air Monday through Friday. During the show I stood near Clyde at the announcer's delight so as not to miss any of his button pushing. The vitally important network buttons were touched only at the open and close or, in radio parlance, the top and bottom of the show. But throughout the broadcast, Clyde had to push a certain button to open his microphone (known as the announcer's mike) each time he spoke and a different button to disengage it afterward. Likewise, he had to hit a specific button to open what was called the studio mike (in this case to pick up the sound of the two pianos) and yet another button to cut it off. I watched intently. As the two ladies' fingers nimbly plied their keyboards, Clyde's hands appeared to be almost as busy working the announcer's delight. After the Pollack and Lawnhurst program finished, Clyde had more work to do. The 8 o'clock show, called *Organ Rhapsody*, was scheduled to use the same studio. It featured Dick Leibert at the giant Wurlitzer originating in the Radio City Music Hall.

Here the "announcer's delight" is quite prominent. I'm on the air doing Omar, the Swingmaker *in 1938.*

While Dick was at the organ console across the street in the Music Hall, Clyde Kittel, did his stint in Studio 8C. The routine went like this: After Dick played the organ theme, Clyde pushed the announce button and did the opening announcement during which he, while seated, exchanged general pleasantries with Dick Leibert. During the half hour that followed, Dick did his own announcing until the closing theme, when Clyde opened his announce mike again and engaged in closing ad-lib jollities with Dick. End of program. I had a lot to learn!

15

THE RED AND THE BLUE

If it seems the description of my third day on the announcing staff reads as if it happened only yesterday, the reason is simple. I've kept the daytime program logs for that day, Monday, May 21, 1934, all these years. There was a log for WEAF and the Red Network and one for WJZ and the Blue Network. The reason I still have those two is that they were the first of the daily logs having my name and my schedule on them. So, being the sentimentalist that I am, I kept them. Those logs listed the programs, the studios they aired from, and the announcers assigned. Of the thirteen announcers working that day, covering both networks, one of them, Don Wilson, would eventually reach the top in radio and television as the announcer for the *Jack Benny Show*. On that Monday in 1934, Don did three five-minute newscasts. According to my log, his final assignment that day was to give the correct time at 6 P.M. over WEAF, New York, which was the key station of the Red Network.

An announcer was always present to cover a standby studio, regardless of where the program was originating. In the event of a line break he would be there to go on the air with a proper apology which usually ended with "Please stand by." If the trouble wasn't corrected shortly, there would be another apology. At that point, if the announcer had information from the master control room that it might take a while to locate and remedy the problem, then he would alert the pianist standing by in the studio for just such a possibility. Until normal programming resumed, the pianist would fill the break with music of his own choosing. Some of the finest pianists in the

business were on the NBC musicians staff. But part of their job was to put in lots of time in a standby studio, just as the announcers did. Morton Gould was a young man about my age when I first knew him as a staff pianist. A great talent, he went on to become a noted conductor.

A word about the familiar sound of the NBC chimes, although they have been used much less often in recent years. Since 1927, when you heard the chimes you knew you were listening to NBC. The sound was made by an announcer striking a hammer on a set of seven chimes, each with a different musical note:

Bong—Bong—Bong—Bong (Pause) Bong—Bong—Bong.

When a program ended and the announcer had concluded with "This is the National Broadcasting Company" (always the full name—the initials NBC were to come later), he would lift his hammer and strike each of the seven chimes. Later it was cut down to three. Eventually the chimes sound was electronically wired into the announcer's delight. How was it activated? It became one more button to push, an added delight for the announcer.

According to the program logs of that long ago day, I was not the only novice being instructed. Another new arrival on the staff, Don Lowe, was being tutored by Lyle Van in Studio 8D, right next door. Their program aired at 7:30 A.M. to the Blue Network. Our program fed the Red Network at 7:45. While this was my third day working under Pat Kelly, it was probably Don Lowe's fifth or sixth day. He had been brought to the New York staff from NBC's Washington station, WRC, and very soon, having absorbed all the instruction possible, he would be on his own. The usual time to break in was a week. So in four more days, I too would solo. As a matter of fact the more I thought about my good fortune, the prouder I felt. I knew if I just sort of kept a low profile and minded my P's and Q's, before long I would be promoted to a regular announcer. Without specifying any time limit, Pat Kelly had as much as told me that.

As time went on, more junior announcers were brought in, from either the page staff or the guides. Two that come to mind were Ellis Andrews, who was promoted three or four months after I was, and Jack McCarthy about a year later. The word about Ellis Andrews was that he came from "an awful lot of money," which, unless you were a Rockefeller or a Vanderbilt, was seldom heard in those financially dark days of the Great Depression. It also was said that he had done lots of traveling, had gone to schools in France as well as the United States, and had as one of his pastimes buying and selling boats. This particular bit of gossip I inadvertently found out was true. One day sometime after he had joined the staff I happened to be in the announcers' lounge for the purpose of using the facilities. The lounge was quite a large room with a desk and telephone right inside the door and the washroom a good distance away. When I entered, the lounge was empty, as was the washroom. In a little while, however, I became aware from my perch that someone else had entered and was using the phone. There was nothing unusual about that, what with twenty-seven announcers, each with his own key, in and out all the time. In the privacy of my quarters, like the proverbial fly on the wall, I couldn't help overhearing what was being said, and by whom. The voice was that of Ellis Andrews, and the conversation was about buying a boat. The most interesting thing was that when, after indicating he would like to close the deal, I heard him say, "You'll have my check for $20,000 in

the morning." Twenty thousand dollars was an awful lot of money at that time so hearing what I did convinced me that the talk going around about him was indeed quite true. He and I never had the kind of friendship I came to enjoy with others. He always seemed remote and distant, without much humor. Even so it came as a terrible shock when, a year or so later, Ellis Andrews committed suicide.

Jack McCarthy was the complete opposite of Ellis. He was sharp as a tack and fun to be around. His reputation as a great storyteller became legend, especially his gift for Irish stories. Inevitably they brought the same result—his listeners screaming with laughter. Having been brought up in an Irish household myself, my ear was well attuned to the sound of Irish brogues rolling off the tongues of a few relatives. But the accent Jack could affect while telling a story was on a par with the natural brogue of the great actor from the ould sod, Barry Fitzgerald. A brief word about Jack McCarthy: He eventually made it from junior to senior announcer and sometime in the mid-forties joined WPIX-TV in New York City. In the early fifties the station began covering the annual St. Patrick's Day parade from 12 noon straight through until whenever it ended late in the afternoon. The management of WPIX-TV, which was owned by the New York *Daily News*, made a very intelligent programming decision in my opinion when they assigned Jack McCarthy to describe the first of the parades they aired. His efforts were so well received by the viewing audience, the sponsors, and the station management that for the next forty-some consecutive years the New York St. Patrick's Day Parade became synonymous with the name Jack McCarthy. An interesting thing about Jack was that you never knew when his sense of the ridiculous might take over. Once on St. Patrick's Day I decided to stop by and surprise him—one Irishman to another kind of thing. I think it was the fifth year he had been doing the parade, and it was my intention to

The author relaxing in the control room between his opening and closing announcements of the soap opera Mrs. Wiggs of the Cabbage Patch *in 1937 (photograph by Norman Sweetser).*

George, standing here beside me, has really made it. He's the only millionaire announcer I know. God bless you George, God bless your father, and God bless all the grand people of County Mayo." I was utterly speechless. What do you say in such a situation? I had come as an old friend to visit and offer anniversary greetings, and I now found myself groping for a reply to Jack's preposterous foolishness. The best I could do was to affect my own version of an Irish brogue with: "On this day everyone expects the great McCarthy to stretch the truth a wee bit. But that statement, my dear old friend, is ridiculous." I was soon to learn that my parents just happened to be watching when that little moment occurred. They almost fell off their couch. Their phone began to ring immediately with relatives and friends, Irish and otherwise, offering congratulations and such talk as, "Why have you kept this grand news about George such a secret?" Jack McCarthy, my fun-loving friend, had caused a mild earthquake for me to explain away and to live down.

wish him happy anniversary. He greeted me effusively and was as usual "sharp as a tack," noting that at that very moment the Mayomen's Association from County Mayo was marching by. Suddenly affecting his Irish brogue, Jack proclaimed to the TV audience: "All the good people of County Mayo are so proud of one of its grand members, John Ansbro, because his son,

Don Lowe had just become engaged

before he came to New York. Lillian, his fi-ancée, had been a pianist and receptionist at WRC, Washington. Don's promotion to the New York announcing staff was reason enough for them to change their plans, so she quit the station and arranged to stay in the Bronx with relatives temporarily. The local parish church her folks attended was agreeable to the date they had set for their wedding. Meanwhile, Don and I, having in common the fact that we were the newest kids on the block on the announcing staff, became pretty good friends. So much so that he invited me to be an usher. Eventu-ally the big day arrived. The wedding, the church, the reception—everything went off without a hitch. The bride was beautiful, the bridesmaids gorgeous. All in all it was a banner occasion, a great send-off for the newlyweds.

Shortly after the happy couple had re-turned from their honeymoon and had moved into their apartment in the Bronx, they invited three of the younger announc-ers and me to join them for dinner. The others were Bob Waldrop, who had very re-cently joined the staff from the NBC affiliate in San Francisco, and Ed Herlihy and Jack Fraser, both of whom had come down from NBC in Boston. With me, the only native New Yorker in the bunch, acting as guide, the four of us took the uptown subway; we were warmly greeted upon ar-rival, especially so because our host and hostess let us know that we were the very first guests to cross the marital threshold and, this said with tongue in cheek, we would be expected to behave with proper decorum. With all of us having so much in common, radio in general and NBC in par-ticular, in no time at all we were off and running, conversationally. Lillian served the first round of drinks, which was Scotch, for us four guests. Don was a ginger ale man, while Lillian begged off from the opening round, pleading that she had to get dinner started. I had forgotten, until then, that Don drank nothing but ginger ale at his wedding. He was obviously a teetotaler, but

it didn't bother him when others drank. It had already been my opinion that with his sense of humor he didn't need a drink to be good company. After a while Lillian re-turned with more of the same for us and a bourbon for herself which, I couldn't help but notice, seemed to disappear very rapidly—almost before we got started on ours.

While general conversation was going on, she said something about setting up a bar on the sideboard so we could help our-selves while she looked after dinner in the kitchen. But in setting up the bar she had forgotten ice. Trying to be helpful, I stuck my head in the kitchen door to ask where the ice bucket was so I could set it up in-side. But I held my tongue for a moment. Lillian, with her back to the door, was just then tossing down a generous belt of bour-bon. Making some throat-clearing sounds as if I had just come in and not seen a thing, I asked about the bucket, trying to appear as nonchalant as possible. Without batting an eye, she handed it to me along with a bag of ice. All this took only a few minutes, so I wasn't missed in the living room. The sight of the ice-filled bucket brought action at the sideboard bar, and we guys settled down for more talk. And more talk. After a while the action at the bar had slowed down considerably, but there were still a lot of topics to discuss. By now, as interesting and pleasant as our chatter was, I began to realize I was get-ting hungry and the others must feel the same. I got to thinking, where is Lillian? It must have been more than an hour since we had seen her. Why didn't Don find out? Surely he must be starving too. As if he could read my mind, he interrupted what-ever was being discussed and said he had better go out to the kitchen to check on how dinner was coming along. When he got there, we heard him exclaim, "Oh, my God!" With that, we all made a beeline after him to see what was the matter. There was Lillian lying prone on the floor, a half-empty bottle of bourbon nearby.

The dinner, of course, was ruined. Some of us helped Don lift her up, carry her into the bedroom, and put her on the bed. We thought he would be better off coping with this sad situation by himself, so not knowing exactly what to say except to commiserate with him, the four of us—Mr. and Mrs. Don Lowe's first guests after their honeymoon—went back downtown and ate a very quiet dinner in a restaurant. While we were eating, Bob Waldrop reminded us of what Don and Lillian had kiddingly said when we had arrived at their apartment, and suggested it might be best if we would treat the entire evening's experience "with proper decorum." Amen.

16

ON MY OWN

Now to get back to my first week learning the ropes in my new job, tagging along with whatever announcers Pat Kelly assigned me to. As with all fledglings, the day finally arrived when Pat trusted me enough to fly alone. The previous week of training had worked out just great, and it was not as though I was meeting the various performers for the first time because I had had a pleasant relationship with most of them from my page boy days. And not just performers and musicians, but engineers and production men as well. So it was that during those first several months I found myself quite at home going from one show to the next. For quite a while my day began early. In the spring and summer of 1934, I found myself announcing many different types of programs, from the two-piano team of Muriel Pollack and Vee Lawnhurst to a Japanese xylophone player, Yoichi Hiraoka. Of course, as I learned on my first day of instruction with announcer Clyde Kittel, when you did Pollack and Lawnhurst you also did the follow-up show with Richard Leibert, joining him in conversational pleasantries while he was at the organ console in the Radio City Music Hall and you were at the mike in Studio 8C. Dick Leibert fed the Red Network from 8:00 to 8:30. Another organ program fed the Blue Network from 8:30 to 9:00. Lew White was at the console of the huge "dual organ" in the Center Theatre across the street on the southeast corner of 49th Street and Sixth Avenue. But when assigned to Lew White, you actually went into the Center Theatre to engage in friendly chitchat at the organ console. Why those two organ shows were set up that way, I never could

understand. I mean, to announce and chat with Dick Leibert you stayed in the studio, but to do likewise with Lew White, you would physically join him in the theatre. The end result to the listener of both programs was exactly the same—an organist and an announcer making small talk about what the next number would be. But, I must confess, this was probably the first of many, many inconsistencies in broadcasting I was to encounter during the decades to come.

Jolly Bill and Jane was a daily morning program aimed at the kiddies. It featured Bill Steinke, a large Santa-type of a man with a "Ho, Ho, Ho" personality. He was teamed with a young lady of preteen age named Peggy Zinke, who played Jane. During their many years on the early morning air, they enjoyed a sizable audience of youngsters. The show eventually went off when Peggy Zinke grew out of her teens and quite definitely lost that little girl sound. This was what caused Bill Steinke to end the show, pull up stakes, and retire to Maine instead of looking for a replacement for the character of Jane. Peggy became a very busy actress, playing mostly ingenue roles on the radio scene all around town.

Breen and De Rose was a program I felt especially at home doing. May Singhi Breen and her husband, Peter De Rose, had something about them that would make anyone feel at home. She was known as "the Ukulele Lady," and he was a composer. Their act consisted of songs and chatter, with May playing the ukulele and Peter the piano while both joined voices in song. Being with them was always a pleasant

71

experience, whether on the air or socially. Aside from their radio program, Peter had achieved quite some renown as a composer of popular songs. One morning just after we went off the air, he told me he had been "fooling around on the keyboard last night" and had put together something and he wanted to know how I liked it. He then sat down and played what to me sounded beautiful. And of course I told him so. Not too much later the whole country would be enjoying that same melody, enhanced by lyrics written by Hoagy Carmichael. It has long since been considered a standard among pop tunes. Looking back, I've always felt kind of privileged being in at the birth of "Deep Purple."

Another morning show that was fun to do was *The Honeymooners, Grace and Eddie Albert.* They filled up fifteen minutes with sprightly songs and patter, not unlike May Breen and Peter De Rose, but younger. For the year or so that they were on the air, I took it for granted that Grace and Eddie were a newly married couple. After all, why should I think otherwise when they were billed as the "Honeymooners." It wasn't until their program went off the air at the time Eddie made his mark on Broadway and later in Hollywood that it became known around NBC that Grace was really Grace Bradt, a singer who just happened to team up with Eddie Albert, and they called the act *The Honeymooners.* Interestingly enough, some twenty years later a fellow named Jackie Gleason did pretty well when he put together an act for television using the same title. Now about Eddie Albert making his mark on Broadway. It seems that one day the playwright Garson Kanin appeared as a guest on their program and was quite impressed with Eddie's talent, so much so that he cast him in his play *Brother Rat.* I can still remember the joyous excitement in the studio on the morning following opening night of *Brother Rat.* The New York papers had unanimously acclaimed the show a big hit and Eddie Albert the newest star on Broadway. His

theatrical success pretty much spelled finis, however, to his nice little morning radio show. Movie scouts spotted him, and, after his next Broadway show *Room Service*, Warner Bros. signed him up. He starred in the movie version of *Brother Rat*, then returned to Broadway for the Rodgers and Hart musical *The Boys from Syracuse.* During World War II, he saw action in the South Pacific, and when the war ended and he had become a full lieutenant, Eddie continued his career in motion pictures. Somewhere along the way he married the actress Margo, best remembered as the Shangri La dweller who aged dramatically when she left her Himalayan paradise in *Lost Horizon.* Their son, Edward Albert, Jr., is a chip off the old block and also a success in movies.

Some years after our association in the early radio days I had occasion to be present at a preview of *Roman Holiday* in which he starred with Audrey Hepburn and Gregory Peck. Eddie was also present, and we enjoyed a delightful reunion after the showing. The preview was held aboard the S.S. *Andria Doria* while it was docked in New York harbor, the same ship that later suffered the terrible tragedy of being rammed by a freighter and sunk, causing the death of many passengers.

In early autumn of 1934, I crossed two new thresholds in my life—my first soap opera and my first remote broadcast. The soap opera was *Home Sweet Home* and it starred Harriet MacGibbon. The sponsor was Procter and Gamble, which was promoting two soaps, Chipso and Chipso Granules. The program was among the very first soaps on network radio to be broadcast from New York. The only others already on NBC at that point were Oxydol's *Ma Perkins* and *Clara,* and *Lu and Em,* sponsored by Palmolive Super Suds and broadcast out of Chicago. I never did know how I was put on the *Home Sweet Home* show. There was no announcer's audition for it, nor did Pat Kelly even talk about it with me. So whether I was requested for it or

Pat just decided to assign me I never did find out. All I do know is that I was mighty pleased to be on a sponsored show, especially with such a prestigious sponsor as P & G every morning at 11:00 five days a week. My call was to appear for the rehearsal at 10 A.M. in Studio 8D. When I arrived the first day, I met with Cecil Secrest and Harriet MacGibbon, who were the two leads, Billy Halop who played their son, and Joe Latham, who was Uncle Will. The series related "The dramatic struggle of Fred and Lucy Kent and their son for a home sweet home of their own." I also met another announcer, a freelancer, John Monks, which surprised me. For a moment I thought Pat Kelly, or somebody, had made a mistake and I shouldn't be there at all. But things were made clear when the director, John Taylor, gave me a full script of the show, including the opening and closing Chipso commercials, and another set of opening and closing commercials but for Chipso Granules. It was explained to me that while John Monks would be doing commercials for plain old Chipso in Studio 8D to the regular network, I would be selling Chipso Granules downstairs in Studio 5B to the New England leg of the network. It was the sponsor's desire to first introduce Granules to the New England market as a sales test before offering the new product to the rest of the country. So following rehearsal in 8D, I would go to Studio 5B on the fifth floor which was a tiny cubicle, squeeze myself into a chair next to the engineer, cross my fingers, and hope all would go well because I did have a worry. Although the commercials which Monks and I would be reading simultaneously were written to the same exact timing, I worried that he might read faster or slower than I. So it became incumbent upon me to wear headphones and monitor him while I was reading. This was so I could gauge my tempo accordingly and be sure to end exactly when he did. When Monks finished, he would pause five seconds before leading into the story line with "And now, *Home Sweet Home*." During that pause my New England network leg would rejoin the regular network. And, oh yes, it was also incumbent that I sound convincing to the good people of New England while rattling on and on through a page and a half of Chipso Granules copy. But as time went on such fears lessened and I found myself looking forward to the pleasantries of being with the cast and John Monks during rehearsal before going below to Studio 5B.

Many years later Harriet MacGibbon became a regular cast member on television's *Beverly Hillbillies* with Buddy Ebsen, while Billy Halop appeared in movies with such stars as Humphrey Bogart and Joel McCrea and as the leader of *The Dead End Kids*. *Home Sweet Home* ran about a year and a half. It went off the air in early 1936. It was really a wonderful experience for me, a very different experience, especially the business of pacing myself to the tempo set by someone else. In all my subsequent years in the business, such a situation happened very seldom, but when it did I was always glad I had had the *Home Sweet Home* background.

The other new threshold I crossed in the fall of 1934 was my first remote. A remote was a broadcast originating outside of the studios. This one occured on a Saturday afternoon following the football game, and as on every Saturday during football season on NBC, it came from the Central Park Casino, which in later years became the Tavern on the Green. The program featured the celebrated Eddie Duchin, his piano, and his orchestra. In 1934 Eddie Duchin was at the height of his fame and success. The Central Park Casino was one of the most glamorous spots in New York, and it was mighty exciting for me to be assigned there. It was my understanding that the first thing you did upon arriving was to find the orchestra leader and, if he was not at that moment doing what made him famous— leading the band—you would show him the music sheet you had brought with you from the announcers' office master book. If your sheet jibed with the selections he was scheduled to play on the broadcast, you had nothing more to do until air time, which, depending on when the football game ended, could be anywhere from ten minutes to an hour. If he had planned any changes in the music, that was when he told you. While waiting for the indeterminate moment when the game ended, you stayed pretty close to the engineer. He was in constant touch with master control back at NBC in Radio City, and when the time came to start the broadcast, he was the fellow who threw the cue to the band leader to start the theme music. This particular show was like every other program Eddie Duchin had done. The engineer threw the cue to Duchin, who then gave the downbeat to the musicians. Next, he nodded to the announcer, in this case me, to give the introduction announcement over the theme music and then inform the listeners what I'm sure they had all been waiting for with bated breath, the title of the first number. At any rate that occasion was a whole new experience for me. Where I had felt right at home on shows with Breen and De Rose, Richard Leibert, Lew White, and Grace and Eddie Albert, with Eddie Duchin, it was just different. He treated me respectfully. He was professional. When I brought him on at the opening of the show, he said, "Thank you, George Ansbro." But he lacked warmth. It was just the way he looked at me when I first introduced myself to him, and on and off during the entire time I was there. Maybe it was my youthful imagination working overtime, but I couldn't get over the feeling that he resented NBC sending this young kid to put the great Eddie Duchin on the air from the magnificent Central Park Casino. To be truthful, I was glad when it was over. When leaving I waved "so long" to him, but there was no response. On the subway ride back home, my mind went back to the time one year earlier at the formal opening of Radio City when Deak Aylesworth asked if I would be good enough to guide William S.

Paley, the CBS chairman, and his wife through the new NBC Studios. I remembered the feeling of honest appreciation they had openly displayed, both during the tour and when they said good-bye. During the remainder of the 1934 football season, while Duchin was still playing at the Central Park Casino, I was assigned there two or three more times and each time the situation was a little more comfortable. And for that I felt much better about him. So much so that, not too many years later, I felt great sympathy and quite some grief when he was taken from this life at such an early age.

My next band remote after Eddie Duchin was at the Great Northern Hotel on West 57th Street. The music of Angelo Ferdinando and his orchestra, and also the hotel's elegant dining room were quite popular and very "in" for several years during the thirties. I found myself doing the dinner-hour broadcasts on Tuesdays and Thursdays during the fall and winter of 1934–1935. Before what I'm about to relate occurred, I had been there several times, and liked it better each time. As soon as I would arrive, the maître d' would seat me at a table close to the bandstand and leave a dinner menu. When assigned to do Angelo Ferdinando's program, dinner for the announcer went with the territory, courtesy of Mr. Ferdinando. It didn't take me long to appreciate how gracious and generous he was. One Tuesday evening after the broadcast, I was having dinner at my usual table when he sat down with me and proceeded to engage in pleasant small talk. He seemed really interested in such things as whether I liked announcing and where I lived. I told him I lived in Bay Ridge, Brooklyn, with my family, and I went on to say that in two more days, on Thursday, February 14, Valentine's Day, my parents would celebrate their thirty-fifth wedding anniversary. Also I said that I knew I was scheduled to do his show Thursday evening but wouldn't be able to stay for dinner because I would be wanted at home to help with the preparations for the surprise anniversary party we siblings were giving my parents. My oldest sister, Madeline, was handling the arrangements, I said, and I just hoped that by now she had come up with a plan for what to do with Mother and Pop to get them out of the house for a while so that when they returned all the guests would be there and they would be genuinely surprised. He then asked if I would mind if he put in his two cents? "Be my guest," I said. What he then came up with was further proof of what a nice person he was. And thoughtful. He said he had a plan that should solve my sister's problem. Simply stated it was this: Forget about dashing home after his program to help out. Instead I should invite my parents over to the Great Northern "to actually see you, for the first time, working in front of a microphone to a coast-to-coast audience. And what better day to do it than on their anniversary. It's a great reason to get them out of the house, have dinner, and then return home, with no reason to expect anything further when they get there."

Madeline and the others thought the idea was super. And so it came to pass that on Valentine's Day, their big day, Mother and Pop drove over from Brooklyn, pleased they were going to see a radio broadcast for the first time. But most especially they were actually going to see me announcing "over the radio" for the first time. I walked up from Radio City and met them, as we had planned, in the hotel lobby. In the dining room we sat at my usual table. There were about twenty minutes to go before air time, which explained why the musicians weren't on the bandstand yet. Mother and Pop were chattering away on this, their big special night out. It was time for me to check over the musical numbers with Angelo Ferdinando so I stepped into the lobby to look for him. Sure enough he was there, and he was in conversation with someone I could swear looked just like Hugh James, my fellow guide who was one of the bunch that had auditioned last May and who had such a great voice. As I got closer, sure

enough it was Hugh and before I had time to figure out what he was doing there he spotted me and, noticing the look of curiosity which I guess was written all over my face, came over with Mr. Ferdinando to explain. Hugh said he was still on the guide staff, which I of course knew, and, through Pat Kelly it had been arranged that he be considered for a job opening in Washington, D.C., as an announcer at the NBC affiliate WRC. Late that afternoon Kelly had set it up with Mr. Berkeley, the WRC station manager, to have him make the decision by listening to Hugh announce tonight's program.

Kelly had told him, he said, to explain the situation to me and to ask me for the program's music sheet so he could check it out with Mr. Ferdinando. Wow! In a thousand years who could ever have been faced with a situation like this? My parents had driven over from Brooklyn on their anniversary to, for the first time, watch me announce a well-known band and then have dinner as the band leader's guests, when suddenly this seemingly impossible situation happens. And not a thing in the world I could do about it. Knowing it was getting close to air time, I quickly assured Hugh that I understood and wished him luck on his audition. I gave him the music sheet, which he double checked with Mr. Ferdinando while I had the embarrassing job of going back to my parents' table to try to explain why I was going to sit with them during the broadcast. Instead of watching me perform on the bandstand, they would hear an old friend of mine, probably with his heart in his mouth as mine once was, hoping and praying Mr. Berkeley listening down in Washington would like what he heard and hire him—which is exactly what happened. In hiring Hugh James, Mr. Berkeley facilitated the beginning of what proved over many years to be one of the most illustrious announcing careers in broadcasting.

The party waiting for us at home was a huge surprise for Mother and Pop and was a great success, too. Ironically, even though my parents both lived into their nineties, they never did see me announce any shows, although of course they listened.

Angelo Ferdinando continued at the Great Northern for another year or so, but I was sent to announce his dinner dance program only once in a while, not nearly as often as before. The Big Band Era was now well underway and big name bands and soon-to-be big names were vying for broadcast spots on NBC and CBS as well as the newest network, Mutual, with its big local outlet WOR. I guess my work with Eddie Duchin and Ferdinando encouraged Pat Kelly to see how I might do with other bands. So as time went on I saw less of the Central Park Casino and the Great Northern Hotel and more of other remotes.

17

BIG BAND REMOTES

Expanding my schedule to do other orchestras did not mean no more morning shows. It meant, maybe, shows not quite as early in the morning. But as long as *Home Sweet Home* continued, even if the particular remote I might have been doing the previous night didn't end until 1 A.M., I would have to be at rehearsal for that, my very first soap opera, at the usual 10 A.M. In this expansion of my schedule, I so well remember my first late-night dance remote. It was the Dorsey Brothers Orchestra at the Glen Island Casino in New Rochelle, New York.

I had known Tommy and Jimmy Dorsey on a "hello, how are ya" basis from my page boy days when they were both on the NBC musicians staff. Knowing that bringing a date to a remote was quite okay with Pat Kelly as well as band leaders, I decided to invite a young lady of my acquaintance who sold tickets for the guided tours from a booth close to the NBC elevator bank in the lobby of the RCA building. I first knew her when I was guiding. Her name was Mary Jane Hassman. She lived with an aunt on West 57th Street, which made it easy for me to pick her up on my way to the West Side Highway for the drive to New Rochelle.

We arrived plenty early, like an hour before the broadcast was scheduled. I had planned it that way so we might get a little dancing in before I got down to the business of announcing the Dorsey Brothers program for thirty minutes beginning at midnight. Pleased as Mary Jane was to be at the Glen Island Casino, a nationally known spot in the thirties because of all the broadcasting done from there, she was nev-

ertheless not the type to swoon in the presence of celebrities. That made it that much more pleasant when Tommy or Jimmy would join us for brief snatches of conversation at our table situated close to the bandstand. Working as she did in the NBC lobby, Mary Jane had become quite accustomed to seeing and often chatting with the famous and near famous.

Midnight arrived. I did what I was sent there to do—announce the program. When it was over, the Dorseys thanked me and invited us to stay and dance some more, which we did. Somewhere in the post-broadcast period, Mary Jane mentioned that we were having such a good time she hoped I had not forgotten I had to be in Studio 8D at ten o'clock in the morning, which, of course, I hadn't. So it was agreed that after we enjoyed one more dance, I would drive her back to West 57th Street and then return home to Brooklyn.

It was at that point that Mary Jane told me she had another aunt who lived in a house in New Rochelle no more than ten minutes away. She frequently visited, she said. So often that her aunt had given her a key to come and go as she liked. In order to save both of us the long trip to the Big City and then to Brooklyn, and most important, to give us a few more hours sleep, she suggested, "Why don't we go there? I'll sleep in the other bed in my aunt's room and you can sleep in the guest room on the third floor. I'll set the alarm clock for seven o'clock and go upstairs and waken you. How does that grab you?" Talk about manna from heaven. It had been a long day, and, quickly, before she might change her mind, I let her know her idea really grabbed me, as she probably knew it would.

We said goodnight and thanks very much to the Dorsey brothers, got into the car, and in hardly more than five minutes we pulled into her aunt's driveway. Quietly opening the front door with her key, Mary Jane stealthily led me into the hallway, which was lit only by a dim night light, and motioned for me to follow her upstairs. By peeking into her aunt's bedroom, it was easy to determine from the nocturnal sounds therein that the good lady was quite happy in dreamland. Next flight up was what, by now, I sure was looking forward to—the bed in the guest room. By the faint illumination of another night light, Mary Jane was feeling around on the wall right inside the open doorway for the light switch when she suddenly froze. No more feeling for the light switch. As she turned to me, from the look on her face I couldn't tell whether she was going to laugh or cry.

In a whisper she said there might be a problem. She had forgotten that her aunt had told her sometime ago that Uncle So-and-So from St. Louis might visit for a night or two when he was next in New York. And the reason for her consternation was that Uncle had obviously chosen today to visit Auntie. She whispered: "if you'll peek in, you'll see him, sound asleep, where you're supposed to be and what in heaven's name can we do about it?" What we did about it was this. After a brief whispered discussion, I said that under the circumstances I had better get moving because it was a long drive to Brooklyn. She replied that at this hour such talk made no sense and I was going to stay come hell or high water or she would never forgive herself. With that she entered the room for a few seconds to make a closer inspection of the situation. And thank God she did, because she could just about see in the dim light from the hall that Uncle was occupying only the far side of the double bed and that there was plenty of room for me. It didn't take me long to buy her argument, I

was that pooped. So downstairs she went to the other bed in her aunt's room after reminding me she would come up to rouse me at 7 o'clock. I was left to strip off my shirt and pants and quietly climb into the unused portion of the bed, and join in sleep this total stranger, the St. Louis brother of Mary Jane's aunt.

True to her word, promptly at seven, Mary Jane shook me and I woke up. But Uncle was already awake and, I suppose, had been trying to figure out, before Mary Jane arrived, what was going on here. Like who might this sleeping beauty be who was occupying the other side of his bed. And why? I had to admire the way Mary Jane handled things with such cool detachment. Because the next thing I knew, after greeting her uncle and welcoming him to New Rochelle, she kind of laughingly said, "I would like you to meet my friend, George Ansbro." With that, still in bed, we shook hands. She went back downstairs. I put my clothes back on, and said, "Nice meeting you, Mr. So-and-So," walked out of the room, went downstairs, had a cup of coffee with Mary Jane, got into my car, and drove down to NBC, arriving just in time for the rehearsal of *Home Sweet Home*. End of story. Except I never did meet my hostess, Mary Jane Hassman's aunt.

This is an appropriate moment to enumerate, as memory will allow, band remotes I covered during the remaining years of the 1930s and all throughout the 1940s and 1950s when the Big Band Era was at its peak. Actually because of the continuing inroads being made by television at the end of the fifties, that historic period was rapidly coming to a close. And by quite early in the sixties, it's safe to say it had become just a memory. But for much of those three decades, it was part of my job two or three times a week to hie myself to yet another spot where yet another famous leader and his band were playing and put them on the air for yet another half hour.

It would be impossible all these years later to be specific about the dates when I announced any of these big bands. I've already mentioned my association with Eddie Duchin, Angelo Ferdinando, and the Dorsey Brothers. Ferdinando, however, never did achieve the fame of Duchin or the Dorseys. Of the many other orchestra leaders I worked with, one pops into my mind instantly, Chick Webb. Despite his hunchback, he was a fantastic drummer who had the good sense and astute musical taste to hire a young vocalist who, though only seventeen, would in the ensuing years prove to be a talent that seemingly went on and on and on. When I first went uptown to the Savoy Ballroom in Harlem, Chick Webb had just hired her. Her name was Ella Fitzgerald.

Another great sound originating from the Savoy Ballroom was Lucky Millander and his orchestra. I looked forward to going up there, not only for the unusually good music, but there was an added attraction for me and that was the view from my perch on the bandstand of the remarkable spectacle in front of me on the dance floor—fabulous jitterbugging by the paying guests, the like of which I had never seen before.

About Lucky Millander. My friendship with him continued for a long time after our initial meeting at the Savoy. He was a delightful person to be with, really good company. As time went on, he retired from the business of actively conducting an orchestra and subsequently became known as the unofficial mayor of Harlem. Some ten years into our friendship, shortly after I was married to Jo-Anne, Lucky invited both of us to join him on a tour of Harlem, at night, with him as our personal escort. "And please leave your money home," he said, which I took to mean that the evening was on him, and I was right. Not that Lucky had to dig into his pocket to actually put out money as we progressed from one place to the next. It was simply that, no matter where he took us, nobody would accept his offer of payment, he was that well liked. They seemed thrilled to have him. And he took us to a lot of places. Fancy places and, shall we say, less than fancy places. In every one of them, the house seemed quite flattered that Lucky Millander thought enough of them that he would bring his guests from downtown into their establishment. After that night on the town in Harlem, we could very well understand why Lucky Millander was called the unofficial mayor of Harlem.

More now about the big bands I had the fun of covering during what are now called the "old-time radio" years. Guy Lombardo and his Royal Canadians seemed to hold forth forever at the Hotel Roosevelt Grill. Guy's brothers, Carmen, Victor, and Lebert, as well as his vocalist sister, Rose Marie, were all part of the Lombardo orchestra. To millions of holiday radio listeners, New Year's Eve wasn't complete without the sound of the Lombardo orchestra playing "Auld Lang Syne" at midnight. Glen Gray and the Casa Loma orchestra and Ray Noble and his orchestra were featured alternately in the Rainbow Room atop the RCA building. To get to the very posh Rainbow Room, I didn't even have to leave the building—I would just go to the main lobby via the NBC elevators and walk to the special elevators servicing only the Rainbow Room. Then, whoosh, in no time at all, I would step out onto the 70th floor and go to work, if you could call it that. The Starlight Roof of the Waldorf Astoria was where, for a long time, the Latin rhythms of Xavier Cugat and his orchestra held forth. Another musical attraction at the Waldorf, broadcast at lunchtime, was Jules Lande, the troubadour of the violin in the Sert Room just off the main lobby. Besides offering music much more sedate than the flamboyant Cugat sounds broadcast upstairs later at night, Mr. Lande always graciously offered an invitation to lunch no matter who the announcer was. I feel safe in claiming that his offer was never turned down, at least not by me.

After the Dorsey brothers decided to go their separate ways in the musical world, Jimmy, his saxophone, and his orchestra made frequent appearances at the Cafe Rouge of the Hotel Pennsylvania, while Tommy with his trombone and band returned often to the Glen Island Casino and various other spots. Interestingly, each one hired male vocalists who were young, handsome, quite talented, and practically unknown. With Jimmy it was Bob Eberle. Tommy took on a fellow named Frank Sinatra.

Others who come to mind when I think of announcing from the Pennsylvania Hotel's Cafe Rouge are Glenn Miller, who played there a lot with his orchestra in the late thirties, and Benny Goodman, the "King of Swing," his clarinet, and his orchestra. I had never heard the name Benny Goodman until shortly after I became a member of the announcing staff in May of 1934. The following fall the National Biscuit Company joined the growing ranks of important sponsors by purchasing six continuous hours on NBC every Saturday night. Actually it was a three-hour program from nine until midnight with a live repeat to the West Coast following immediately, from midnight to 3 A.M. It was called *Let's Dance* and, in appealing to terpsichorean types, the sponsor put together a package of three wonderful orchestras. But only one of the leaders, Xavier Cugat, was a big name, and throughout the duration of the program, *Nabisco Show,* the Waldorf Starlight Roof replaced him with other bands on Saturday nights. In my page boy days at 711 Fifth Avenue, I had known Kel Murray, another of the three leaders. Back then he was an NBC house musician and his name was Murray Kellner. The third was Benny Goodman, equally as unknown as Kel Murray. In looking back now from a vantage point of time elapsed, it's hard to imagine that Benny Goodman was ever unknown. The *Let's Dance* program was his springboard to greatness, where he was first called the "King of Swing."

Having so recently arrived on the announcing staff, I understood, of course, that I should expect the short end of the stick when it came to lousy hours. So when Pat Kelly assigned me to cover the full six hours of the *Let's Dance* program, I must confess I winced a little and swallowed hard, not knowing what to expect. I did know that at the end of each hour I would give what was called the system cue, "This is the National Broadcasting Company," which I did. I also knew that when 12 o'clock came around I would give the local station's call letters, WJZ, New York, which I did. Then, after an appropriate pause, still during the 30-second station break, and in a style that would have put John Barrymore to shame, I gave a dramatic recitation of the mundane and totally unimportant information, "The hour is midnight."

But enough about the little nothings I did. It turned out that just being in that studio on Saturday nights was an experience not to be forgotten. It was NBC's largest, 8H. On the huge stage was the setup for each of the three orchestras: stage left, Benny Goodman; stage center, Kel Murray; stage right, Xavier Cugat. Two staff announcers were busy on and off doing cookie commercials and whatever else the National Biscuit Company happened to be pushing at the moment. They were Howard Petrie, who would later go on to Hollywood for a stint in movies, and George Hicks, who later crowned his broadcasting career when he described the almost indescribable action while crossing the English Channel with the Allied forces on D-Day. In Studio 8H the first ten rows of seats were removed to accommodate dancing by the studio audience. I would often spot others kicking their heels on the floor—pages and guides off duty in mufti, dancing with their dates. Likewise off-duty hostesses and receptionists. Also an occasional NBC vice president was spotted. The party atmosphere never stopped. And what was I doing when I wasn't doing the things I was sent there to do? Before I answer that, it's important that you should know that each band played for twenty minutes and had the next forty minutes off. Where to go? What to do in off time? They had three choices: A) stay seated in place on the stage, B) retire to an anteroom backstage for rest or recreation, or C) drop down to Hurley's Bar on the corner of Sixth Avenue and 49th Street for possibly needed liquid refreshment. Hardly any of the men chose "A" for the first three hours, but by the fourth hour, the hour right after midnight, a few of the onstage seats were occupied. Then more in the fifth hour. When the sixth hour came around, I would say three quarters of the musicians who were not playing were back sensibly resting their weary bottoms in their chairs. Why were they weary? Because most of them had earlier opted for "B" or "C." The big attraction in the backstage anteroom was a continuous crap game. I spent most of my off time in there utterly fascinated by the goings on, although I would occasionally stop by Hurley's for a beer. What little I knew about shooting craps I had learned from kids I knew in high school, which was definitely not enough to even think of handling the dice with these sophisticated players. At least not at first. After three or four weeks working the *Let's Dance show* and with a little good-natured prodding from the likes of Gene Krupa or Kel Murray, I decided to take the plunge and roll the dice. I kind of remember that after I had had the dice two or three times and was out five dollars I decided it was time to quit. Five dollars was one-fifth of my junior announcer's salary, one-fifth more than I could afford to lose. So on subsequent Saturday nights I disciplined myself by merely watching the game, which, in a way, was more fun than playing because there was no worry involved. Also by not joining in I was free to look around at the others in the room, players and nonplayers, and contemplate the wealth of musical talent I was privileged to rub elbows with. Benny Goodman himself, I guess for want of something better to do during those off periods, frequently dropped in for a look-see but never picked up the dice. I couldn't help but like him because of his pleasant personality, off stage as well as on. He was a nice man who was also an amazing virtuoso of the clarinet and, in my opinion, surely deserved the great success he achieved.

18

MORE BAND REMOTES

Vincent Lopez with his piano and orchestra made his radio debut in 1921, and he continued to be heard until the early sixties. I first listened to him on my family's crystal set about 1923. He next entered my consciousness when I began working as a page at NBC in 1931. At that time he and his orchestra were on the air from the St. Regis Roof, an elegant room featuring dining and dancing, at the hotel on Fifth Avenue opposite 711 Fifth Avenue, where NBC was then located. When I would cross 55th Street to cash my paycheck in the St. Regis lobby, the Lopez face was always prominently displayed there as a promotion for his appearance upstairs. And I heard him on the radio at home. With all those years of radio work behind him, he was, to say the least, very well known. So I looked forward to my first assignment with him at the Hotel Taft and, indeed, my expectations did not go unrewarded. The name of his program, *Luncheon with Lopez*, rang true as far as I was concerned. When he heard that I remembered listening to him on the old crystal set, he pulled up a chair when the broadcast was over and joined me for lunch and much pleasant chatter. Yes, "luncheon with Lopez" became a reality on that day and on many others down the line.

Some more band remotes I covered way back then included Blue Baron, who was a staple fixture at the Hotel Edison for a long time. Harold Stern held forth at the Hotel St. George in Brooklyn Heights. The Hotel Statler featured *Music in the Morgan Manner* by Russ Morgan and his orchestra, with vocals by Lou Julian. Lou had been an NBC guide when I was on that staff, and we had remained good friends. He was one of the first to be drafted after Pearl Harbor. Before he reported for duty, Lou had me to his apartment on East 58th Street for a farewell drink. Before leaving, he told me he would like it if I would live in his apartment until he came back, whenever that might be. He had known, he said, that from little things I had said—probably unconsciously—that I was becoming increasingly burdened by the long subway ride to and from our house in Brooklyn, what with the crazy hours I was working. For instance, he reminded me that I had told him how generous some of the other bachelor announcers had been by inviting me to sleep on their living-room couches. Among these friends were Ben Grauer, who lived alone in the Des Artistes Apartments off Central Park West, or Ed Herlihy and Frank Gallop who lived in an apartment on West 45th Street Lou flattered me by saying I would actually be doing him a favor because he felt sure I would take proper care of the place.

As for my thoughts on the subject, I knew my mother and father were constantly worried about my riding the subways, especially late at night, and if I were to accept Lou's kind offer, they would have one less worry. So the deal was struck. I wanted to take over full payment of his rent, but he insisted I accept the offer as his guest, with no money involved. We finally settled that I would pay half the rent until he came back. At home my folks understood and were relieved. The postscript to this is indeed a sad one. Lou Julian never did come back. He became a very early casualty in the war when his company was advancing during the fighting in Italy. It was a difficult meeting

I had with his brother when I returned Lou's key.

When Horace Heidt and His Musical Knights were in New York, they played at the Hotel Biltmore, near Grand Central Station. When they weren't in New York, at least during the late thirties and early forties, their replacement was Ray Heatherton and his orchestra. Ray had been a singer of pop tunes on his own fifteen-minute daytime program and, like Breen and De Rose's and Grace and Eddie Albert's, I had been assigned to his program a couple of times a week. We were good friends.

One night we double-dated and brought our ladies to dine and dance at the Hotel Astor Roof Garden, where the big attraction was the music of Rudy Vallee and his orchestra, with vocals by Alice Faye. The girl who was Ray's date was later to become Mrs. Ray Heatherton. My date's name was Evie, but my mind goes blank when I try to remember her last name. Be that as it may, I think I'll always remember how the evening ended. Evie lived across the river in Jersey City, and Ray very generously offered to drive her home first and then drop me off at Ben Grauer's, because I had made arrangements to stay with him. Needless to say he didn't have to twist my arm to accept. His car was quite new, with a convertible top which he lowered because it was such a nice summer evening. On the way down Seventh Avenue nearing the Holland Tunnel, I was enjoying the starry night in the backseat of Ray's new car when I became aware that my fellow passenger hadn't said a word for several minutes. Closer scrutiny indicated she was, to say the least, uncomfortable. By now we were inside the tunnel with nowhere to go except straight ahead. Evie indicated to me, by holding her index finger to her lips, not to let Ray know about her queasy situation. So in deference to her wishes, I held my tongue. This went on for what seemed an eternity until, as we were exiting the tunnel, the tide could no longer be stemmed and the upchuck the poor girl had been holding back erupted

like Niagara all over the backseat and us. A moment like that can be very panicky not just for the poor soul who loses control but for others close to the situation. Thank the good Lord Ray was able to pull into one of those gas stations that line the road after the tunnel exit in New Jersey, and we were able to get a supply of paper towels to attempt a temporary clean-up job. Evie was mortified. I'm sure she was happy when Ray pulled up at her front door in Jersey City. Happy so she could get inside fast and get out of her clothes. Very little time was wasted on embarrassed good-byes.

One night a couple of years later as I walked into Hurley's Bar, an NBC hangout, someone called my name. I turned around and was pleased to see my friend Evie. She was just leaving the ladies room and looked great. I was starting with the "What're you doing here?" kind of talk when she took me by the hand and led me to a table in the back where I recognized two well-known people sitting there, Ed Wynn, who was nationally known as the Perfect Fool, and his son Keenan. She then introduced me to "my husband, Keenan Wynn, and my father-in-law, Ed Wynn." I didn't stay very long, but while I was there Evie told me she and Keenan lived in California and had come east to visit his father. I was glad she had the good sense not to mention l'affaire Holland Tunnel. That was the last time I saw Evie, but I did read about her sometime later in a gossip column. The story was that she had divorced Keenan Wynn and married his best friend, Van Johnson, a very big movie star at the time, which I couldn't help but think was verrrry interesting.

One more big band leader I must mention was Charlie Barnet, who was in a class with Harry James when it came to playing the trumpet. Charlie and his orchestra held forth at the Hotel New Yorker, on 34th Street and Eighth Avenue. Once, I think it was in the early forties, I had just finished announcing Charlie Barnet's program on a

New Year's Eve when I was approached by the maître d.' He asked if I would please follow him to a table where a friend wanted to wish me Happy New Year. The friend turned out to be Florence Freeman, the star of the daily soap opera I had begun a few years earlier in 1938, *Young Widder Brown*. Florence was with her husband Rabbi Sam Berman and a group of close friends, and she invited me to join them to help ring in the New Year. I couldn't have been more pleased with her surprise inasmuch as I don't think I had ever seen the Widder Brown outside of the studio before. But on that New Year's Eve, there was no way I could have known that, as fate would have it, I would continue to see her in the studio five days a week for more than ten years to come, with me as the announcer and Florence as an oh-so-brave-but-much-put-upon character: "Young Widder Brown with two fatherless children to support. The story of the age-old conflict between a mother's duty and a woman's heart."

In 1937 and 1938, I was frequently assigned to do dance programs from a nightclub in Greenwich Village named El Chico, where wonderful Latin music was the attraction. I especially remember that it was a fun place to go. Much later, around 1943 and 1944, I was part of Sammy Kaye's *Sunday Serenade* beginning at 1 P.M. for a half hour every Sunday. The show was done in front of an audience from the stage of a small theatre in the Barbizon Plaza Hotel. My good friend John Cleary was the producer/director of that program. I was the announcer, and Sammy Kaye, as well as leading the orchestra, liked to read romantic poetry. Much later, throughout the sixties when television had become thoroughly established, John Cleary came up with one of the biggest TV hits of that decade, *College Bowl*, which he produced and directed.

Along with my big band work, I had occasion to know some individual musicians. Among them was a virtuoso of the xylo-

phone, Yoichi Hiraoka. Yoichi, a native of Japan, did the first program following the sign-on announcement Monday through Friday at 7:30 A.M. on WJZ, the key station of NBC's Blue Network.

One morning when Charles O'Connor was assigned to announce Yoichi's show, Charlie, who had a sense of humor that was clearly off the wall, decided to have a little fun. It was at the expense of none other than Yoichi himself who unfortunately had a speaking problem—a very heavy Japanese accent encumbered by a cleft palate. Once on the air Charlie told the radio audience that he thought it might be nice if Yoichi added his personal touch to the program by not only announcing his own show but also telling a little bit about the composer of each selection. With that Charlie joined the director and engineer in the control room, leaving the star of the show, who was highly flattered by Charlie's request, jabbering on and on almost unintelligibly about the classical composers. Yoichi was in heaven fulfilling Charlie's request, while in the control room Charlie and the others were practically on the floor in hysterics. Charlie had all he could do to pull himself together and go back into the studio with a straight face to sign the program off. Fortunately for him, there were no repercussions.

Yoichi, who happened to live near me in Bay Ridge, shared an apartment with a fellow countryman named Akira. I had grown to know and like both of them. Once while discussing sports in general with two boyhood chums, Clayton Doherty and Joe McCarthy, I happened to mention the unusual strength these two Japanese gentlemen possessed in spite of their small size. I could tell that my friends, who both over six feet, well built, athletic, and cocky, were very skeptical and seemed to have adopted a "show me" attitude. When I mentioned this to Yoichi, he very politely invited me and my two friends for tea one afternoon. While there, I must say my friends really embarrassed me by baiting their hosts to the inevitable showdown of who was stronger—two huge men or two small men. Well, Yoichi and Akira, without actually hurting them, made mincemeat of my old buddies. Obviously Clayton and Joe had never heard of karate!

Many times during that period Akira would drive Yoichi to work, and on mornings when I was going to announce his program, he would stop by my house and pick me up. One day when nearing the approach to the Brooklyn Bridge, Akira thought he had been deliberately cut off by another car. Wasting no time, he took off after the culprit and reciprocated in kind, only much more so. At the next intersection, the light turned red, so while we were stopped the other driver in this cut-off game pulled alongside us, jumped out, stepped up to Akira's open window, and quick as a flash reached in, grabbed the car keys, got back into his car and sped away. Stunned, we didn't know whether to laugh or cry. There we were stranded just short of the entrance to the bridge. In short order a policeman appeared to find out why we were holding up rush-hour traffic. When he heard Akira's story, he couldn't help laughing. But he did call a cab for Yoichi and me, enabling us to make it to NBC by the skin of our teeth. Akira had to wait quite a while before a tow truck finally rescued him from the terrible spot he and his car were in.

Some years later on Sunday, December 7, 1941, Pearl Harbor was attacked. The next morning the listeners of WJZ did not hear Yoichi Hiraoka playing his xylophone. Instead, they heard an announcer offering an apology for his absence followed by a substitute program featuring the staff pianist who was to have been Yoichi's accompanist. Calls to his apartment went unanswered that Monday morning and throughout the week. It was as if, coincidentally with the Pearl Harbor attack, the earth had opened up and swallowed Yoichi and Akira. A lot of speculation went on around NBC about whatever became of them. The awful word *spy* found its way

into such conjecturing. But to this day the why and where of their disappearance to my knowledge have never been answered. Jo-Anne, my wife, remembers something that was quite similar to the mystery of Yoichi. At the time of Pearl Harbor, she and her family were living in an apartment uptown in Washington Heights. In the same building lived a Japanese family. They were well liked by their neighbors in that they appeared to be pleasant, decent people. But they too disappeared as if into thin air. They dropped out of sight the Friday before Pearl Harbor. Could it be that they had advance knowledge? And, perhaps had been spirited away? And since it was on that same Friday that Yoichi was last seen at NBC, those questions might be applied to him and Akira, his roommate. Speculation again. But it sure makes you wonder.

Seth Parker was a program of small-town humor and hymn singing which was extremely popular in the mid-thirties. It was written and created by Phillips H. Lord, who also played the starring role. The setting was Jonesport, Maine. When I was still conducting tours through the new studios, part of the deal was to drop in on any program you might find in rehearsal. We would go not into the studio itself but into what was called the "clients' room" on the floor above which looked down through a glass partition at whatever was happening in the studio. We guides would identify the actors and the program they were rehearsing. Of course the clients' rooms were equipped with loudspeakers so the tours could hear everything going on below. Once when I was in that room describing to my people, who included two nuns and a priest, the activity in the studio and was explaining what the program was about, I suddenly became aware that the program's star, Phillips H. Lord, was yelling at another actor and using a frightful burst of profanity. He was really letting him have it, using every four-, five-, six-, seven-, and eight-letter word in the book, leaving nothing to the imagination. When this happened,

I had not yet arrived at the part of my spiel where I tell my folks the names of the actors in the cast. Somewhere during his tirade, Mr. Lord must have furtively glanced in our direction and realized he had a large group of eavesdroppers. Without changing his angry tone of voice and without batting an eye, but with no more bad language, he wound it up with "I'm not going to let this thing end here. As soon as Phillips Lord gets back, I'm gonna tell him all about it," and stepped out the door and out of sight. I guess that proved how creative and what a fine actor Mr. Lord really was. When the priest, obviously upset at what they had all witnessed, asked, "Young man, who was that vulgarian?" I should have prefaced my answer with "Bless me Father, for I am about to sin." For that is exactly what I did when I replied, "Father, I'm afraid I've never seen him before. He must be the new director of the *Seth Parker* program, and I'm sure Mr. Lord will be furious when he hears about his disgraceful exhibition. On behalf of NBC I would like to apologize for what you've all just witnessed."

19

INTERESTING REHEARSALS

In the 1930s, especially after I joined the announcing staff, I became what today might be called a rehearsal junkie with impeccable taste. Because at the top of my list and the rehearsal I most frequently dropped in on, when I had the time, was that of the NBC Symphony Orchestra with its celebrated conductor, Arturo Toscanini. Ninety of the world's finest musicians were assembled on the great stage of NBC's largest studio, 8H, several times a week in preparation for the Saturday night broadcast. As impressive as it was to attend the broadcast, it was far more interesting, and much more fun, to sit in on an afternoon rehearsal.

The Great Maestro, Mr. Toscanini, was a tough taskmaster. As charming as he was socially, once he stepped onto the podium he was all business. I guess part of his genius was that he could detect a false note instantly, whenever it happened, from any one of the ninety top musicians seated before him. And woe be unto him, or her, who made the same musical mistake twice. Of course, everybody knows that nobody is perfect. As great and as talented as the individual members of the orchestra were, mistakes were just bound to happen—and they did happen once in a while. And that's where the fun came in. I was lucky enough to be there a few times when a fiery Arturo Toscanini would bring down the wrath of God on such a poor soul in one and a half languages, Italian and broken English. And all the while waving his baton at the wretched musician in a seemingly threatening fashion. I have to say that while such occasions were memorable to those of us who were there as witnesses, my heart would go out to the victims who had to suffer such embarrassment in front of their peers. However, such errant behavior on the part of one musician had a different ending.

I've always been so glad I was in 8H that day because this tale has become legend. An oboe player was having problems, it just wasn't his day. After he had made the same mistake twice, the Maestro read the riot act to him. When he erred the third time, Toscanini really let him have it with both barrels. But the fourth time was too much. The terrible-tempered Toscanini in all his fury ordered him to pack up his instrument and to leave the studio forthwith, or the Italian equivalent of same, and to never return. Instead of appearing distraught as one might expect in such a situation, Mr. Oboe Player was seemingly calm, cool, and collected and was taking forever to pack his oboe. Deliberately so. Meanwhile on the podium stood the Great One, arms folded and breathing fire, silently staring at the musician's laborious closing of his instrument case. Finally the ejected one left his place and sauntered, almost casually, with his beloved instrument in one hand in the direction of the door. As he was passing the podium, he paused, looked up at the Maestro, raised his free hand toward his mouth and very loudly gave him the Bronx cheer, which, for the uninitiated, is a noisy expulsion of the breath through nearly closed lips with tongue protruded. The almost apoplectic Arturo Toscanini nearly fell off the podium as he screamed, "Iss a too late for apology! Too late for apology!"

The charming soprano star of such old

radio shows as *American Album of Familiar Music* and *Waltz Time*, Vivienne Della Chiesa, got a big laugh from our audience with another Toscanini-ism when we both sat on a panel at an old-time-radio convention a few years ago. It seems that the short-in-stature Maestro was upset with a very tall, physically well-endowed soprano. In front of his podium, as a matter of fact, she still stood at least an inch above him. She had not been performing to his satisfaction during rehearsal. It would be putting it mildly to say he had become agitated while insisting she sing the same part over and over again until she got it right. He got so excited he actually slipped and was about to fall off the podium, when in desperation with both hands he grabbed onto the ample endowments of the soprano. In spite of his precarious situation and still furious, he yelled, "If only these were brains!"

During the years he was at NBC, the Maestro was frequently accompanied by Mrs. Toscanini. I say accompanied, but the truth is that whenever they were walking together it was not the togetherness the average person, at least the average American, understands. For the Toscaninis, walking together really meant walking about ten feet apart. She was in front while he brought up the rear—ten feet directly behind her. If she would stop to chat with someone, he would join in. But as soon as the conversation ended, he would wait until she got the ten-foot lead before he would resume walking. It was, indeed, fun to watch.

The *Fleischmann Hour*, starring Rudy Vallee, his orchestra, and prominent guests, was sponsored by Fleischmann's Yeast and was on the air every Thursday at 8 P.M. coast-to-coast on NBC's Red Network. This extravaganza was broadcast out of Studio 8G, which was across the hall from 8H but less than half its size. Accordingly its seating capacity suffered by comparison, but a far greater sense of intimacy seemed to prevail, especially during the afternoon

rehearsals. The *Fleischmann Hour* was rated as one of NBC's top shows at the time and was credited with boosting many talented performers from the vaudeville stage to national stardom. After a few appearances on the program, such acts as George Burns and Gracie Allen, Edgar Bergen and Charlie McCarthy, Milton Berle, and many others were in such demand that they went on to star in their own shows on radio and later on television. Dropping in to 8G during the Rudy Vallee rehearsal always proved fruitful to somebody like me because I remembered having seen and sometimes even met some of the performers when I was a kid, and my neighbor, the vaudevillian Will J. Ward, took me along with his two children when he was playing in Brooklyn or Manhattan. In visiting the rehearsal, you also never knew when established movie stars from Hollywood might be on the bill.

One day as I took a seat there I found I had arrived just in time to catch the last few minutes of rehearsal of a dramatic sketch featuring Edward G. Robinson, who was then starring in a motion picture called *Little Caesar*, which portrayed the life of the notorious Chicago gangster, Al Capone. When the sketch was finished, the program's director in the control room could be heard speaking over the public address system to Mr. Robinson, advising him that the dress rehearsal would begin in another half hour or so and he shouldn't wander too far off. Acknowledging that advice, Robinson left the stage with one of the actors, aimlessly wandered down the aisle and wound up moving into the empty row in front of me where they both sat down, lit up cigarettes and relaxed.

Onstage, meanwhile, Rudy Vallee had started rehearsing his orchestra. So, having to kill some time and having nothing better to do, Edward G. Robinson and his actor friend just took it easy and watched. At this point I must interject that it was pretty generally known around NBC that the "Vagabond Lover," as Rudy had been known in his earlier days, had quite a temper and a very foul mouth. Mother Teresa herself might be sitting in on his rehearsal, and he couldn't care less. Almost always the butt of his nastiness was the orchestra, en masse or individually. Maybe he was trying to emulate Toscanini's outbursts. But the Maestro was never known to have used gutter language in his occasional tirades. Rudy's cursing, swearing, and vile tongue got under Mr. Robinson's skin. So much so that after fifteen minutes of it, I heard him complaining to his fellow actor: "I can't believe what I'm witnessing here. If his public ever knew this side of Rudy Vallee, he'd be finished tomorrow. Let's go out in the hall where we might get a breath of cleaner air. And I wish with all my heart I didn't have to come back for tonight's show." But, of course, he did. Little Caesar would not defy the showbiz dictum "The show must go on."

Speaking of off-color language, the last person on earth you would have expected to hear it from was Edward MacHugh, the gospel singer. Mr. MacHugh's daily morning program, sponsored by Procter and Gamble, had a national audience for several years. Ed MacHugh was a nice man. He loved life and enjoyed being with friends and making them laugh. His pleasant Scottish burr added to the stories he had such fun telling. He had no studio audience, so all his lighthearted patter during rehearsal was never heard by anyone other than those connected with the program. He made sure that the loudspeakers in the clients' room above were turned off during rehearsal so the visiting tours couldn't eavesdrop. When rehearsal ended and the broadcast began, the loudspeakers were turned back on. Many of the tourists watched with seemingly reverential interest as Edward MacHugh mesmerized large numbers of the radio audience with his stirring renditions of old, familiar hymns. Of course they had no way of knowing that as soon as the program was over, he would more than likely continue his amusing, but

off-color, routine in the studio. The big difference between him and Rudy Vallee was that Ed MacHugh was always good-humored, even though what rolled off his tongue didn't exactly balance with the sacred songs coming out of the same mouth. Whereas with Rudy his outbursts were mean-spirited, and he didn't care who overheard.

As I approached the NBC bank of elevators in the main lobby one day in the thirties, there happened to be one person already standing there waiting. It was Al Jolson. Right after I arrived two middle-aged ladies, obviously tourists, also appeared. Realizing there was no elevator on the ground floor yet, they were continuing their conversation when one of them suddenly became aware of the identity of the gentleman standing near me, on the opposite side of the elevator bank about twenty feet across from where they were. Excitement takes different forms with different people. With this lady I guess it showed in her attempt to give the impression of being real cool. This she did by raising her hand and moving her index finger in sort of a "come hither" fashion as she called his name, "Oh, Mr. Jolson." She was also indicating, by the beckoning movement of her finger, that she would like him, this world-famous and beloved entertainer to come over to her, probably to hear what pearls of wisdom she might impart to him. Until that moment he appeared to be daydreaming. When he realized that the stranger on the opposite side of the elevator bank was summoning him as she would a porter, he let the startled lady have it with both barrels. He told her off like I'm sure she had never been told off before. I remember his tirade began along these lines, "Madam, you need to be taught some manners. The nerve of you calling me to approach you as if I were a child. I am not your lackey." No expletives. No profanity. And when he got through, he stepped on an elevator after it finally arrived, as did I. The tourist, probably feeling disgraced in front of her companion, very definitely did not get on. Inside the elevator I couldn't resist letting Mr. J. know how much I approved of his performance. I quietly feigned applause. With that the great Al Jolson smiled from ear to ear. Angry no longer, he looked at me and mouthed the words "Thank you."

Long before Julia Child became the queen of cooking on the airwaves, there was a daytime radio program all through the thirties and into the forties called *The Mystery Chef*. Why the star chose to appear under a pseudonym I never did know because there was no mystery why his program was so popular. It was simply because his approach to cooking was entertaining as well as instructive. There was also no mystery about what his name was—Angus MacPherson. Everybody in radio knew it. On occasion one or another of the radio columnists would mention his name, thereby letting the cat out of the bag insofar as any mystery about him was concerned. Such an unintended gaffe was usually committed right after Thanksgiving, Christmas, or New Year's Day. The reason was that on those three holidays Mr. and Mrs. MacPherson had open house all day long for members of the NBC announcing and engineering staffs at their beautiful apartment a few doors west of the Plaza Hotel on Central Park South. If it was a working day for you, you sandwiched your Mystery Chef turkey buffet in between shows. Another thing there was no mystery about was the food. In a word it was scrumptious. And no matter when you dropped in, it was hot. This was decades before the advent of the microwave oven. As I look back now, yes, there was a mystery. How did Angus MacPherson manage to keep that delicious holiday repast hot all those many hours? Maybe that's why he called himself the Mystery Chef.

20

FIRE THE ANNOUNCER

One day sometime in the thirties while having dinner in Hurley's, I suddenly looked up and who was standing there smiling at me but my old friend, my mentor actually, C. J. Ingram, who helped get my career started when I was a page at 711 Fifth Avenue. I knew he still wrote a column and was radio editor of the *Jersey Journal*. He joined me for dinner, and it was indeed a pleasant reunion because I had not seen him in quite some time. He had looked for me in the announcers' office and learned I was through for the day but to try Hurley's.

Then he told me why he was glad he found me. He hoped I could join him on his press pass to see the show at the Radio City Music Hall while Amos 'n' Andy were playing there. Of course, I accepted his invitation. But instead of entering through the usual front entrance, Mr. Ingram took me through the stage door and up in a backstage elevator to their dressing room. It seems he had an appointment with them to discuss their appearance on his *Stardust* program on WAAT, Jersey City, the following Sunday. It was indeed quite a thrill to sit down in private with those two giants of radio comedy. I left most of the talking to C. J. Ingram because, after all, it was his appointment. However, they did indicate they remembered me as the page who used to sit in the control room with Deak Aylesworth when they would pop in from Chicago from time to time. Whether they meant it or not, it sure made me feel good. As Clint Eastwood might say, it made my day. Then, as the call came that show time was coming up, they put the icing on the cake. They asked if Mr. Ingram and I would like to watch their show from backstage. They were two very nice men. Freeman Gosden and Charles Correll, whose performance as Amos 'n' Andy on NBC kept all America in stitches every night at 7:00, were now causing the rafters to rattle in the Radio City Music Hall. And I was standing in the wings watching them.

In 1936 there was a strike against the radio networks by ASCAP, the American Society of Composers, Authors, and Publishers. ASCAP members wanted more money for allowing the networks to play their music. Therefore, during the strike the networks stopped playing all ASCAP tunes. One morning on a program I was assigned to, *Allen Prescott, the Wife Saver*, the pianist Joe Kahn played a song which had mistakenly been placed on his piano by a clerk from the music library. An executive at the NBC station in Cleveland, WTAM, happened to hear it and realized it was an ASCAP number so he called John F. Royal, the vice president of programming, to complain. Royal had been manager of WTAM before coming to New York. His immediate reaction was, "Fire the production man." He soon learned no production man had been assigned that day and that the only other program department employee on the show was the announcer, who had nothing at all to do with music. Needing a scapegoat, however, he called my boss, Pat Kelly, and ordered him to "fire the announcer," which Kelly had to do to me, however reluctantly, that very afternoon.

In utter disbelief at what had happened so suddenly, I tried to get work on other stations, to no avail, during the next week. I was completely devastated. Fortunately, I

Columbia University
in the City of New York

DEPARTMENT OF ENGLISH
AND
COMPARATIVE LITERATURE

PHILOSOPHY HALL

23 July 1936

Miss Margaret Cuthbert,
Program Department,
National Broadcasting Company,
Rockefeller Center,
West 49 Street,
New York, New York.

Dear Miss Cuthbert:

Will you send me the name of the
announcer for my program last Monday, WEAF, 2:30-
245? He is quite young and, so far, unspoiled.
He sounds not only like a human being but really
like an American and yet withal very pleasant.
His voice in real life has an edge which comes
through the tubes as a very pleasant resonance
indeed. He possibly would profit by a caution
not to be too emphatic in phrasing; for example
his rendition of "not only ... but also" seems a
bit formal. But if instruction means that he may
become self-conscious, he should have none at all.

I should like to have his name in
order to watch his progress (I trust).

Yours truly,

Cabell Greet.

The kind of letter that pleases the heart and swells the head.

learned it was common gossip among the executive secretaries that Alfred H. Morton, manager of the program department's purse strings, thought I had been given a raw deal, as did the trade papers, *Variety* and *Zits*. Losing no time, I got Morton's secretary to pencil me in for an appointment the next day. Mr. Morton listened to my side of the story and impressed upon me the responsibility my job entailed, etc., etc. He then called Pat Kelly and told him to put me back on the schedule immediately, thus countermanding John Royal's edict.

Realizing I now had nothing to lose, I explained to him that two years earlier when I was hired from the guide staff I had been promised that if I worked out okay I would be promoted to the regular staff. I strongly suggested to Mr. Morton that by now after two whole years I had either proven myself or I hadn't. Having just given me my job back, there wasn't much he could say. He had no argument. So as events turned out, he acted accordingly. The very next payday my check reflected my new status, that of regular announcer.

Forgetting the fact I had been doing the same work as the other announcers for two years, I couldn't have been happier at the turn of events. In those awful Depression days of 1936, so many millions of people were jobless. Heads of families were reduced to selling apples on the streets if they weren't waiting in endless hunger lines to receive a handout from charitable organizations like the Salvation Army. Hope mixed with despair was the order of the day for those poor souls. In the face of that, it's easy to see why I had good reason to be thankful for my good fortune. By a strange twist of fate, I found myself unemployed one day and within a week I not only had my job back and was paid for the days I was out but my salary was almost doubled, from $25 to $45. In 1936 that was not to be sneezed at.

I was reminded of all this when, in the

New York Times of April 20, 1974, I was saddened to read that the man who had been my benefactor thirty-eight years earlier had died from smoke inhalation in a fire at his Connecticut home. I couldn't help but think if it hadn't been for the fairness, understanding, and decency of Alfred H. Morton, qualities which John F. Royal demonstrated he was quite lacking in, who knows what different course my life might have taken.

Now that I was no longer a junior announcer, it was decided to send me on a remote that was quite different. Every weekend from late June to early September of 1936, I traveled to Chautauqua, New York, to announce the Chautauqua Symphony Orchestra. Chautauqua, a summer resort town in western New York on beautiful Lake Chautauqua, was, and still is, the seat of a summer educational association offering lectures, concerts, etc. On Friday nights I would catch the overnight train out of Hoboken, sleep in a Pullman car, and get off in Jamestown, New York, where I was met early in the morning by a limo and driven the twenty miles to Chautauqua. Talk about VIP treatment.

While there, I stayed at the St. Elmo Hotel, a warm and inviting relic of the nineteenth century. The symphony orchestra was presented in two programs. One was a half-hour broadcast on Saturday mornings at 10:30. This was a "children's concert," music appealing to the younger set. On Sunday afternoons at 3:00, the orchestra appeared for a full hour in a regular concert of memorable music by the great masters. Operatic stars as well as famous instrumentalists appeared. The conductor was the celebrated Howard Hansen. I must confess I felt awed doing my bit while looking out at five thousand music lovers from the stage of this huge rotunda. I must also confess that for me it was not all work and no play, no way. Between the Saturday morning and Sunday afternoon shows, I had lots of free time on my hands, and much of it I took advantage of by trying to improve my swimming in beautiful Lake Chautauqua.

Sometime during that summer of 1936 I was approached by Ford Bond, one of the staff announcers. He was trying, he said, to arrange time off from his busy schedule of commercial programs so he and his wife could get away for two weeks. He asked if I would go up with him to Studio 8C to meet Martha Atwell who was the director of *Just Plain Bill* and read the announcer's copy for her. If she approved, he could relax because *Just Plain Bill* a soap opera, was the last of the six commercial shows for which he needed a substitute. His other five were the *Cities Service Concert* on Friday nights, *Manhattan Merry-Go-Round* on Sunday nights, *Easy Aces*, on three nights a week, and *David Harum* and *Stella Dallas*, both Monday-through-Friday soap operas. His substitute announcers for those shows had all been approved by each of the different directors. Now it just remained to be seen what Miss Atwell thought about my reading. Naturally I was flattered to be asked by this important announcer and agreed to accompany him to Studio 8C.

That Mr. Ford Bond should come to little old me probably inspired just the degree of confidence I needed to do a reading satisfactory enough to be accepted by Martha Atwell, which is what happened. When I finished, she said from the control room, "Suits me fine." Coming into the studio, she told Ford to have a pleasant vacation and said, "I'll see you in two weeks." To me she said, "I'll see you on Monday, and thank you very much."

Looking back from my present vantage point, six decades later, that was a moment when I might have thrown my arms around the good lady and professed that it was I who should thank her for agreeing with Ford Bond's judgment of my work. The few minutes it took me to audition that day in the summer of 1936 was the foot in the door which opened into twenty years of uninterrupted association with Air Features, the soap opera "factory" owned and operated by Frank and Anne Hummert. More about that later.

I neglected to mention earlier that when I was still a kid and hoping that when I grew up I would have a singing career, I became a fan of the "Silver Masked Tenor" on WEAF, around 1925. Aside from the fact that he sang stuff I knew and loved, there was an aura of mystery about him which got to me. As it was intended to. Whenever his picture appeared in the papers, his face was always covered by a silver mask. I guess I was too immature to stop and figure out that this was an advertising gimmick. Goodrich Silvertown Tires sponsored his program. The orchestra, conducted by Jack Shilkret, was the Goodrich Silvertown Orchestra. The nameless Silver Masked Tenor made listeners happy, and listeners made the sponsor happy by buying lots and lots of Silvertown Tires. After several successful years, the Goodrich Company, for whatever reason, dropped its sponsorship. At that point the nameless tenor dropped his silver mask and his anonymity and continued singing on NBC. No longer sponsored, his billing became straightforward and brief—Joseph White, tenor.

It was at this phase of his career that I had the pleasure of meeting Mr. White. It was during my page boy days at 711 Fifth Avenue and I was thrilled because he had been one of my singing idols before I ever knew what his name was. After I joined the announcing staff and found myself doing his program from time to time, my friendship with Joseph White as well as with his wife and children continued. His son Robert in later years proved to be a chip off the old block. He too is a wonderful tenor. His success has been, and continues to be, mostly on the concert stage. He also teaches at the Juilliard School of Music in Lincoln Center.

In 1994 Robert and I had a most enjoyable reunion at the Juilliard bookstore, where our friend Tom DeLong had invited us to a book-launching party to celebrate

97 Elm Street
Oberlin, Ohio
February 15, 1937

Mr. George Ansbro
Care of the N. B. C.
Radio City
New York

Dear Mr Ansbro:

This is not a fan letter, but I am writing to tell
you that some people do listen to the program which
comes at 10:00 A.M. E. S. T. over the Red Network
of the N. B. C. who are critical enough to detect a
flagrant misuse of the English language, which you
have made at least three weeks in your Monday morning
commercial. You say that "dust lays on the floor"
and I wonder just what it lays.

I listen to the program largely because it follows
a news cast and I am too busy to change it. I am a
semi-invalid, but rather well-educated, and this
repeated mistake annoys me more than I can tell you.
Probably your sponsors do not listen in or correct
it, and perhaps the majority of your listeners do not
notice it. But I am sure that a great many of them
do, and that it would make a better impression if
you spoke correctly.

                    Very respectfully yours,

                        (Mrs.)
                        E. W. Chamber

Mrs. Chamber is quite right. This definitely is not a fan letter!

the publication of his *Biodiscography of the Golden Voice of Radio, Frank Munn*. Munn, also a tenor, was one of the all-time great singers of radio. Robert and I enjoyed wonderful reminiscences of his father and mother from when he was just a kid and I was a very young announcer. I had known and worked with Frank Munn, so it was great getting together at the party with other old friends who had also known him. Friends such as Felix Knight, another leading tenor of those early radio days, who

Sept 26-1936

My Dear Mr. Ansborough,

I have listened to you on the radio for a few years, and think there is nothing like your voice. It has such fine quality.

Would you be kind enough to answer these questions

1. How tall are you?

2. What color eyes and hair?

3. Are you married?

4. Do you do anything besides announcing?

5. How old are you?

6. Do you go out with girls?

7. Would it be possible for me to get a picture of you in some way?

I heard you on "Mrs. Wiggs of the Cabbage Patch".

Patricia Cash

There is no doubt about this letter though.

was there with his wife of many, many years, Ethel Blume. I had known Ethel as a child actress and hadn't seen her since. Jean Dickenson, a soprano who had sung with Frank Munn on the *American Album of Familiar Music* program, was also there. The biggest surprise of the evening and the only guest I had never met was the all-time great star, Hildegarde. Although I had never had the pleasure of speaking with her, I had seen her perform several times in the forties and fifties when she was featured at what was then perhaps the most elegant supper club in New York, the Persian Room of the Plaza. She had been billed as the "Incomparable Hildegarde." Later, as Tom DeLong's guest at dinner, she was seated between Robert White and me, and she indeed lived up to her billing of those long-ago days. She proved how incomparable she was by good-naturedly tapping the side of a glass with her knife to get the attention of the table and announcing that in exactly one week she would reach her 88th birthday. And that furthermore, she would celebrate by working that night at a club in Greenwich Village. Not only was Hildegarde still "incomparable," she was also delightful.

Looking back, the year 1936 turned out to be quite a milestone in my career. Things happened which would have lasting effects. As I mentioned earlier, the first event was my being fired, and unfired a week later. I say unfired instead of rehired because, as it turned out, even though I was not actually on the air during those worrisome days, the event was a blessing in disguise, the proof of which was NBC's paying me during my enforced absence and raising me to the ranks of senior staff announcers. It would be incorrect to say that I was rehired when I was never "not paid." That's why I prefer coining the word *unfired*. Semantics aside, I feel quite sure NBC would not have sent a junior announcer twelve straight weekends during that summer to do the Chautauqua Symphony Orchestra. Nor, by the same token, would Ford Bond have suggested a junior announcer as his vacation replacement on the soap opera *Just Plain Bill*. There's never been any doubt in my mind that gesture led directly to my being selected by Anne Hummert as the announcer for a new show which the Hummert soap opera "factory" was about to air on NBC.

Martha Atwell, the director who had okayed me to do two weeks of *Just Plain Bill*, undoubtedly influenced Mrs. Hummert in selecting me for that program, *Mrs. Wiggs of the Cabbage Patch*. I had strong feelings that that's how things worked out because when I walked into Studio 3D at 9 o'clock for rehearsal that first day of *Mrs. Wiggs* in early September of 1936, I was happy to see Martha Atwell smiling at me through the control room window. The only cast member I knew was Peggy Zinke, who had played Jane on *Jolly Bill and Jane*. The name of the character Peggy played was Australie, Mrs. Wiggs's daughter. Her romantic interest was played by a young actor about my age, twenty-one at the time, whose name was Van Heflin. As countless

fans will remember, Van became a top movie star not too long after his appearances on radio. The leading role of Mrs. Wiggs was played by Betty Garde. Betty was thirty-one, and our friendship continued until she passed away at eighty-five in 1990. She had been retired and living in California for quite some time.

Mrs. Wiggs was one of the few daytime shows which aired a live repeat to the West Coast. We would rehearse at 9 o'clock, drop down briefly to the Kaufman-Bedrick Drugstore to enjoy coffee and small talk with members of that day's cast, and then return to 3D in time to go on the air at 10. The program, live repeat and all, ran for two years. In those days repeats to the West Coast were performed live because of the networks' hard-and-fast rule against putting any kind of recording on the air. In later years the rule was dropped.

21

AFRA BEGINS

At this point I would like to tell about the other announcers at NBC in the 1930s. Some of them I've already mentioned, like John S. Young, Jimmy Wallington, Don Wilson, Graham McNamee, Ford Bond, Don Lowe, Charles O'Connor, Clyde Kittel, and the ill-fated poor little rich boy who took his own life, the second junior announcer, Ellis Andrews. As I look over the roster of NBC announcers which I've hung onto over this long stretch of time since 1935, I'm reminded that the oldest of the group, Graham McNamee, was born in 1889. Not only was he the oldest and most famous of the twenty-seven NBC announcers, but he was indisputably the most famous in all America. He was the first political announcer, the most renowned of the early sportscasters, the first announcer of big variety shows, and the first "second banana" on shows starring big-name comedians. He played foil to Ed Wynn in Texaco's *The Fire Chief* beginning in 1932. In the attractive and spacious quarters for our exclusive use, the announcers' lounge, I frequently found myself during the thirties and into the forties enjoying a game of Chinese checkers with Graham McNamee. It was a variation of the regular checkers game I had known since childhood, and it was quite popular at the time. Graham would occasionally remark that this game was being played by two men at the opposite ends of the announcers' age spectrum, he being the oldest and I the youngest. Had this been in the later era of the great comedy writer, Neil Simon, Mr. McNamee might have referred to us as "the odd couple."

The next oldest announcer was Alois Havrilla, who was born in 1891 in Prague, Czechoslovakia. For someone who had come to this country at the age of four when his family emigrated to Bridgeport, Connecticut, his later command of the English language was remarkable in that he had no trace of an accent. He was one of the most sought-after commercial announcers on the NBC staff. Two other things about Alois stand out in my memory. One was the mystery of his eating and drinking habits. He kept a bottle of Scotch in his locker at all times for that moment when he just plain felt like a nip, which I witnessed many times. He was not one who frequented bars or cocktail lounges. To my knowledge he was never seen in Hurley's, the Down Under, or the English Grill, the busiest watering holes in the building, where the NBC crowd congregated. Where he ate lunch or dinner nobody ever knew, and no one ever caught him eating out of a paper bag in our lounge. The other thing about him that amused us all then as it does me now was simply this. It seems that in 1932 he won the award of the American Academy of Arts and Letters for good diction on radio. A direct result of his receiving this prestigious accolade was his less-than-subtle attempt to impress whomever he might be talking to. This attempt was particularly amusing when it involved a certain word. A cuss word. His occasional descent into speaking blasphemously would cause double takes followed by titters from anyone within earshot. When he would take the name of the Lord in vain, profanity would come out like so: "For Christ-tss sake," the "tss" sound so audible it became a second syllable. Without realizing it, Alois Havrilla created his own trademark. Sort of.

Milton Cross was the third oldest NBC announcer. He and I were the only native New Yorkers, both of us being from Brooklyn. Besides shepherding us kids through his Sunday morning *Children's Hour*, he was recognized for his distinctive voice on several classical and semiclassical programs. The best known of these was *The A & P Gypsies*, which began on WEAF, New York, in 1923, four years before the birth of the National Broadcasting Company. For quite a while, Milton was the butt of good-natured teasing based on a blooper he once made when he said on the air, "Presenting the A & G Pipsies." But no one could ever come close to his remarkable record as host of the Metropolitan Opera broadcasts originating in the Metropolitan Opera House in New York. The series began on Christmas Day 1931 and was heard during the opera season for forty-four years. In all that time, Milton prided himself on never missing a broadcast performance of the Metropolitan Opera.

For several years beginning in February of 1940, his Sunday nights were occupied when he acted as "chairman" of *The Chamber Music Society of Lower Basin Street*, which featured swing music, singers such as Dinah Shore, and Milton's tongue-in-cheek commentary in the long-hair style. It was a complete departure from anything he had ever done before, from his usually staid and somber approach to the spoken word. Just to hear the sonorous tones of Milton Cross announce that "The Chamber Music Society is dedicated to Three B's: Barrelhouse, Boogie Woogie, and the Blues" was an experience in itself. I often wondered how he could do it with a straight face. Without breaking up. For Milton was a giggler. I had heard him a couple of times when something he was reading struck his funny bone and he became hysterical. Fortunately on those few occasions he

was reading short, unimportant promotional announcements. I say "fortunately" because he was also a worrier. Most importantly to me, who had known him since I was twelve, Milton Cross was a genuinely nice person.

Howard Claney and Alwyn Bach, both born in 1898, were in the army during World War I. Alwyn fought in France, while Howard never even got seasick because he was saved by the armistice. He had been in a few plays on the New York stage and joined the NBC staff in 1930, a year before I became a page. During my page and guide days and later as a junior announcer, I listened to and concentrated a lot on the announcing style of each of the NBC announcers. I concluded, to myself of course, that if anyone were ever to tell me I sounded even slightly like Howard Claney, I would be more than happy, even if he didn't win a diction award. Speaking of which, Alwyn Bach did win it. He was the third NBC-er to achieve the honor, after Milton Cross and Alois Havrilla. But, unlike Havrilla, when Al Bach said, "for Christ's sake" he didn't pussyfoot around. It came out as it generally does, "for Chrissake." He wasn't out to impress with his excellent enunciation. No extra sibilant sounding syllable was added. His listener might have thought "tsk, tsk," but never tittered, like Havrilla's.

Al Bach was a fun guy. You could always be sure there would be something to smile about, if not have a real belly laugh, when he was around. Thinking of him brings to my mind his expertise at ping pong. He and George Hicks were, without a doubt, the best players on the announcing staff. They were evenly matched even though Bach was seven years older. Until I became a member of the announcing staff, I had never held a ping pong paddle. But, thanks to the kind patience of Bach and Hicks and a few of the others, after I had been part of their group for a couple of years I found that I was enjoying the game tremendously and doing a lot better than

Milton Cross and I at a company affair in 1948. And our pretty companion? I can't remember her name, but I'm sure if Milton were still around, he would!

when I first started. There were some who never played, like McNamee, Havrilla, Cross, Bond, and Kittel, but they liked to watch. Others, like Charlie O'Connor, Ben Grauer, Ed Herlihy, or Don Lowe would occasionally grab a paddle and suggest a game. I happened to be there with nothing to do, I would quickly hop to the opposite end of the table.

One of the announcers who played once in a while was Nelson Case. He had been transferred to NBC, New York, from KFI, Los Angeles, sometime in 1934 after I had been promoted to the staff. By 1936 or 1937 I had come to the conclusion that Nelson, for whatever reason, was cool toward me. I had the feeling he resented me, a young

whippersnapper who, unlike him, had no background to speak of. No college degree. No well-to-do family. No father like his, who owned a newspaper in California. He had had his own orchestra, had a fine baritone voice, and was an excellent announcer. So it's understandable that I was pleased when one day while I was alone in the lounge he walked in to use the facilities and when he was finished, as he was nearing the door to go out, he suddenly suggested a game of ping pong. Of course I said yes, and while walking toward the section where the ping pong table was I tried to figure out why he had had this sudden change of heart toward me if in fact that's what it really was. Or was he planning to show this kid how the game was really played? Taking our places at the table, we volleyed for a few minutes to warm up and then started.

Understandably, after these many years, I don't recall the exact scores. But what I do remember, what I will never forget, is that he couldn't conceal his unhappiness when I took the first game. And then the second. By the time we got into the third game, he had become openly hostile, with plenty of abusive language to make his point. Somewhere along the line Graham McNamee and Alwyn Bach came in and stayed because they were amazed by Nelson's poor sportsmanship. And was I ever glad they happened in. Because when the third game ended with still no victory for Mr. Case, he really exploded by actually throwing his paddle at me. Then he rushed across the room, fists clenched, ready to fight. McNamee and Bach quickly interceded by blocking his way, which I guess caused him to realize that if he continued against those two, especially Graham McNamee, he would be in real trouble. Muttering a very low "I'm sorry," he moved toward the door and, obviously embarrassed, left the room. Needless to say, he never suggested a ping pong game again. However, I'm pleased to say that the incident, strangely enough, had the effect of improving the relationship between Nelson Case and me. It seemed that as time went on, he wasn't just civil to me but genuinely friendly. And I was happy to respond in kind.

Ed Herlihy made the leap from Boston radio to the NBC New York announcing staff in the mid-1930s at the same time that his close friend, Frank Gallop, left Boston. Gallop came here to join CBS. Both became so successful that eventually the demands of that success caused them to reluctantly leave their respective staff jobs to freelance. It was the networks' policy that staff announcers could not work on the opposition networks or on independent radio stations even in their free time. It was a rule that was strictly adhered to. But as freelancers they were fortunate in that many new opportunities opened up. Each enjoyed the pleasure of being about as busy as it was possible for an announcer to be in New York.

One of the better-known NBC announcers in the 1930s was Kelvin Keech. He was born in Honolulu in 1895, so I suppose it was only natural that he took to playing the ukulele as a youngster and became quite accomplished at it. During World War I, he was with the U.S. Signal Corps, and after the war he organized his own band, which took him to France, Monaco, Greece, Turkey, and England. There he befriended the youthful Prince of Wales, who later abdicated and became the duke of Windsor. During his association with the prince, Kelvin taught him how to play the uke. During an engagement with his orchestra in Constantinople, Kelvin met a Russian refugee. It was love at first sight, and they got married. Much later he liked to tell the story that he married her when he learned she couldn't say no in English.

Toward the late 1930s there were more announcers employed by NBC in New York than at any subsequent period. Twenty-eight in all. Here, in alphabetical order, are their names: George Ansbro, Alwyn Bach, Bill Bailey, Ford Bond, Nelson Case, Howard Claney, Milton Cross, Neel Enslen, Ben Grauer, Gene Hamilton, Alois Havrilla, Ed Herlihy, Kelvin Keech, Pat Kelly, Alan Kent, Clyde Kittel, Frank Klode, Don Lowe, Graham McNamee, Charles O'Connor, Howard Petrie, Dan Russell, Charles Tramont, Lyle Van, Robert Waldrop, James Wallington, Don Wilson, John S. Young.

And here are the names of our friendly competitors at CBS, as memory will allow, during the same era: Mel Allen, Andre Baruch, Norman Brokenshire, Bill Cullen, Paul Douglas, Ralph Edwards, Larry Elliot, Frank Gallop, Art Hannes, Harry Marble, Tony Marvin, Bert Parks, Ken Roberts, David Ross, Dan Seymour, Warren Sweeney, Harry Von Zell.

At my mother's insistence (she never really did get over my not finishing college), I started taking a weekly course in public speaking at NYU. After two or three classes, I decided it was a waste of time because I was learning far more on my job so I stopped going. Sometime later I was flabbergasted to see my professor in Pat Kelly's office applying for an audition to get a job. He in turn damn near dropped dead upon meeting me because I had been very careful while attending his class not to let him, or any of the students, know what I did for a living. I still remember how bad I felt for his embarrassment.

Since the weather bureau began giving names to hurricanes one doesn't hear much about storms that happened earlier. One I have in mind is known simply as the Hurricane of 1938. It comes to my mind now because in reminiscing about NBC in the old days I see myself, and many others, standing at the windows of our announcers' lounge looking across at the Radio City Music Hall while that terrible storm was raging. Our lounge was situated on the second floor directly opposite the huge Music Hall marquee, the largest in New York, and everyone watching had little doubt but that the entire marquee would be blown off before the hurricane was over. Word had passed around that the announcers' lounge was the best spot in the building to view a disaster that seemed inevitable. And so the door was left open for the curious throughout the company to have a front-row seat. Thank God that unbelievable wind never did win out. In spite of its swinging and swaying, the marquee beat the odds and held fast.

Other places, however, were not so fortunate. Long Island was among them, especially Westhampton, situated right on the Atlantic Ocean. Three different families I knew lost their Westhampton Beach homes, which disappeared into the ocean. Two of them had fortunately closed up right after Labor Day and were not there when the storm struck. But the young wife of my friend Peter Campbell Brown had decided to stay at the beach with her baby a bit longer and return home later when Peter came out to pick them up. Tragically, mother and child were both lost, along with their house. Mrs. Brown's remains washed up on another beach a week later, but the child was never found. Thanks to the nameless Hurricane of 1938.

In 1938 the performers' union was established. The American Federation of Radio Artists, AFRA, officially came into being when working conditions were agreed upon and contracts were ratified between the radio networks and AFRA. Independent radio stations across the country had their own individual discussions leading to agreements and eventual ratifications with AFRA. There is absolutely no doubt it greatly improved actors', singers' and announcers' working conditions. The union did not include musicians, however, who already had their own union. Some of the points covered by AFRA were minimum wages and the setting of rehearsal hours. My personal financial situation began to improve markedly, as did every other member's. It's an honor to be known as a charter member of AFRA, which in 1953 became AFTRA when the "T" for television was added.

For a short spell in the thirties, I found myself on a program, Monday through Friday, called *Peables Takes Charge*. Even though it was quite amusing, it didn't last very long, probably because it never had a sponsor. Besides my opening and closing of each day's program, I had the fun of engaging in conversation with the lead character, an elegant butler named Peables, discussing the most recent foibles of his sour-tempered employer, played by Alfred Swenson. Peables, who referred to himself as a gentleman's gentleman, was Mark Smith. Both actors were veterans of the Broadway stage. Thinking back, that show was head and shoulders above a lot of the stuff on the air then and later.

In the summer of 1938, Pat Kelly

Chatting with Mark Smith as Peables, an elegant butler, was most enjoyable. We did Peables Takes Charge *weekdays at noon through 1938 and 39. Peables lent charm to the show and many a smile to 1930s listeners.*

notified me that beginning the following Monday I would be doing a new sustaining program called *Omar Herth, the Swingmaker* at 8 A.M. on WEAF and the Red Network. For several months previously I had been the *Esso News* reporter reading news at 7:55 on WJZ (without NBC's Blue Network), so I asked Kelly if I was being dropped from *Esso News*, which in my mind was a logical question because I couldn't see how I could be on WJZ until 8 and start something else on WEAF and the Red Network immediately. He said not to worry, "As you know, you do the news for

four and a half minutes, until 7:59:30, and during the next thirty seconds master control does the switching as long as you push the right buttons on the announcer's delight." I heaved a sigh of relief to hear I wasn't being dropped from *Esso News* because since the very recent agreement with AFRA the *Esso News*, being a commercial program, was now paying me a fee of $5. It was quite understandable that I didn't want to lose it because I was the daytime *Esso News* reporter four times every day, five days a week. So at this time my income had increased $100 a week over and above my

Omar Herth, the Swingmaker consisted of Frankie Froeba, Dick Ridgely, and Milt Herth with me as spokesperson. We dressed up in silly costumes for the picture because it was a silly show. The trio nevertheless provided sensational swing music six mornings a week at 8 o'clock for several years in the late thirties and early forties.

base salary which, also because of AFRA, had jumped from $45 to $60. Nelson Case was in the same position at night doing four nighttime Esso reports. He and I were the very first *Esso News* reporters, long before the Standard Oil Company changed the name to Exxon.

As flush as I felt with my new prosperity, I must confess I had been disappointed when *Mrs. Wiggs of the Cabbage Patch* had suddenly gone off the air a month or so earlier. Already I missed the enjoyment of getting together twice each day with the cast members and Martha Atwell, the director. I also missed the daily experience of doing the commercials for Old English No Rubbing

Liquid Floor Wax. I had been looking forward to receiving a fee for *Mrs. Wiggs.* So too were the actors looking ahead to increases over what they had already been getting. In addition, for the first time, we all would have received payment for the repeat show to the West Coast. The newly established scale payment for a repeat program was 50 percent of the first show. In my case, if *Mrs. Wiggs* had not been dropped, I would have really been in clover. Having done the show for two years for no fee, I would suddenly have found myself being paid $15 per show, or $75 per week, plus half again for the repeats, $37.50, for a total of $112.50. But unlike the actors, I had my staff job, plus *Esso News*, which was now paying a fee. By the way, a word of explanation. The reason the *Mrs. Wiggs* program, had it stayed on, would have paid $15 per show while the *Esso News* paid only $5 was simply because *Mrs. Wiggs* was fifteen minutes in length, whereas *Esso News* was only five.

The next Monday I picked up my news copy, plus Esso commercials, in the newsroom and went to the studio where *Omar Herth, the Swingmaker* (Milt Herth) and the other members of his trio were rehearsing. Milt played Hammond organ, Frankie Froeba piano, and Dick Ridgely drums. I was put at ease right away when I saw that Frankie Froeba was one of the trio because I had already become a fan and a friend of his at the club he worked at on West 52d Street. In those days 52d Street between Fifth and Sixth Avenues was known as Swing Alley. It was Frankie's fabulous fingers knocking out sensational jazz that attracted me to the club, plus his pleasant personality. In the studio I learned that this was to be a very different announcing experience for me. One look at the script told me that.

At 7:55 the trio quit rehearsing while I began on WJZ with "This is George Ansbro, your *Esso News* reporter." For four and a half minutes, I continued with news and weather. Then, I switched off WJZ, and at 8:00:00 switch on WEAF and the Red Network. The very first thing heard on the new show was a loud Chinese gong. As the note cleared, affecting an exaggeratedly pontifical voice, I proclaimed, "Omar Herth, the Swingmaker." Theme music, an eerie oriental sound, was established and then lowered as I, with tongue in cheek, continued:

No loaf of bread, no jug of wine, but thou
Beside me, swinging in the wilderness.
And wilderness were paradise—AND HOW!

A little more theme and then I continued: "Gilded lines from the Rubaiyat, Byzantine Barrelhouse from the wastes of Kurasan. All this scrap [the word "crap" could not be used on the air then] and Milt Herth too. Take it Omar!" For the rest of the program, Milt Herth and the boys beat their brains out with swing music.

I would recite a silly poem before each number, the idea being to connect the thought in the last line of the poem with the title of the song. Here's an example:

> Bring me musicians! Let them play
> Madrigal, serenade, roundelay
> Sonata, scherzo, and saraband.
> Skip it! I'll take a ragtime band!
> (Music: Alexander's Ragtime Band)

The program would end with me reading, again over eerie oriental music with a beat, something like this: "And so reluctantly we leave the Garden of Allah. But there will be more of these gracious moments of melody tomorrow. And this? This is George Ansbro, your Potentate of Poesy. And this is NBC, the National Broadcasting Company."

The program over, it was out of the studio in a hurry to the newsroom to pick up the *Esso News* for the 8:30 spot on WEAF. Now that *Mrs. Wiggs* was a thing of the past, I usually had plenty of time for a leisurely second breakfast downstairs in the drugstore at 9:00, joining the likes of Peter Donald, Van Heflin, Karl Malden, Dinah Shore, Richard Widmark, other assorted announcers, actors, singers, or musicians who happened to be there.

22

HORSING AROUND WITH HOOVER

If I still had time to kill, I would try to find a partner for ping pong in our announcers' lounge, which was really quite sumptuous. Private showers, four or five leather easy chairs, two large leather couches, a telephone desk, a writing desk and large individual lockers surrounding the ping pong table. In one, remember, Alois Havrilla always kept a bottle of Scotch. Lots of bright daylight too, what with four good-size windows looking out onto Fiftieth Street.

During that era a lot of NBC shows like *Vic and Sade* and *Little Orphan Annie* originated in Chicago. Therefore I would spend some afternoon hours in a standby studio with a house pianist, like Morton Gould, Vladimir Brenner, Earl Wild, or others. These men were excellent musicians, who enhanced some of NBC's finest programs, as well as filling in at an unlikely line break (loss of sound from point of origin). Morton Gould went on to become a celebrated conductor. Earl Wild is to this day playing to packed concert houses like Carnegie Hall. Because the Great Depression was still in full swing, it is my guess they chose the safety net of a steady job at NBC during those unsettling days rather than the uncertainties of the freelance musical world. While on duty in a standby studio, I would either listen to Chicago's programs, read, use the telephone, or shoot the breeze with the pianist on duty. Or, better still, sit quietly and listen while he would practice. I think it was Morton Gould who told me the joke which he said was old even then. Question: What are the three best ways to get into

Carnegie Hall? Answer: Practice, practice, practice.

One night in the thirties NBC was carrying a speech by Herbert Hoover. No disrespect intended, but the former president was never regarded as one of the world's best speakers. If anything, quite the opposite. His dreary sound probably helped Franklin Roosevelt defeat him in 1932. That night in my standby booth I was monitoring his speech from somewhere out west. Seated next to me was the standby pianist, Milan Smolen. I think Milan and I were on the verge of being put to sleep when I suddenly became aware of a certain pattern in Mr. Hoover's delivery which began to interest me. When he would end a thought and was applauded, he would not resume speaking until about five seconds after the applause stopped. Such a pause was referred to in the radio business as dead air. I became fascinated. Applause ends, followed by dead air, then Hoover resumes speech. Same thing over and over.

About now a mischievous idea entered my head. I began to realize it was within my power to add a little something to Herbert Hoover's speech, to experiment, so to speak, and at the same time fill up the dead air spots. And no one would be the wiser. My announce booth was supervised by the master control room, as were all studios. But only the announcer could open and close his mike without detection. This was done simply by pushing the on-and-off button labeled "announce" on the announcer's delight box. By now you might have guessed what's coming. No. No four-letter words or anything like that. What I did worked quite well: each time the applause ended I opened my mike, forcefully cleared my throat, and then stopped one second before Hoover resumed speaking. Continuing this throat clearing game until the end of his speech, I deceived the listening audience into believing Hoover himself was clearing his throat. And nobody knew the difference. Except of course Milan Smolen, who by now was practically on the floor. It's a good thing there was no technical trouble on the line because I doubt I would have been able to do a serious apology without completely breaking up and joining Mr. Smolen in hysterics.

When Air Features, which was also referred to as the Hummert Office, discontinued *Mrs. Wiggs of the Cabbage Patch* in the summer of 1938 shortly before AFRA came into being, I was a bit let down, for reasons I've already mentioned. I had no way of knowing, however, that fate had a very pleasant surprise in store for me. Pat Kelly called me in one day in mid-September to inform me that the Hummert office had requested me to be their announcer on a new soap opera. It would begin Monday the 26th and would be on the air at 4:45 P.M. five days a week. I was to be in the studio for rehearsal at 4 o'-clock. It was to be called *Young Widder Brown*. They had tried out this show on the Mutual Network for a year or so. Having given me this good news, he then congratulated me, not just for getting a new show without having to go through the audition process but because, thanks to AFRA, I would receive the minimum fee for such a program, $75 per week, which, of course, I had been well aware of since my disappointment when *Mrs. Wiggs* was dropped. One other thing fate must have been aware of but, understandably, had no way of letting me know in advance was the fact that this "goody" would be part of my life, continuously, for the next eighteen years. The $75 fee was increased several times over those years in accordance

with each new minimum scale negotiated by AFRA.

On that first day, besides Martha Atwell, the director, I was pleased to find that I already knew at least one member of the cast, Bud Collyer. Bud was playing Dr. Peter Turner, a young doctor in love with Ellen Brown. Ellen was Florence Freeman. Florence had played the leading role on the Mutual Network as Ellen Jones. Why the name change from Jones to Brown, nobody ever told me. Nor would I have cared if the Widder's name had been changed to Smith—it would not have diminished my happiness at being there. I'm sure everybody else in Studio 3D that day felt the same excitement at being in on the ground floor of a new soap opera.

My opening announcement spoke of "Young Widder Brown, a woman as real as her friends who listen to her. The dramatic story of a very human mother's duty to her children, in conflict with the dictates of her heart." A few years later that was changed to "the dramatic story of attractive Ellen Brown, with two fatherless children to support. The story of the age-old conflict between a mother's duty and a woman's heart." With this somber thought established as a lead-in, I would then proceed into the commercial for whichever of the Sterling Drug products was scheduled for that day, such as Bayer Aspirin, Phillips Milk of Magnesia, Haley's M-O, and others. The commercial over, next I would establish the opening scene for that day's pathos.

And so it went, day after day until June 29, 1956. As some wag once wrote of the show, it was "eighteen years of the most excruciating radio torture ever devised by Frank and Anne Hummert." Over those years there were numerous cast changes. The first occurred in the early 1940s. Dr. Peter Turner, who since the beginning had been proclaiming his ardent love for Ellen Brown, had developed a brain tumor or some such thing and had become a less than pleasant person, to say the least. As a

December 14, 1975   G R I T *Family Section*   31

RETURN WITH US TO...   *by* Don Showood   Bill Owen 18

Young Widder Brown

YOUNG WIDDER BROWN, THE STORY OF THE AGE-OLD CONFLICT BETWEEN A MOTHER'S DUTY AND A WOMAN'S HEART.

ELLEN BROWN RAN A TEA ROOM IN "SIMPSONVILLE." THE ROMANTIC INTEREST CENTERED ON ELLEN AND DR. ANTHONY LORING. *YOUNG WIDDER BROWN* BEGAN ON NBC IN 1938.

FLORENCE FREEMAN PLAYED ELLEN. HER OTHER RADIO CHARACTERIZATIONS INCLUDED THE TITLE ROLES IN *WENDY WARREN* AND *VALIANT LADY*. SHE ALSO PLAYED DOT IN *DOT AND WILL*.

GEORGE ANSBRO WAS THE PROGRAM'S ANNOUNCER FOR 18 YEARS... A RECORD FOR SOAP OPERAS. HE BEGAN HIS RADIO CAREER AS A PAGE AT NBC IN NEW YORK AT AGE 16.

ORGANIST JOHN WINTERS PLAYED THE THEME "IN THE GLOAMING." IN THE FINAL YEARS OF THE PROGRAM, THE THEME WAS CHANGED TO "WONDERFUL ONE."

In 1975 readers of Grit *were asked to look back to those* Young Widder Brown *days which had ended almost two decades earlier in 1956.*

became so believable that it caused an avalanche of mail protesting his nasty change of character, brain tumor or not. This caused the Hummerts to have second thoughts about the advisability of continuing with Dr. Peter Turner. It had been their plan to have the good doctor recover completely from his cranial condition and rejoin his neighbors in the midwestern town of Simpsonville as the same upstanding chap he had been before the scriptwriters had caused him to sink so low. But the thousands of letters from irate listeners made them decide otherwise. So Peter Turner never recovered from his tumorous troubles. He was "killed off," as they used to say in radio land, and was replaced by Dr. Anthony Loring.

Anthony's character soon became well liked by the show's listening audience. Anthony, played by Ned Wever, became Ellen's most persistent admirer. For most of the remaining years, he and Ellen were on the verge of getting married; their marriage plans were on again, off again. But somehow the big day never arrived. Ellen seemed forever doomed to raise those

matter of fact, the story line during that period had reduced him to doing some terrible things, like belting Ellen around once in a while. Because Bud Collyer was such a fine actor, Dr. Turner's unpleasantness kids alone. With each drastic development, Anthony seemed to slip farther and farther away. The complications ran the gamut, as recalled by *Newsweek* in June of 1956, when the magazine bid adieu to Ellen and friends when they were leaving the air-waves forever: "a false accusation of mur-der, amnesia, innumerable broken bones, addiction to a 'powder of forgetfulness' slipped into her drink (nonalcoholic, of course) by an unscrupulous painter, and blindness brought on by an allergy to chocolate cake (an affliction cured when a cake flour advertiser complained)." But for all their ups and downs, romantic and oth-erwise, during those almost two decades, in the final scene on the last day Anthony and Ellen fell into each other's arms.

"Will you marry me, Ellen?"

"Yes, I will, Anthony!"

And so another radio soap opera bit the dust after an unusually long run.

I would like, however, to recall some things that stand out in my memory con-cerning the *Young Widder Brown* show. In its eighteen years on the air, Ellen Brown was played by three different actresses. The first, and by far the best, was Florence Free-man. She did it the first fourteen years. She was fired by Frank and Anne Hummert when they got panicky because the ratings had dropped a little and they thought hiring a younger actress might help. Millicent Brower was chosen by the Hummerts to re-place Florence, but she sounded like a col-lege girl—completely miscast. After a year of her and no improvement in the ratings, they decided to replace me. I only learned of this through the grapevine, so I ap-proached Dick Leonard, who was directing the show. He had taken over when Martha Atwell, to everyone's sorrow, committed suicide in 1951. Dick was also the producer of the NBC Symphony Orchestra con-ducted by Arturo Toscanini. He was quite sympathetic to me, and as a good friend he tipped me off that an audition was being scheduled to decide on my replacement and that I had nothing to lose by appearing

at the audition, even though the Hummerts had not even notified me of my intended dismissal. Inasmuch as he was to handle the audition (with Mrs. Hummert making the decision), there was no problem about my being allowed to read.

I remember Mrs. Hummert smiling courteously at me from the control room. What it boiled down to was that I was audi-tioning for something I had been doing successfully five days every week for the previous fifteen years. On the day of the competition, I faced many of the top an-nouncers of the day, including such impres-sive names as David Ross, Frank Gallop, Ed Herlihy, Jack Costello, Nelson Case, and Ken Roberts. The fascinating conclu-sion to this little saga is that I continued doing the show. For the next week or so, I kept expecting to hear from the Hummert office that I was through and would be re-placed by announcer so-and-so. But such a message never arrived. Whatever made the Hummerts decide to keep me I never learned. Needless to say, it was a good thing for me that I had found out about the audition. Perhaps the Hummerts finally re-alized how miscast Florence Freeman's re-placement was and that better they should replace her and leave me be, which, of course, is what happened. They hired Wendy Drew, who played the leading role the final two years. Wendy was no Florence Freeman, but she was a big improvement over her immediate predecessor.

Speaking of Frank and Anne Hummert, their company, Air Features, owned and produced an incredible number of radio shows back then. Frank Hummert was one of the founding partners of a Chicago-based advertising agency called Blackett-Sample-Hummert. While there, he started Air Features and guided its growth into be-coming a giant of the industry. Blackett-Sample-Hummert became the agency that represented every show out of the Air Fea-tures factory, thereby getting the agency commission. So Mr. Hummert had the best of two worlds. As an agency partner he shared in the agency commissions, and as sole owner of Air Features he reaped the fantastic harvest from all the shows his production house turned out.

When he was forming Air Features, he married his much younger secretary and elevated her to equal partnership with him. Accordingly, in the credits at the end of every one of their shows, the phrase "Written and produced by Frank and Anne Hummert" was heard. Mr. Hummert, himself, was the majordomo of their nighttime shows. For many years I did what were called "cowcatchers" and "hitchhikes." These were twenty-second product plugs other than the commercials in the body of the show itself, which were done by the program announcer. A cowcatcher was done at the very beginning of the show, before the theme music started. Hitchhikes were at the very end, when the theme ended. I did these on *Waltz Time* and *The American Album of Familiar Music* featuring Frank Munn, the golden voice of radio on Friday and Sunday nights. And on *Manhattan Merry-Go-Round* on Sunday nights. So on almost every Friday and Sunday night, I would find myself exchanging "how-do's" and small talk about the weather with the old man, and sometimes his wife, in the control room where he would sit quietly and observe. Oh, I almost forgot. I did cowcatchers and hitchhikes on *Easy Aces* with Jane and Goodman Ace, and on *Mr. Keen, Tracer of Lost Persons*, which were also Hummert shows. A non–Hummert program which used me in the same capacity featured Larry Clinton and his orchestra with vocals by Bea Wain. My announcements were for Pall Mall cigarettes. Bea Wain later married Andre Baruch, the famous announcer who, among many other shows, did the very popular CBS program *Your Hit Parade* for many years.

In addition to *Young Widder Brown* and *Mrs. Wiggs*, the production team of Frank and Anne Hummert turned out more major soap operas than any other producer. Here's a partial list: *Amanda of Honeymoon Hill, Backstage Wife, David Harum, Evelyn Winters, Front-Page Farrell, John's Other Wife, Just Plain Bill, Lora Lawton, Lorenzo Jones, Nona from Nowhere, Orphans of Divorce, Our Gal Sunday, The Romance of Helen Trent, Second Husband, The Stolen Husband, Stella Dallas*—quite a record. From time to time, I was used as a substitute on those programs, which were on NBC, when the regular announcer was sick or on vacation.

Amanda of Honeymoon Hill ran for five years in the early forties. Frank Gallop was the regular announcer, and his occasional tendency to almost break up but still manage to hang on for dear life while on the air was the giggly gossip of New York radio. The reason was the opening announcement which, as on all the Hummert soaps, was written by Anne Hummert. This particular lead-in indicated how truly naive Mrs. Hummert must really have been: "We bring you now the story of Amanda of Honeymoon Hill, laid in a world few Americans know. The story of love and marriage in America's romantic South, etc., etc." The attention-getting word remained for the entire run of the program because, evidently, none of Anne Hummert's subordinates at Air Features had the temerity to approach her about deleting the double entendre and replacing it with a word or phrase less suggestive. Rather than chance it, they skipped it. But by substituting for Gallop myself once in a while, I found out what it must have been like for poor Frank to not break up. And for five years yet.

23

CALLING ALL MEN
TO BARNEY'S

Sometime in 1939 I was asked by Bill Farren, an announcer who had been on the staff a year or so, if I would like to move in with him and share the rent. His offer had much in its favor, no more sponging off my fellow announcers by sleeping on their couches. My first visit showed that his apartment was quite satisfactory—a good-size living room, kitchen, two bedrooms, all nicely furnished. Bill's monthly rent was $80, which was quite right for West 56th just off Sixth Avenue. I recall giving the idea a lot of serious thought. Much as living so close to NBC would make life a lot easier for me, I worried that my family might be hurt if I were to officially move out of the house where I had lived since I was 12, exactly half my life. A discussion with Mother and Pop took care of that. Their feeling was that if it would be beneficial to me, then by all means go for it. This understanding attitude went a long way toward putting me at ease when I accepted Farren's offer.

In those days it was pretty much accepted that sons and daughters didn't leave home until they got married, possibly even more so in an Irish Catholic household. That is why I was concerned that even the thought of such a move might upset my family, especially since I was the youngest. Of my three brothers and three sisters, only one, Kathlyn, had married two years earlier. Two of my brothers had become priests, Jim in 1931 and Jack in 1932. So, besides me, those still living at home with Mother and Pop were Madeline, the oldest; Ray, the next oldest; and Dolores. Both

Madeline and Dolores were employed in Manhattan. Ray, a perennial bachelor, was a dentist practicing in downtown Brooklyn. So, having my parents' okay, I wasted no time in transferring my belongings to West 56th Street. If my siblings had any serious thoughts about my leaving, they never expressed them.

Bill Farren was a unique character. He was much older than I, by at least twenty years. He had been divorced much earlier. He had a fondness for soda, as long as there was Scotch in it. He contributed regularly to the upkeep of his bookie's lifestyle. That is, when he wasn't at the track during the racing season. Working mostly at night gave him time to pursue the horses, his favorite hobby when he wasn't pursuing the ladies. Until I became his roommate, I really knew nothing about him except his apparent age. But it didn't take long for me to discover all of the above.

I had first made the acquaintance of Bill Farren three years earlier when I had been "fired" and before I was reinstated at NBC. During that dreadful week, among the other radio stations I approached in New York for a job was WNEW, which had recently started in business under the ownership of Ed Wynn, the famous comedian I spoke of earlier. As a matter of fact, the EW in the call letters WNEW were Ed Wynn's initials. Farren was the chief announcer at the station. When I met with him in his office, he wasted no time turning down my request for an audition, using the old excuse "We're not hiring right now." I was in and out of the place in two minutes flat. A couple of years later when Ed Wynn sold the station the new owners let Bill go, but Pat Kelly hired him on the NBC staff. I could tell he didn't remember the two minutes he had spent with me, nor did I expect that he would, so I never brought the subject up. The unpleasant first impression I had gotten in our brief earlier meeting soon disappeared as I began to find that he was personable and had a good sense of humor, which is why I had no qualms when he suggested I share his apartment. Even though I thought he was a bit of a nut, I could see no reason we shouldn't hit it off well. Also I liked the apartment, my room in it, and my share of the rent, $40.

Bill's voice was familiar to New York radio listeners because of a commercial he had made promoting a well-known downtown men's store, Barney's. I guess Mr. Barney considered the commercial successful because it ran for years. Bill had done it in a deliberately sing-song monotone style. Except for the words, it sounded like a friar soloing during matins in an abbey. The message was short and to the point: "Calling all men, calling all men to Barney's—Seventh Avenue and Seventeenth Street!" It was among the first recorded commercials, and it was played constantly on most New York radio stations.

One Saturday afternoon I was enjoying myself in the company of six or seven other NBC friends, including my roommate, Bill Farren. We were sitting around the big table in the back of Hurley's Bar. I had been there close to an hour, but no doubt others had been there much longer. One such person was Jack Fraser, a fellow announcer, who after a while suddenly exclaimed that he had almost forgotten he had promised his wife he would buy a new suit so he had better be on his way. He was going over to Saks Fifth Avenue, and he said he might see us later. Saks was a block away. Farren immediately got into the act, telling Jack he would save money by going to Barney's instead and that he

would go along with him just to make sure. He distinctly gave the impression that because of his celebrity doing the Barney's commercial, if he simply accompanied Jack, or anybody, they would get a hefty discount, which impressed all of us. So much so that in no time at all we got out of Hurley's, squeezed into a couple of cabs, and were on our way down to Seventh Avenue and Seventeenth Street to the mecca of men's bargains.

After at least an hour in Barney's the liquid happiness we had imbibed in Hurley's had worn off considerably, which dampened the mass enthusiasm for buying new suits, especially trying them on. But what really caused the sobering of us suit seekers was the information which Jack Fraser had gleaned from the section manager: Barney's prices were already as low as the management would go, regardless of what poppycock (translation: B.S.) Mr. Farren might have told us. So we all, except Bill Farren, walked out empty-handed and returned to Hurley's. Very embarrassed, mortified as a matter of fact, Bill remained behind and bought two suits. Jack Fraser had a quick drink in Hurley's, went down the street to Saks Fifth Avenue and did what he intended to do in the first place—buy a suit. To think that Barney's has over the years become one of the most ultrachic and expensive stores in Manhattan absolutely boggles my mind.

My new living arrangement seemed to be working out okay as I had a day schedule and Bill worked nights. My two days off (no more six-day weeks thanks to AFRA) were Saturday and Sunday because of my Monday through Friday commitment to *Young Widder Brown* and *Omar Herth, the Swingmaker*. Indeed, I considered myself very, very lucky at that stage of my career to have weekends off. Bill was doing a lot of band remotes, but mostly at Frank Daly's Meadowbrook, which was on the Pompton Turnpike, Route 23, in Cedar Grove, New Jersey. It was a place where the biggest of the big bands appeared. It was on the air so often on NBC, CBS, and the Mutual Network that it had become nationally famous. And I could tell Bill really loved going out there.

Bill spent his two days off, which were midweek, in the apartment drinking and cavorting with various women. One especially became a real fixture, with frequent overnight stays. When I found out that she was Mrs. Frank Daly, wife of *the* Frank Daly, owner of the Meadowbrook, I got scared. Scared enough to want out of the apartment posthaste. Not just because of Mr. Daly's jealousy if he found out, but because of what he might do about it. Frank Daly was reputed to be very closely connected to the Mafia. No way did I want to remain in residence with that worry on my mind.

Talk about great timing. As it turned out, I was able to leave Farren's place almost overnight and move two blocks closer to NBC, 54th Street just east of Sixth Avenue. It was indeed fortuitous that just a few days earlier George Putnam, who had been sharing an apartment with Radcliff Hall, left to get married. Both men were fellow staff announcers. I was as happy to move in with Rad as he was to have me split the rent. No big gap in age, as with Bill Farren. Rad was a year or two older and had a great sense of humor; we hit it off just fine.

When I was rooming with Rad Hall, we would occasionally cohost cocktail parties. Once, our good friend and fellow announcer Doug Browning was a guest. There's very little doubt he had been elbow bending elsewhere before dropping in on us. His normal good humor, which increased with each intake of booze, outdid itself when he approached me to complain facetiously that there was no more club soda in the cupboard for his next drink of Scotch. I replied in the same vein that a courteous guest should overlook the shortage and take water from the tap. Next he sought out Rad with the same alleged complaint. Rad's answer was much like mine.

With that, Doug opened the French doors to the small balcony overlooking 54th Street, turned around to us, yelled, "All right you cheap bastards, I'll go buy my own club soda," and jumped off. Thank God we were only on the second floor so he wasn't splashed all over the sidewalk. Doug picked himself up, made it to a store around the corner, and returned to the party carrying a couple of bottles of club soda. Jovial as ever and with only a slight limp. Whoever said "God takes care of drunks" sure knew what he was talking about.

During that same period, an NBC flying school was formed. It was started by four or five fellows from various departments in the company who were licensed pilots. They had access to a couple of biplanes at Flushing Airport and were offering flying lessons at minimal cost to interested employees. No official memo was sent out. It was simply a word of mouth deal.

I learned of it from Cracker Williams. His first name was Bill, but everyone called him by his nickname because he came from Georgia. He was a studio engineer at NBC and was one of the pilots-instructors. We saw each other almost every day while working on one program or another, and when he first asked if I would be interested, I agreed immediately, thinking it would be just great if I could look forward to flying my own plane someday. Students had to coordinate their available daylight time with their pilot, in my case with Cracker. No problem there, as he had weekends off too. So for the next I don't know how many Saturdays and Sundays, I would meet with him at Flushing Airport, each time learning a little bit more about the ins and outs, to say nothing of the ups and downs of flying an airplane. My confidence increased with each lesson. I mean by that the confidence and enjoyment I had while flying over Manhattan. It was quite a thrill to maneuver a dip above the Empire State Building. Sort of a tip of the hat to the new building that was the tallest in the world. Then over New York Harbor to look down upon the ever-graceful Miss Liberty, and the many ocean liners contributing to New York's reputation as one of the world's greatest seaports. The return to Flushing Airport was made easier, especially for a student flyer like me, by the sight of the Trylon and Perisphere looming up over the World's Fair grounds like a beacon. Such casual flying above Manhattan was permitted then. But these many years later, because of the tremendous increase in commercial flying and the danger small private planes would pose in such a busy aerial corridor, they have long since been prohibited.

Much as I loved flying that little biplane, I began to realize the confidence I thought I had gained during my instructions was simply because Cracker Williams was sitting next to me ready to take over the dual controls if necessary. I had to admit, both to Cracker and to myself, that flying up high in the sky was great but coming down for a landing just plain scared me. I had built up a thing in my head about getting caught in telephone wires near the airport, even though he patiently insisted my landings had improved with each next lesson. One Saturday after we got through he told me, "Tomorrow's the big day. You're ready to solo!" I thought I might be ready, if a little shaky. He thought I was ready, actually overdue. That night brought very little sleep. What kept going through my head over and over was me doing the usual flying routine the next day and then coming in for a landing without my faithful friend and instructor, with his always reassuring attitude, sitting beside me.

In the morning—very nervous, upset, and most of all embarrassed—I called Cracker and explained as best I could about my fear of the wires and told him that after much contemplation and worry it was my decision not to solo. Not that day, or in the future. He took it very nicely, like the gentleman he was. He said that even though those wires might seem like a silly bogeyman to some people he could very well understand my worry and therefore my

decision. And so I chickened out. The sad postscript to this story is that Cracker lost his life when he was shot down over Germany during World War II.

Those were busy days in Flushing Meadows Park, the location of the World's Fair of 1939. The combination of the tall and stately Trylon standing high next to the huge and magnificent Perisphere was a symbol of the future and was recognized everywhere as the official logo of the World's Fair. It's easy to see why that 700-foot spike and accompanying 200-foot ball were so plainly visible to me returning from flying over Manhattan. Endless crowds, people from all over the world, poured in every day and night to inspect the "wonders of the future," of which television was undoubtedly the most outstanding. The amusement section had every conceivable contraption imaginable to enhance one's pleasures. Restaurants featuring international delicacies abounded.

The World's Fair seemed like a giant, never-ending party. My friend Betty Garde, who played Mrs. Wiggs on *Mrs. Wiggs of the Cabbage Patch*, being a great party lover herself, decided to round up a group of guys and gals, all actors, actresses, and announcers, to meet regularly every two weeks for "fun and frolic," as she put it, at the Fair. Besides myself, other announcers who showed up frequently were Ben Grauer and Frank Gallop. Deciding where to meet was made easy when Agnes Moorehead let it be known that her husband was the manager of the Cuban Village and he would be happy to have us meet there. The suggestion was well taken and word filtered through the radio crowd in New York that when you visited the Fair, you should be sure to make the Cuban Village the first stop because you never knew whom among your peers you might join for a fun outing. Karl Swenson, who was well known to the radio audience then as "Lorenzo Jones," was probably the most frequent of the radio fun-lovers at the Fair. It seemed from the moment he would arrive at the Cuban

Village, a big smile just never left his face. Of course, I can make that observation because I was there a lot too, and I loved every minute of it. Other radio friends I remember being with back then are: Bennett Kilpack, who was Mr. Keen on *Mr. Keen, Tracer of Lost Persons*; Walter Kinsella, of *Dick Tracy* and many other programs; Vicki Vola, who played Miss Edith Miller, secretary, on *Mr. District Attorney*; Bret Morrison, who played the lead on *The Shadow*; Richard Widmark, who played the lead on *Front Page Farrell* (after making the picture *Kiss of Death*, he became a big movie star); Evie Juster, a member of the cast of *Amanda of Honeymoon Hill* and many other shows; Jackie Kelk, who played Homer Brown, Ezra Stone's pal on *The Aldrich Family*; Eleanor Kilgallen, sister of famous gossip columnist Dorothy Kilgallen (Eleanor and Jackie Kelk were an "item"); Lucille Wall, who starred in *Portia Faces Life* and also starred as Belle, Lorenzo's wife, in *Lorenzo Jones*; Staats Cotsworth, who followed Dick Widmark as the lead in *Front Page Farrell*; Alice Frost, who was Pamela North of *Mr. and Mrs. North*; Ed Begley, who was the lead in *Charlie Chan* and later acted in many movies; Van Heflin, who made his radio debut on *Mrs. Wiggs of the Cabbage Patch* (he later became a big star in Hollywood); Fran Heflin, Van's sister, who played in *On Borrowed Time* on *The Theatre Guild on the Air* (later, on TV, she played Susan Lucci's mother for many years on *All My Children*); and Ben Grauer, who announced Arturo Toscanini on the *NBC Symphony* and later the *Jergens Journal* with Walter Winchell.

Speaking of the World's Fair, another friend I would occasionally run into was John S. Young, he of my freezing midnight drive to Albany seven years earlier with Al Binney when Al and I were pages. Young had left NBC's announcing staff when Texaco decided to move the Ed Wynn show to CBS, and Graham McNamee, Mr. Wynn's straight man, wouldn't go because of his exclusive NBC contract. When Texaco said

it would be happy with John Young as McNamee's replacement, he had to resign from NBC in order to do it. And because the program aired only once a week, he found he had lots of time on his hands, time which proved quite valuable to him later. He spent much of it in the company of some old political pals, the most important and powerful of whom was Grover Whalen, who had been the "official greeter" of the city of New York during the twenties and thirties. Whalen had become a household name because of his high visibility during the regimes of several mayors, most notably that of Jimmy Walker. When such homecoming heroes as Charles Lindbergh and Gertrude Ederle were feted with huge ticker tape parades on lower Broadway in appreciation of their accomplishments, Grover Whalen was always there, seated in a prominent position in the open touring car with the mayor and the celebrated visitor. He not only rode in the parades, but did the advance planning for every one of them, and there were many. In the mid-thirties when ideas and suggestions were being formulated for the World's Fair, there can be little doubt that Grover Whalen's high profile as New York City's official greeter and the very unusual experiences that went with such a job had a lot to do with his appointment to the top position, chief executive officer, of the New York World's Fair of 1939.

The Ed Wynn program didn't last very long on CBS, so when it was dropped by Texaco it might have been expected that John S. Young would seek other employment as a freelance announcer, actor, straight man, or what have you. But fate had something else in store for Mr. Young. It seems Ed Wynn's show left the CBS schedule at around the same time Grover Whalen was made CEO of the forthcoming World's Fair. And so Whalen put Young in charge of all radio and television at the Fair, a pretty big assignment for someone who had never had executive experience of any kind. Mr. Young had become well

known through his expertise as a radio announcer. Now, in his new position, American radio executives as well as those from
all over the world had to go through him
for permission to broadcast to their home-
lands from the World's Fair. Quite a heady
experience, to say the least.

Undoubtedly Mr. Young's most important behind-the-scenes achievement was his
handling of the visit to the World's Fair of
the king and queen of England and President Franklin D. Roosevelt, who was host
to the royal couple. Their visit took place
not too long after the Fair had opened, and
of course it commanded front-page attention in newspapers everywhere, thus giving
the Fair such a tremendous boost that its
success was practically guaranteed. The
fact that television made its public debut
there with the stars of TV's first program
being the royal couple and the president
sparked additional interest universally. This
was sufficient proof that not only sound
could be transmitted through the air, but
now video, actual live images, could too.
Even though there were only a handful of
TV receiving sets in all of New York, it
worked. The few owners of sets actually
saw Roosevelt greeting his distinguished
guests and accompanying them around the
Fair. Saw it all in their own homes. It was
incredible at the time. For which feat, John
S. Young, being the person in charge of
radio and TV, accepted the plaudits.

It has been said that that wasn't all he
accepted. The strong rumor was that John

S. Young became a rich man through the
power given to him by Grover Whalen.
Simply put: it was rumored that all radio
stations, both American and foreign, that
wished to broadcast directly from the Fair
were required to pay a "user's fee" to Mr.
Young. During the two years the Fair occupied Flushing Meadows Park, there were an
awful lot of broadcasts to all corners of the
globe, and according to the rumor, a sub-
stantial amount of user's fees went into the
pocket of John S. Young.

When the Fair ended in 1940, Young embarked on a year-long, round-the-world trip
to personally thank all the individuals in
countless countries for their participation
in the Fair. During the trip he mailed an interesting communication to Howard Petrie,
who was still on the NBC announcing staff.
Howard got such a kick out of it that he
posted it on our bulletin board, which is
where I saw it. John had mailed it from an
island in the South Pacific. I think it was
Samoa. But there's no doubt in my mind of
what made Petrie and all of us who saw it
laugh. It was a postcard with a picture of
four gorgeous, native Polynesian young
ladies surrounding a tanned and handsome
John Young, who was smiling from ear to
ear. His companions, looking equally
happy, had not bothered to cover the upper
portions of their anatomies. In a word, they
were bare-breasted. John's written message
to Howard: "Having a wonderful time, glad
you're not here."

24

WINCHELL

From the mid-30s well into the mid-40s, the highest-rated radio program was on the air only once a week and for only a brief 15 minutes. Its star was Walter Winchell. His fame grew from his daily newspaper gossip column. The show was essentially a radio version of the column. His announcer was Ben Grauer. Besides putting him on the air and signing him off, Ben's main job was to try to convince Winchell's listeners, who numbered over 20 million, to use Jergens Lotion. Grauer had been announcing the *Jergens Journal* since it first started on WJZ, New York, and NBC's Blue Network every Sunday night at 9 o'clock eastern time. Undoubtedly he was aware of the prestige that went with the assignment. Accordingly, I was quite surprised and highly flattered when he approached me one day to say he was planning a three-week vacation and would I be interested in substituting for him if the advertising agency approved. (Shades of Ford Bond a few years earlier arranging to have me spell him on *Just Plain Bill*.) It's not hard to imagine what my answer was. So the next step was to read the commercial copy for the agency man whose name I've forgotten but whose agency was Lennen and Newell. Grauer suggested I stop by Studio 8C, the Winchell studio, on Sunday night so the agency man could listen to me read the Jergens commercial. Sunday I got there early enough to have Grauer introduce me to the agency man, who took me into the small hallway behind the studio and listened while I read the copy. Next Grauer had me join him in the control room during the broadcast, and when it was over, he brought me into the studio to meet Winchell. I guess the agency man thought it was important that Winchell be given the opportunity to approve or disapprove of whoever was going to replace Grauer. The great Mr. W. then went into the control room, where he listened as I addressed myself to the microphone, giving my all to the Jergens commercial. When he came back into the studio, he said it was okay with him and he would see me next week. As we all went down in the elevator, he told Grauer he would see him next month and to have a great vacation.

That's how my acquaintanceship with Walter Winchell began, although I had seen him around for quite a while. In the years prior to this meeting, I had heard and read all kinds of things about him. About how he had started in showbiz as a grammar school dropout when he was thirteen. He, Eddie Cantor, and Georgie Jessel were teamed in a kid vaudeville act in 1910 produced by the impresario of kid acts, Gus Edwards. Others who got their early training under Mr. Edwards's stewardship were people like Milton Berle, Hildegarde, Ray Bolger, Groucho Marx, and many more. After some off-and-on years in vaudeville as a not too busy song-and-dance man, Winchell found himself less inclined toward performing and more inclined toward journalism when he was hired to write reviews of new acts for a trade paper called the *Vaudeville News*. He soon added gossipy items and other assorted tidbits to his writing. New York tabloids took notice, and before long he had a regular column in the *New York Evening Graphic* where his efforts reached a much larger reading audience. Eventually, he and his column moved to William Randolph Hearst's *New York Daily Mirror*. It was his great success at the *Mirror* that brought him into radio in 1932 on the *Lucky Strike Magic Carpet* program, where his main function was to introduce name bands broadcasting from cities all over the country and his trademark, after introducing the band leader was to blow a whistle and shout into the microphone, "Okay, America." But unlike the gossipy stuff which he successfully featured later on the *Jergens Journal*, on the Lucky Strike show, he did little more than introduce each band. But the Winchell name became more and more familiar to the radio audience. Earlier in these remembrances I mentioned having seen him at work on the Lucky Strike program shortly after I had started as an NBC page. The lady who was on his arm one night was Jean Harlow, the big movie star, who had me go downstairs to get a pack of cigarettes for her, which I've never forgotten.

Needless to say I enjoyed subbing for Ben Grauer those next three Sundays. Winchell was cordial but preoccupied before the broadcast, making sure all his items were in the correct order. Once we were on the air, he was seated at the microphone with his fedora at a rakish angle, jacketless, and his tie loosened. He also opened his fly to give his midsection greater flexibility as he gyrated all over the chair with each syllable. Immediately following my introduction, this is how he opened: "Good evening, Mr. and Mrs. North and South America and all the ships at sea ... let's go to press."

Operating a Morse-code signal key to accent his dramatic, rapid-fire, breathless delivery he would then take off like a rocket. When my closing commercial was over, he would sign off: "And that, Mr. and Mrs. North and South America, winds up another Winchell until next Sunday. Until then and with lotions of love, this is your favorite newsboy Walter, telling you to take good care of yourself, because if you don't, ain't nobody else who will. Goodnight now."

His attempt to sound syrupy when he said "lotions of love" was to me exactly that—an attempt to sound syrupy. But as long as the clients liked it, that was the name of the game.

Grauer returned from his vacation refreshed and happy, the Lennen and Newell Agency was happy with my substitution, and I was happy that they were happy. And hopeful that Grauer might have had such a good time that he would entertain the idea of taking more frequent vacations. Once established as Ben Grauer's substitute, I continued spelling him for the next six or seven years for vacations and occasional illnesses until eventually Jergens was replaced as sponsor by Richard Hudnut Cosmetics. At that point, Ben Grauer was replaced by announcer Dick Stark, and I was replaced by whoever substituted for Stark.

As usually happened in such situations, that was the end of my on-the-air connection with Mr. W.W. (which reminds me, WW was the only marking on his N.Y. license plates). For many years after his Jergens show, he was cordial when we would cross paths in an elevator or in the newsroom, but mostly at the Stork Club, a former speakeasy which, when Prohibition ended, had become internationally famous as a social meeting place for members of high society and what was then called cafe society, with numerous politicians and showbiz folks. He spent an awful lot of time at the Stork, always holding forth (he never stopped talking) at what was known as the Winchell table, table 50.

My introduction to the glamorous Stork Club was in 1937 with a small group of Brooklyn friends who had been there many times before. The reason they kept returning was because for some reason or other the owner, Sherman Billingsley, mistakenly thought they were celebrities or at least important people. At any rate they always seemed to receive what I later found out the waiters, maître d's, and Billingsley called "the treatment." Maybe it was just because Billingsley liked the way they dressed and comported themselves and by lavishing the treatment on them he hoped they would continue to come back. My friends had been telling me what great fun it was to be on the receiving end in such a posh and famous club. So when I got to join them one night, I saw for the first time exactly what they meant and enjoyed every minute of it. The treatment consisted of bowing and scraping and much more attention from the waiters than ordinary mortals received. Bottles of champagne on ice would appear shortly after their arrival. The ladies usually received gifts of fine perfume, the gentlemen red "Stork Club" suspenders. But one never knew for sure when, upon leaving, the waiter would quietly drop the word that there was "no check, compliments of Mr. B." Not all the time, but at least often enough to make going there an interesting game. Will tonight be on the house or won't it? Regardless of the outcome, the champagne and the perfume invariably appeared.

Table 50 was just inside the very exclusive Cub Room and was quite visible from the main room, with its orchestra and dance floor. Obviously Winchell liked being seen by everyone in the place, which helped to feed his enormous ego as top politicians, theatre and movie people, and others paid court to him. James A. (Big Jim) Farley, the postmaster general of the United States and the person credited as the brains behind President Roosevelt winning his first two elections, was a frequent visitor to table 50. As a matter of fact, the rumor was widely circulated that, because he backed Roosevelt in the column and on the radio, Walter Winchell was the only person in the media with open access to FDR's oval office. There was little doubt he wallowed in the attention.

Once, not long after *Gone with the Wind* had made Clark Gable a bigger star than ever, there he sat chatting with W.W. at table 50. As I was passing by, Winchell, after nodding to me, suddenly said, "I would like you to shake hands with Clark Gable." Gable was as surprised as I was, and under the circumstances, with Winchell obviously not remembering my name, was more than gracious. He stood up, bowed slightly and shook hands. But that was it. No invitation from the host to join them, which of course I didn't expect. So I shuffled right along to my own table. Joining my party, I jokingly told them that if they were nice to me I would let them shake the hand that just shook the hand of Rhett Butler.

Not everyone I became close to while relaxing at Hurley's Bar was a member of the radio crowd. One of my friends was a much older man than I, Bill Elliot, who was a vice president of the Irving Trust Company's Radio City branch. It was his habit to drop in when his day at the bank ended and partake of a liquid refreshment or two before his subway ride home to the Bronx. His working day ended when my *Young Widder Brown* show got off the air, 5 o'clock, at which time I would often stop by Hurley's looking forward to pleasant chitchat with him. On occasion Walter Winchell was topic A, especially since I had become his substitute announcer. So I regaled my good friend with an account of the Winchell/Clark Gable story the day after it happened. And, as is usually the case, one story led to another. I pointed out to Bill that what we were really doing was repeating to each other gossip about the man who was the foremost scandalmonger of our time. The man who had become very rich, famous and, most especially, powerful in the pursuit of his trade. When I finished making that unremarkable observation, Bill got a curious look on his face. I asked him if I had said something I shouldn't. His answer was, "No, but I think I'm about to." He then explained that his position as v.p. of the bank included, among other things, "being bossman of safe deposit boxes and vaults." Then he told me, "Mr. Winchell has a vault containing seven million dollars in cash." And, as I nearly fell on the floor, he wound up his thunderbolt with, "Please don't ask me how I know, but I know."

This highly interesting piece of information seemed to jibe with what Winchell himself had claimed many times in his column, that even though he frequently touted stocks, he never bought any. The same with racehorses. Even though he would give tips on horses, he never bet on them. And he was a notorious cheapskate. He never put out a dime at the Stork Club, or for that matter, anywhere else. Rumor had it that he and Sherman Billingsley had a deal whereby Mr. B. granted him carte blanche in return for constant Stork Club plugs in the column and on the radio. So considering the above, together with his huge income, what did he do with all his money? Bill Elliot had just told me. And him I believed. In my opinion this was pretty solid proof that Walter Winchell trusted no one but himself.

About 1940, Tom Mann, a friend of mine who was a Wall Street broker, got me financially interested in a project he had become involved in. One day he took me to the Aeolian building on West 57th Street to meet someone he had been telling me about, Jay Fonda. For a long time Fonda had been experimenting to find some way to record sound other than on cumbersome discs. He had finally devised a method to record audio electronically on cellophane tape, and he had leased space there to demonstrate the result of his efforts to prospective investors. Tom Mann had already invested some money in the Fonda Company and was so enthusiastic about its possibilities that he wanted me to see firsthand Jay Fonda's remarkable invention so I could decide for myself about investing in it. After witnessing Fonda's demonstration, I was flabbergasted. There was no doubt I was witnessing the beginning of the end of discs.

Others who were there that day were every bit as impressed as I. People like William L. Shirer and H. V. Kaltenborn, both famous radio commentators. And Dr. Frank Black, the noted music conductor. I don't know what they put up—probably far more than I did because I was single and didn't find it easy to hang onto a buck. "Young and fancy free" I guess was the best way to describe me at the time. However I scraped together a thousand dollars, a lot of money then, and took the plunge.

What should have made millionaires of us early backers turned into a disaster when Jay Fonda took to celebrating his invention much too soon. What began as a celebration became a perpetual bender. As a result he blew everything. He drank himself out of his company, his invention—and our money. Even as I reminisce about his great fiasco all these years later, I'm still angry because his invention was the beginning of the biggest technical revolution in the business—audio tape followed by video tape. I must confess, it still leaves a rotten taste in my mouth when I think what my thousand dollars, if left untouched, and with Fonda not stupidly celebrating, would have accrued to by now. How sad that nowhere in the industrial history books can his name be found—Jay Fonda, the man who actually invented tape recording.

25

WANNA BUY A NETWORK?

One night in the early 1940s I was on my way out to Bay Ridge for a weekend visit with my folks. I had been dining with friends in a restaurant on Lexington Avenue so, after bidding them goodnight, I entered the Lexington Avenue subway station at 60th Street. As I descended the stairs and was nearing the bottom, I saw a drunk weave dangerously near the platform edge and then topple off onto the tracks. Racing as fast as I could to where he fell, I could see he was conscious and muttering a lot of drunken gibberish.

All I could think of was to get him out of there, and get him to safety. It was about 11 P.M. The station was almost empty, just three or four women, all excited, and one fellow about my own age. I was pretty excited too, and with very good reason, because I knew I was going to go down there to try to help the poor soul. I also knew that in no way could I handle the situation alone. And that whatever was going to be done had to be done pronto, before the train became visible in the tunnel after its trip from Queens under the East River. The other fellow must have sensed what I had in mind and wanted no part of it, which he showed by slowly walking away as I anxiously told him I would need him down there. Not wanting to waste another second I lowered myself down to the unfortunate man on the tracks. What I had in mind was to move him into the space under the platform overhang and to huddle close to him so that in case we were still there when the train came through we wouldn't be touched. While this was going through my head as I was glancing into the tunnel, I could see that up on the platform the ladies

were trying to shame the other fellow into coming down to help me, and they succeeded. The next thing I knew he had climbed down and was there with me. Another glance into the tunnel. Still no train. I lifted our drunken friend by the arms while my newfound helper took him by the feet, and when I counted to three, we swung him up onto the platform, where the women took over, making sure to immediately pull him away from the edge and to safety. Now to get ourselves up. Of course we realized we were on our own—there was no way we could help each other. I soon found out the trick was to grab hold of the edge above and then, because there was nothing to step on, alternately pull and shinny yourself up until you had achieved enough leverage to force your body onto the platform and while going through these contortions hoping and praying the train wouldn't arrive at the station until you were out of its way. Of course that's what happened or I wouldn't be around to tell about it. The same was true for my helper, who indeed turned out to be a great help once he overcame his initial fear of joining me on the tracks.

A word about the fiftyish man whose lack of balance was the cause of all this. If he hadn't been as drunk as he was, I have no doubt he would have been quite seriously injured instead of just pretty well shook up, shook up and scared. Such a combination has been known to have a sobering effect and that's what seemed to happen. At least he was sober enough to sit next to me on the platform bench and, with tears rolling down his cheeks, thank me profusely. I was able to extract from him where he lived and the station he wanted to get off at, Union Street in Brooklyn, which was several stops before mine so I was glad I would be able to keep an eye on him and make sure he got off without any problems.

As the train finally entered the station, I stood up and was happy to see that my friend was able to do likewise—his earlier drunken wobble had just about disappeared. For the first time since climbing back onto the platform, I took stock of myself and realized I was a mess. My face and hands were filthy, my suit was ripped in a couple of places, and my shoes were scuffed to a fare-thee-well. And, without going into specifics, my traveling companion was far, far filthier. When the train stopped, I took Mr. Dirty by the arm and stepped into an almost empty car, almost empty because of the late hour. Steering him to a seat, I saw a gentleman peer over the top of his newspaper at me. At the same time, I heard him say, "Hi, George." Of all times to have such a thing happen. Talk about embarrassing moments—I was mortified. The passenger was a radio actor I had been slightly acquainted with. I had never really known him on a social basis, and as best I could remember, I had never worked with him on a show. His name was Francis de Sales. So, in answer to his greeting, I quietly said, "Hello, Francis, good to see you," and kept moving, with my newest and foulest friend, to a further section of the car. When we arrived at Union Street, I saw to it that he got off safely and hoped he got home just as safely and got a good night's sleep, which is what I was looking forward to. I never saw Francis de Sales again, for which I was very sorry. I had always hoped our paths would cross sometime when I might be in a better position to explain what he undoubtedly thought was pretty strange behavior. And who my scrungy companion was and why we didn't stop to join him and engage in pleasant chitchat.

The above subway episode brings to mind another adventure I inadvertently found myself involved in. In this one, a couple of years later, the scene was the Rockefeller

Center station during the height of the rush hour. Once again it began as I was descending the stairs, but any similarity between the two episodes ends there. It so happened that I chose the stairway at the front end of the station for no particular reason that I remember. And a lucky thing I did. As I neared the bottom of the stairs, the train I had hoped to catch was just closing its doors. Suddenly I saw something which obviously no one else had. On the platform in front of one of the doors of the first car I saw a young woman. Her arm was caught in her twisted purse strap—with the rest of the strap and her purse closed tight on the other side of the door. Realizing the train would start to move and that in seconds, she would be crushed against the wall at the end of the platform, I flew down the remaining few steps, caught up with her, grabbed her arm and pulled it free of the strap. A quick thinking passenger on the inside tossed her purse out of an open window an instant before the car passed the dreaded wall.

This scary little drama happened so quickly that even though the platform was crowded only a few people saw it. Those few were more than kind to me with their kudos and congratulations for the safe conclusion to the near death situation. They also tried to help the still frightened young lady who couldn't stop shaking and crying, but through it all kept telling me how grateful she was. It turned out that, coincidentally, she too worked at NBC. Several of us invited her for coffee, tea, whatever, but she refused, saying she just want to get home safely, which I assume she did. I, too, was pretty shook up so I accepted my own invitation for a little "whatever" before I departed for home.

I continued to use the New York subways for another fifty years without ever encountering another true life drama. However, because of my professional occupation, another kind of drama, those portrayed in radio and TV soap operas, did occupy very much of my time.

In 1941 the Radio Corporation of America, which owned NBC, had been ordered by the Justice Department and the Federal Communications Commission to divest itself of one of its radio networks, the Red or the Blue, on the grounds of "attempted monopoly of broadcasting." So General David Sarnoff, RCA's chairman, made the decision to offer the Blue Network for sale. It was generally understood that he chose the Blue because its affiliated stations were in weaker markets and its programs, with the exception of Walter Winchell, were less popular than those on the Red Network. Before a buyer could be found, however, it became necessary to split NBC down the middle, employee-wise, so to speak. Or, more precisely, to split each department. With those of us in the announcing department, it worked like this: Ray Diaz was to become announcing supervisor of the Blue Network. Ray invited whichever of us NBC guys he wanted, up to a certain number, to switch over with him to form a new Blue Network Announcing Staff. Of course those he invited had the right to decline, with no hard feelings. For instance, of those of us Ray asked to join him, Ben Grauer and Radcliff Hall preferred to stay with NBC.

The split became official in February of 1942. The announcers who comprised the new Blue Network staff were, as best I can remember, myself, Milton Cross, Jack Gordon Fraser, George Hicks, George Hayes, Kelvin Keech, Don Lowe, Jack McCarthy, and Bob Waldrop. No longer did we report to Pat Kelly's space on the fifth floor but to the second floor office of Ray Diaz because, although we were still paid by NBC, we were part of what a potential buyer was going to get when he purchased the Blue Network. On the air we signed off our programs with, "This is the Blue Network of the National Broadcasting Company." Later, when our fledgling company was bought, the sign-off cue became simply "This is the Blue Network."

You may recall that earlier in these recollections I mentioned Charles O'Connor, a young NBC announcer four or five years my senior, who had a sense of humor that was "off the wall" and demonstrated it one day by inviting Yoichi Hiraoka, the Japanese xylophone player, with the cleft palate, to do his own announcing. When the Philip Morris Company sponsored a program on NBC with little Johnny spouting his famous line "Call for Philip Mawrees," Charlie O'Connor was selected to be the announcer. Charlie had a very distinctive announcing style, and his efforts proved to be very successful in selling the client's cigarettes. The show was so successful that a few years later Philip Morris bought time on CBS to present an additional program, and they wanted the same announcer, Charles O'Connor. Because of the agreement among the three networks—NBC, CBS, and Mutual—prohibiting staff announcers from doing announcing chores on any but their own home base, Charlie was faced with a big decision: to turn down the new show on CBS and stay with the NBC staff or to resign from NBC to do the new *Philip Morris Show* on CBS and hopefully pick up more shows elsewhere. I feel sure he had a few sleepless nights before he decided to go the latter route, to leave NBC and go freelance.

Unbeknownst to all of us, Charlie was a quiet drinker. You might say a closet drinker. He was a great guy, lots of fun, a wonderful storyteller. He had a lovely wife and two kids. She had been captain of the Rockettes at the Radio City Music Hall before marrying him. People never thought of him as a drinker, probably because he never hung around or even dropped into Hurley's, the Down Under, or the English Grill—the closest watering holes for the NBC crowd. Some years earlier, I remember, he had gotten loaded at a party at Pat Kelly's house in Long Island and had fallen down the stairs. Not hurt, he got up smiling, but Mrs. O'Connor took the wheel driving home. We all assumed he just didn't know how to drink and had unfortunately polished off much more than he should have that night.

Charlie's decision to leave NBC and freelance turned out to be a bad one because he had too much time on his hands. Even though he had the two Philip Morris shows on NBC and CBS on two different nights of the week and he would spend time during the day knocking on doors at the ad agencies hoping for more work, it became known that little by little he was spending more and more time in other midtown bars so as not to be seen by his NBC cronies. Of course his alcoholism caught up with him. So much so that the Philip Morris people decided they simply had to replace him on both of their shows. When that happened, Charlie went to see his old boss and friend, Pat Kelly, hoping to be taken back on the NBC staff. Kelly had always had a great fondness for Charlie, especially because they shared the same Irish sense of humor, but it was too late. Word that his drinking was the cause of his losing the Philip Morris account had already reached not only Kelly but Kelly's bosses as well, making it impossible for Pat to help. The next morning I happened to be in Ray Diaz's new office when Charlie came in to talk to another close old friend, hoping he would hire him on the new Blue Network staff. Ray greeted him warmly and then closed the door to his inner office, pretty much knowing what Charlie's mission was because he had heard all the stories. But Ray was in no position to hire someone who was a known alcoholic, and as he later told me, he let Charlie know it as gently as he could. No way could he take him on, he said, "After all the Blue Network isn't even a week old and I've got all the announcers they'll let me hire so even if Charlie weren't an alcoholic I couldn't hire him." That was the first week in February of 1942. Everybody felt pretty bad about Charlie O'Connor's sad plight. But six weeks later Charles O'Connor proved how very dark his Irish sense of humor really was. At home alone in the kitchen, he turned on the gas and put his head in the oven. The date, March 17, St. Patrick's Day.

Considering all the staff announcers I had worked with through almost six decades, I think it's interesting that relatively few became alcoholics. Of the names I've remembered, Norman Brokenshire was the best-known announcer who fell into that unhappy trap. Even though he had achieved stardom as a member of the CBS staff in the early thirties, they fired him in 1936 because he had become too undependable. John F. Royal, hoping to capitalize on his celebrity, hired him at NBC, where he stayed dry for almost a year. But when he fell off the wagon, NBC had to let him go. Others on the staff whose heavy drinking caused their downfall, resulting in the loss of their jobs, were Herluf Provensen, Bill O'Toole, Douglas Browning, Bill Farren and Neel Enslen. Of the alcoholics only Enslen and O'Connor ended as suicides. Enslen had done it a few years before Charlie. Strangely, O'Connor chose the same method Enslen had used, the kitchen oven. While on this macabre subject, let me note that announcer Roger Krupp once attempted suicide in the announcers' lounge with a revolver he had sneaked out of the sound effects department. His firing aim was ridiculously, and some thought purposefully, poor, causing only a minor flesh wound and a few drops of blood. He later admitted he had done it because of a love affair gone sour, and he had hoped his action would bring the lady back to him, which it didn't. All it did was create a lot of excitement and get him fired.

Now to a much more pleasant subject. My friendship with Betty Garde had continued since our paths had first crossed when she was the star of *Mrs. Wiggs of the Cabbage Patch* and I was the announcer. That was in 1936. Now let's move ahead seven years. Betty invited me to accompany her mother and stepfather to the opening night of the Rodgers and Hammerstein musical *Oklahoma!* The date was March 31, 1943. The reason we were there was that Betty was in the show as one of the main characters, Aunt Eller. Other performers were Alfred Drake, Celeste Holm, and Howard da Silva. *Oklahoma!* was the first of a long string of great shows by Richard Rodgers and Oscar Hammerstein. Its music was outstanding. Besides the title song, others like "Oh! What a Beautiful Morning," "The Surrey with the Fringe on the Top," "I Cain't Say No," "Many a New Day," and "People Will Say We're in Love," will, as they say in showbiz, live on forever.

After the show was over, we joined Betty and lots of her friends at Lloyd Rosenmund's apartment to celebrate what everybody thought was a big hit. We wanted to be sure by staying up late to see what the critics had to say about it in the early editions of the New York papers.

Lloyd was an executive in Frank and Anne Hummert's organization and a good friend to many of us who worked for them, and that night he proved to be a generous and gracious host. When the rave reviews finally arrived and were thoroughly digested by us all, the party went on until dawn. *Oklahoma!* became more than the hit of the season. Its record run of 2,248 performances in New York and the record-breaking runs of its road companies gave it one of the largest audiences in American musical history. It has been said that the importance of *Oklahoma!* in opening a new era in the American musical theatre will never be challenged. What a privilege to have been present at its opening.

26

MAYOR FIORELLO LA GUARDIA

A while back I had arrived at the point in my story where General David Sarnoff, the chairman of RCA, which owned NBC, had offered the Blue Network for sale because the U.S. government had insisted on it. Out of 42 prospective purchasers early in 1943, the one who knocked the loudest, so to speak, on Sarnoff's door was Edward J. Noble, with his bid of eight million dollars cash. Noble had become a zillionaire through his ownership of Life Savers, the peppermint-flavored candy with the hole in the middle. Even though he was known as a tightwad, a reputation he got a kick out of, he lived in lavish style. The thousand-acre estate he owned in the Thousand Islands area of the St. Lawrence River had its own airport, golf course, tennis courts, swimming pool, and hunting grounds. He also owned a home in Greenwich, Connecticut. When in New York, he stayed at his year-round suite in the Hotel Waldorf Astoria. So Ed Noble became the new owner of the Blue Network. The Blue, as we called it for short, continued operating and broadcasting in the same studios and office space it had been using since the split from NBC had taken place under a ten-year lease agreement—until 1952. This arrangement stayed the same under Noble. Much of the programming remained the same, especially very popular shows like *Walter Winchell*, and *Lowell Thomas and the News*. AFRA negotiated an agreement which permitted any announcer who had been doing a show on the other network before the split to continue doing it. Accordingly, Ben Grauer, who stayed with NBC, could continue announcing Walter Winchell on the new Blue. And I, now employed by the Blue, could still do *Young Widder Brown* on NBC. So, on the announcers' daily schedule posted in his office, Ray Diaz, now our supervisor, penciled me in between 4 and 5 P.M. for the *Widder Brown* studio as Pat Kelly had done before him since 1938. Dress rehearsal was at 4:00, cuts and changes after that, and on the air at 4:45. So far as Ray was concerned he couldn't care less which network my show was on. *Young Widder Brown*, 4 to 5 P.M. Monday through Friday was part of my day, and that was that. No deduction in my staff salary for time spent working at NBC either.

Ray's generosity caused him to decide that the old rule should be completely disregarded. Under his aegis as the bossman of Blue Network announcers, no longer did we have to say no if we were invited to do a show or shows elsewhere, as long as the other shows didn't interfere with our own schedule. So around that time, when *Easy Aces* and *Mr. Keen, Tracer of Lost Persons* left the Blue Network for CBS, I was invited to go along with them—not as a show announcer but to continue doing cowcatchers before and hitchhikes after each show. As I explained earlier, these were twenty-second commercial announcements for a product other than the product which the show announcer was selling. I had already been doing them for a couple of years on the Blue Network when it was part of NBC and then when it became a separate network. These were shows out of the Hummert factory. I also picked up a couple more cowcatchers and hitchhikes on two Hummert musical shows on CBS whose titles I'm ashamed to admit I don't remember.

In addition to these goodies on CBS, I picked up a Monday through Friday show, *Lanny and Ginger Grey*, for Royal Scarlet Coffee, every morning on WOR, which was then the key station of the Mutual Network. All in all a tidy bit of new business which added to my happiness for having made the decision to leave NBC and go with the fledgling Blue Network.

In the spring of 1942, the Hummerts added a new program to their long list. Even though it was on in the daytime at 11 o'clock, it was not a soap opera. Directed by my friend, Martha Atwell, it was called *Chaplain Jim*. Each show was based on actual battle experiences during World War II. The United States had been in the war since Pearl Harbor on December 7, 1941, so there were already many experiences to dramatize from the European and Pacific war zones. Chaplain Jim, played by Don MacLaughlin, was a kindly young man of God who served both war fronts. Because the Hummerts produced the show together with the war department, there were no commercials, which was unheard of for any show coming out of the Hummert office. In my opening announcement before leading into that particular day's story, I would inform the radio listeners that the program was "dedicated to the mothers, wives, sweethearts, and families of the men who wear the khaki of the United States Army." When each episode ended, the good chaplain asked his listeners not to forget to send that "daily cheerful letter" to a soldier overseas. *Chaplain Jim* ran about two years.

About 1943–1944, I found myself selling Standard Oil of California every night at midnight, eastern time. The famous newsman, Lowell Thomas, was the feature. The program was aimed at a West Coast audience which heard us in its prime time at 9 o'clock. This program ran for a year.

Thomas continued doing his earlier news show for Sunoco at 6:45 P.M. I asked him once what he did between his earlier show and the midnight show, and his answer was "just like anybody else in the same situation, my wife and I have dinner and then, hopefully, catch a Broadway show or a good movie." If he wound up at a movie he would invariably hear himself voicing the Fox Movietone News.

I had first become acquainted with Lowell Thomas in 1931 during my early page boy days at 711 Fifth Avenue when he replaced Floyd Gibbons, the famous war correspondent of World War I. Mr. Gibbons had lost an eye covering the war. He felt more comfortable wearing an eye patch than a glass eye, and as a result the eye patch became his trademark, so to speak. The combination of his eye patch, his handsome appearance, and his distinctive voice made him a constant target of cameramen from newspapers, magazines, and newsreels. Because of all this attention, he became much more celebrated after World War I ended. When I first saw him at 711, I was sixteen. I can remember how excited I was just breathing the same air. Whereas when I first saw his replacement—a fellow by the name of Lowell Thomas—I remember thinking to myself, "who's he?" Well, during the next decade I found out. And as I look back from my present retirement perch in the 1990s, I'm firmly of the opinion that during all those years no one in the business became more respected and liked than Lowell Thomas. Having said that, I must describe one foible I had observed over the years, probably his only foible. Lowell had a great habit, a penchant you might say, of arriving at the studio at the very last minute, sometimes with only seconds to spare. Once when I was doing his midnight show to the West Coast he didn't walk into the studio until I was already into the opening commercial. Up until then I had never worried that he might not get there because I remembered witnessing his last-minute arrivals as far back as my page boy days and hearing his earlier announcers, like Jimmy Wallington, talk about his habit. Hugh James, who was his announcer for the *Sunoco* show at 6:45 P.M. for many years, had told me it was not easy to get used to, but once you did you could relax, especially when you stopped to think that in his entire career he never missed being there when his announcer said, "Now, here's Lowell Thomas."

While I'm telling tales out of school about him, I've got to include this one. It's hard to believe that the very staid and proper Lowell Thomas could lose all control when something tickled his funny bone. Once in the early forties an alert engineer who just happened to be listening to the program in the recording room sensed that something unusual was starting to happen and began to record what was left of the show even though it was almost over. It seems that a line in a news story Thomas was reading struck him funny, and whatever the line was, it caused a delayed reaction so that, although he was already into his next item, he began to titter slightly. The titter became a louder giggle as he continued trying to convey the point of the item he was now into. But then hearty laughter replaced speech. His sides splitting with hilarity, he tried to bring Hugh James into the act for the closing commercial and barely got out the words "Now here's Hugh." I'll never forget the opening line of Hugh's commercial. He said, "Lowell, tomorrow's the first of May," and that's as far as he got. Instantly he too burst into convulsive laughter, and for about twenty seconds or so all you could hear was Lowell in the background, as hysterical as before, and Hugh, much closer to the mike, still laughing out loud but struggling to get control, which he never did. The program ended with the normally bass baritone Hugh James blurting out in a high-pitched, still laughing voice, "This is the Blue Network."

Another time I remember Lowell Thomas rolling on the floor with laughter

was when he mispronounced the name of Sir Stafford Cripps (an English statesman). He called the honorable gentleman Sir Stifford Craps.

Someone I first knew in my page boy days at 711 was Norman Sweetser. A bachelor, some twenty some years my senior, he had been a producer/director with NBC since it started. Norman was a veteran of World War I, a pilot under the command of Captain Fiorello La Guardia in the Army Air Corps. When the war was over, La Guardia got into politics, Sweetser into radio, and they remained friends and they stayed in touch. Once, after La Guardia had become New York's mayor, Norman and I dropped into the bar at the old Lafayette Hotel, now long since gone from University Place in Greenwich Village, and a familiar voice called out Norman's name. It was La Guardia himself, seated with a friend at a corner table. His voice had a high-pitched, distinctive sound which made it especially familiar to anyone who ever listened to the radio or paid attention to the newsreels in movie theatres. The two old war buddies greeted each other, introductions were made (me to Fiorello, and his companion to us), and before I knew what had happened, this young celebrity buff found himself seated with Mayor La Guardia and one of his aides as the mayor ordered up a round of drinks in celebration of running into his old friend Norman Sweetser who, unlike me, was quite accustomed to rubbing elbows with famous people. In the course of his work as a producer/director, Norman had traveled the country with two of the biggest: in 1928 with Governor Al Smith as he campaigned for the presidency against Herbert Hoover and in the early 30s with Babe Ruth, on nationwide personal appearance tours. To say nothing of many important early radio personalities whose programs he was involved in.

One Saturday in the late 30s or early 40s I had been to the Aqueduct Race Track with a sporting group of friends. They included Dorothy and John Cleary and a friend of theirs, a young lady named Rae Somebody. John was a radio director who, as I've mentioned earlier, eventually hit it big in television as the owner/producer of *College Bowl*. Norm Sweetser and Ben Grauer completed the group. On our way back to the city, the subject came up as to where we might go to get a few laughs and unwind from our day at the track. Dorothy Cleary, who was pretty much up on such things, said it might be fun to try La Martinique, a popular nightclub in a cellar on West 57th Street. She had heard and read some good things concerning a new young comedian by the name of Danny Kaye who was appearing there, his first time in any big city. None of the rest of us had ever heard of him, so with a "what have we got to lose?" kind of attitude, we headed for La Martinique. When we arrived, we had no trouble getting a good table, I guess because the main attraction was not a big name, and a lot of the usual New York nightclub patrons were in a wait-and-see pattern. If Danny Kaye's drawing power strengthened, then they might take a chance to see what he was all about. To put it mildly, we were not disappointed. I don't know when I had heard an audience so hysterical, including, if not led by, Rae, the Clearys' friend at our table. I found myself laughing as much at her hilarious reaction to Danny Kaye's antics as at Danny himself. Simply put, she was a perfect lady who loved to laugh and her merry sound seemed to spur everyone else to do likewise, much as Mr. Kaye deserved. When he finished, he came over to our table, bringing his pianist, Sylvia Fine, along. He wanted to thank us for being, in his words, so pleasantly receptive to his efforts, and he said he had no doubt that our genial response helped make that particular performance so successful. Then he went on to say that Miss Fine was not only his accompanist but wrote almost all of the material he used. "Oh, and by the way, she's also Mrs. Danny Kaye." Before leaving, he told us he was very excited because when his

stint at La Martinique ended he was booked into the New York Paramount, and he would like it if we all could come. And when we came, to please sit in the first row, if possible, so that our laughter, "especially of that young lady, might be as infectious at the Paramount as it proved to be here tonight." It turned out that some weeks later when he was appearing there only three of us could manage to go at the same time. So Miss Rae Ha-Ha, Norman Sweetser, whose belly laugh could be heard a block away, and I, also no slouch in the laugh department, found ourselves one Saturday afternoon front-row center at the Paramount Theatre, holding our sides once more at the shenanigans of a star in the making, Danny Kaye. We had been at his first nightclub appearance in New York, and now here we were at his first New York theatre appearance. His first movie appearance was still to come, with plenty more to follow.

Before I get too far removed from Fiorello La Guardia, let me say that some months after the pleasant drink Norman Sweetser and I enjoyed with him, I had the occasion to see him again. This time at Gracie Mansion, a large and impressive house overlooking the East River, which was and still is the official residence of the New York mayor. No, I wasn't invited. But he did expect me. To be more accurate, he expected an announcer, and it so happened I had been assigned by my fairly recent new boss, Ray Diaz, to go there to put Fiorello on the air to talk about I don't remember what. Remembering me from the Lafayette Hotel bar encounter with his old friend Sweetser, he cordially asked me to join him in liquid refreshment on the porch after the program. I was very sorry to have to turn him down, but I had to be back at the studios within the hour, and there just wasn't anything I could do about it, much as I wanted to stay. I guess I was hoping to get to know him a little better, to try to determine what made him tick, to try to find out what was behind the mayoral facade if, indeed, such a thing existed. I guess what I wondered, not only about him but about any celebrity, was if there wasn't sometimes just a bit of fakery involved in their public persona. I didn't mean it in a critical sense. But it seemed to me that for such high profile types a little fakery, or acting—to use a nicer word—could come in very handy when needed.

Sometime later, while these musings were still occasionally rambling through my head, a perfect opportunity to find out if my thoughts on the subject had any validity was dropped right in my lap. One evening as I walked into room 281, Ray Diaz's office, the sound coming out of the loudspeaker was the high-pitched voice of hizzoner, the mayor. Those in the office were Reggie Stanborough, Ray's assistant who was in charge at night, and two announcers—Don Lowe and Jack McCarthy. I'm sure they weren't even aware that the loudspeaker was on, much less who was on and, most likely, they couldn't have cared less. But their interest perked up when they heard me wondering aloud about where La Guardia was broadcasting from, Gracie Mansion or in one of the studios. A quick look at the daily program log posted on the wall told me he was in Studio E, the speakers' studio on the eighth floor that Lowell Thomas used. Of course for me to carry out the devilish plan I had started to concoct, he had to be in the building. So far so good. A glance at the clock told me he still had about eight minutes left to the end of the show, so I informed my friends I was going to put hizzoner to a test and I needed their cooperation. Even though they thought I had gone bonkers, they were too curious not to agree. I asked McCarthy and Lowe to go to the eighth floor right away so they would be there when the mayor left the studio. I wanted them to just kind of stand around nonchalantly and pick a good spot within earshot of the page boys' reception desk so they could both see and hear Fiorello when he got on the telephone. Crucial to my test, I told them, was to observe

as closely as possible if he hangs up within seconds after he gets on or if he stays on a while.

As the two of them left on their way to the elevators, Reg Stanborough and I listened as La Guardia finished his talk. Then I called the reception desk outside 8E and told the page: "This is City Hall calling. I have a very important message for Mr. La Guardia so would you please get him to the phone quickly before he takes any other calls. I want you to stress to him that this is quite urgent." In no time at all I heard the inimitable, squeaky voice as he got on. "Mr. Mayor," I said, "I have a really important message for you." "Yes? But first who is this, who is this?" Ignoring his question, I then proceeded to make the sound of a Bronx cheer and hung up. Reggie Stanborough just stood there finding it hard to fathom what had just gone on. He seemed both amused and amazed. Wasting no time to get back to the office were the two I had dispatched to check out and report back what had happened at the other end of my phone call. The report they brought back gave me pause. Don Lowe and Jack McCarthy told me they had positioned themselves separately at a discreet distance but within hearing range of the reception desk when the mayor answered my call. But they couldn't figure out how come I kept the conversation going as long as I did when I had told them earlier it would be either very short or he might stay on a while. To them, as observers, no way could I have had such a short conversation that he would have hung up within seconds because indeed he did stay on a while, like two or three minutes. And from what they could glean, they thought I was doing most of the talking. He seemed to be interjecting into what they considered to be my end of the conversation normal little nothings like "Is that so?" "Really?" "I find that hard to believe," until he wound up with, "I'll get in touch with him first thing in the morning. Take care of yourself. Goodnight."

After a rocky opening when he sounded a little uptight, kind of annoyed, they both agreed that he seemed to have settled down to a pleasant chat. McCarthy and Lowe were flabbergasted when I explained, and Stanborough backed me up, that my part in this little playlet, including the Bronx cheer, lasted no more than 15 seconds and what they witnessed was the distinguished mayor of the city of New York speaking to a dial tone. The whole episode, I think, was proof enough that a mayoral facade did indeed exist. At least with Mayor La Guardia. Fakery, Fiorello?

27

NAKEDSVILLE ON
LEXINGTON AVENUE

During the relatively short period that Edward J. Noble owned the Blue Network, despite his reputation as a cheapskate, he threw an annual company outing on a weekday in May, an all-day affair continuing well into the evening. To enable the golfers, tennis buffs, hikers, etc., to get a full day's enjoyment, Mr. Noble chartered busses to leave the city beginning fairly early in the morning and continuing on a staggered schedule until shortly after 5 o'clock. The big bash was held at the Crescent-Hamilton Country Club in Huntington, Long Island. It was a lovely spot, with ample accommodations for the outdoor sports types as well as those more inclined to favor indoor activities—a card game here, a crap game there, maybe a little elbow bending everywhere. Whether I could go depended on what my overall program commitments were. But because *Young Widder Brown* did not get off the air until 5:00, I had to miss the daytime stuff every year, and catch the last bus at 5:15. That is the way it was the day of the outing I speak of.

Arriving about 7:00, I was able to catch the bar just as it was closing because dinner was about to be served. The bar was in the rear of a huge dining room packed with my fellow Blue Network employees. A quick glance indicated most all the tables were full, particularly those close to the stage, but I spotted Les Griffith, a fellow announcer, alone at a table for ten in the rear. He motioned me to join him which I was glad to do because he looked so lonesome at the large table. As dinner pro-

gressed, I learned he had come out on a noon bus. He hadn't participated in any of the outdoor games but said he had "found enough going on inside to make it enjoyable," a statement I had no trouble believing. I didn't ask him where inside because I had already formed my own thoughts on the subject. I must say it was the only time in my many years of knowing Les Griffith that he showed even the slightest sign of imbibing.

Dinner over, there were signs of activity up on the stage. The orchestra was comprised of house musicians accompanying house singers. The emcee was my good friend Walter Kiernan, a top newscaster who was also adept at projecting the lighter side of things. In a word, he was a fine storyteller. Last but not least was the brass—Edward J. Noble, Blue Network owner and chairman; Mark Woods, president; and Robert Kintner, executive vice president, who, industry gossip had it, was a wanna-be president. When it came time for the speechifying, Kiernan graciously introduced Ed Noble, who stepped to the podium and explained that he had never considered himself a good public speaker so he was going to step aside while "we all listen to our president, Mark Woods." Woods then took over for at least ten minutes. Sometimes in listening to Mark, it was difficult to distinguish between his Southern accent and the amount of liquor he had taken aboard. Tonight was no exception. When he finished, Walter Kiernan introduced Bob Kintner, who was also noted for his boozing, but this night he had obviously abstained. After three or four minutes of pleasantries in which he got some real good laughs, he thanked the crowd and sat down. Walter Kiernan, pursuing his role as emcee, began to inform the audience that the time had arrived for dancing, when Mr. Woods got out of his chair and whispered something to him. Walter then asked the orchestra to hold it a moment, explaining that before the dancing began, Mr. Woods wanted to briefly say something he had overlooked earlier. With that, Woods took over and began to talk. And he talked. And he talked. Titters began, then more audible giggles. At our table Les had remained silent. But he began to shake his head disgustedly as Woods continued to drone on. Les Griffith had come to the same conclusion everyone in the place had—which was the reason for the giggling—and he decided to express himself. Aloud. Very loud. At the top of his voice he shouted, "Sit down, you just gave that speech!" Now there were screams of laughter as all eyes turned in the direction the voice came from, our table. But we were not to be seen, because by the time Les had gotten his last word out I had already ducked under the table and grabbed him and literally pulled him down under with me. A postscript to this story is that before too long Mark Woods "retired." Guess who succeeded him as president.

Up until this point, the anecdotes I have related have had mostly to do with radio, or things connected with radio. Not this one, however. In January of 1942, I had reached the age of 27 and still hadn't heard from my draft board. I, like millions of others of draft age, had had to register two years earlier in compliance with the Selective Service Act of 1940. My official address with the government was with my family in Bay Ridge, Brooklyn. Accordingly, my draft board was near the house on 85th Street. With all that was going on in my life, I still was quite aware that the big thing that might change things forever was getting closer. Everyday I would hear about guys I knew being drafted who were considerably younger than my 27 years. My friend Lou Julian had been about my age, and he had been drafted early. He was with the first wave of GI's to go overseas, where he was one of the primary casualties during combat in Italy. Now another fellow having the same concerns as I was Richard Widmark. Along with those concerns, we had something else in common which caused us to keep in even closer touch. We both had perforated eardrums. We had heard very conflicting stories about how this might affect our draft status. Dick was playing the lead in the soap opera *Front Page Farrell* in a studio next to my *Young Widder Brown* studio on NBC's eighth floor. So practically every day we were able to get together to swap the latest we had heard about other men who had the same disability, if you could even call it such a thing. The reason we were on tenterhooks was that some of those men with holes in their eardrums were accepted into the army whereas others were not. From what we could gather, it was a matter of what ear specialist you happened to be sent to on the day of your physical. A roll of the dice.

Finally, a card dated November 26, 1942, arrived notifying me that I had been classified by my local board as 1-A. So unless I was found to have something physically or mentally out of whack on the day of the physical, I would automatically become a private in the U.S. Army. An order to report for induction, which was dated December 11, arrived, stating that the president of the United States wished to offer me "greeting" (without an s) and further stated that if I was accepted after my examination, "You will then be inducted into the army. You will, therefore, report to the local board at 8410 Third Avenue, Brooklyn, New York, at 7:30 A.M. on the 30th day of December, 1942." The order also instructed me to "bring sufficient clothing for three days." Of course I showed my communiqués from Uncle Sam to

With Mark Woods, Blue Network president in 1942.

Widmark, knowing of his vital interest and especially because he had still not heard from Uncle.

The night before the big day I stayed in my old room at the family house on 85th Street, just around the corner from the draft board. On such a day it was incumbent, by law, upon an employer to give a prospective draftee the day off. Accordingly my good friend and Blue Network boss, Ray Diaz, did just that, so did the people at Air Features, the Hummerts' program factory, who hired a substitute announcer for *Widder Brown* that day.

I was ordered by the induction notice to appear at the draft board's headquarters by 7:30 A.M., so when I turned the corner from 85th Street to Third Avenue at 7:20, I walked into a crowd of what turned out to be sixty fellow draftees. Making my way through the group into 8410 Third Avenue, I was greeted by Mr. Alfred Rickenberger, the head of the local board. Mr. Rickenberger informed me that he and his draft board had decided to put me in charge of the others during the subway trip to our destination, Grand Central Palace, close by Grand Central Station in Manhattan. He said that in draft board circles it was considered quite an honor to be so commissioned and that the honor was given me because of being older than the others, I was more likely be able to maintain the necessary discipline which, he informed me, he was sure I had learned when I was a cadet in military school, Xavier High. My God, I thought, they've checked me out that far back. I found it hard to believe. Next he produced a canvas bag filled with nickels, a hundred and twenty-two of them to be exact. It would also be my responsibility, he explained, to see that my charges each received a nickel (the subway fare in those days) and to please observe that they inserted it before going through the turnstile, making sure none broke the law by ducking under or jumping over same in order to pocket the nickel. I would be required to go through the operation again at Pacific Street station when we changed from the BMT (Brooklyn, Manhattan Transit), to the IRT (Interborough Rapid Transit) which as a Brooklyn subway rider I had known since I was practically in diapers. Having finished instructing me, he brought me outside and told the others, my charges, to please line up. He then introduced me, told them I was in charge until we all reached Grand Central Station, wished everybody good luck, and told them to follow me to the subway station on Fourth Avenue, a block away.

Getting them through the turnstile and down onto the platform wasn't as bad as I anticipated. When the train arrived, it was a problem to make sure they all got on and stayed in one car without wandering throughout the train, but we worked it out. However, changing at Pacific Street was no picnic. By now it was the height of the morning rush hour, with throngs of people in a hurry going every which way as I had to get my sixty young men up the stairs together, over to the IRT turnstiles, give each one a nickel again, watch closely as they put it in the turnstile, and then go down another stairway to the IRT platform. Oh, and while doing all this, I had to keep count, making sure I didn't lose anybody. So far as discipline was concerned I had no problems. By and large they turned out to be good kids, and realizing the unpleasant responsibility which had been handed me, albeit Mr. Rickenberger had called it an honor, they appeared to do their best to cooperate. For which I thanked them profusely when we arrived at Grand Central Palace. In return, it seemed all sixty of them shouted their thanks back to me as I officially dismissed them from my charge before we all entered the vast palace on Lexington Avenue.

Inside, the only skin coverings allowed were shoes, sandals, slippers, etc., with or without socks. Nothing else. Hundreds of young men milling about in the altogether, Nakedsville on Lexington Avenue. Occasional small gatherings attempted conversation, but in most cases it was only an attempt. Small talk seemed not to be welcome in nakedsville. Who cared about the weather when something far more important was about to be determined for each and every naked soul there. The army personnel, doctors and the like, were easy to spot because they were the only ones with clothes on. But compared to the large amount of visible undraped skin, those clothed were few and far between. When we first entered Grand Central, posted signs directed us to a section where our clothes were checked. The only laugh I had all morning was when a boy about 19 asked an army attendant how, with no clothes, he could carry his check stub. With a not quite straight face, the attendant answered, "in your shoe, of course. Where else?"

The nakedness edict was to facilitate the myriad physical exams taking place in every nook and cranny available for such use. It had the desired effect of speeding up the procedure. Many more draftees were examined in a given amount of time when the taking off and putting back on of clothing was eliminated. Of the many, many faces I saw that morning, only one did I think I recognized. I furtively glanced in his direction a couple of times trying to make sure he was who I thought he was—a cousin I hadn't seen or spoken to since I was nine or ten years old. Back then, for whatever reason, there had been a family rift between two factions involving adults, but resulting in estrangements between the little kids, who at the time were not even aware of the situation. He had been standing, or rather leaning on a post when I first noticed him. But it wasn't until he stepped away, and I saw him walking that I knew I was right. Seeing him walk brought back that I had heard he had been stricken with polio. There was the proof of his identification as my cousin right before my eyes: As he walked he was quite lame and he seemed to move with difficulty.

He hadn't seen me yet, so I approached him with "Austin Titus?" He gave me that "I wonder who this can be" look and answered "That's right." When I told him who I was, there appeared that great smile I remembered from our childhood. After a few minutes of general pleasantries, how glad we were to see each other after almost 20 years, he brought the subject around to his feelings about being drafted. I then became rather embarrassed because I couldn't understand how he could possibly have been classified 1–A, although I didn't mention it. Yet if he wasn't 1–A, he

wouldn't have been there. He had high hopes of being accepted, and the more he talked, the more I envisioned the big letdown he was surely going to get when the army said no. His 1–A classification just had to be a mistake, no doubt about it. About my situation he had heard the same stuff I had. Some perforated eardrums were accepted, some not. When we had to break it up for more visits with the doctors, we wished each other well and agreed the final decision about each of us was in the hands of the "man upstairs." Standing in the middle of Grand Central Palace, naked as jaybirds, we two cousins shook hands good-bye and went off to stand on different lines for more examinations.

Of all the doctors who tapped, poked, felt, and peered into various parts of my anatomy, the only one who worried me was the ear man. Sphinxlike he said nothing. It was impossible to read him, pleasant as he was. Nor did I dare ask for his evaluation of my situation. Actually he was through rather quickly; he smiled, scribbled something on a small card, and told me to lay it flat inside my shoe with the others and whom to give it to when I had finished with all the exams. When that moment finally arrived, I gave all the cards I had carried in my shoes to the proper person. When he got through deciphering them, he told me to take my check stub to the dressing room, get dressed, and go out "that door over there," as opposed to a different door in another direction. So, with my clothes back on again, I was about to push open "that door over there" when I heard somebody say, "Here, you might need this." The soldier at a desk I had just passed handed me a piece of paper. On it was typed my name, the address of my draft board and the date, December 30, 1942. Also stamped on it were the words "Rejected by the Armed Forces."

I practically floated out of the door and to the nearby Hotel Biltmore, where I immediately called Ray Diaz and told him I was in such a bad way that the army wanted no part of me, and to add insult to injury they had embarrassed me further by reclassifying me 4-F. Ray got the message immediately in spite of the silly way I broke my good news to him. He wasted no time getting to the Biltmore and brought Doug Browning with him. We spent the next two hours celebrating my good fortune in being spared. A postscript: My physically disabled cousin, Austin Titus, was drafted and soon became a private in the U.S. Army. Will wonders never cease? You figure it out. P.P.S. A few months later Dick Widmark enjoyed the same outcome as I, which undoubtedly hastened his rise to stardom in the motion picture world.

28

THY NETWORK IS BLUE

Sometime in the mid-40s, the Hummerts canceled *Mr. Keen* and *Easy Aces* from their early evening periods on CBS, which also killed my cowcatchers and hitchhikes. Sorry as I was to kiss any commercial work good-bye, I was pleased that the opening in my schedule made me available for a return engagement of *Omar Herth, the Swing-maker*, Milt Herth and his swingin' trio, to be aired five nights a week at 6:30 just ahead of *Lowell Thomas and the News*. Milt had been booked by Jack Dempsey, the former World's Heavyweight Champion, into his restaurant in the heart of the New York theater district. The show had last been on the air in 1938 and 1939 at 8 o'clock in the morning with yours truly reciting the silly rhymes, and I was delighted it was back. From a restaurant yet. Not just any old restaurant, but Jack Dempsey's. And Doris Gilbert, the same talented lady who wrote the nonsensical poetic foolishness back then, was still available to write new stuff for me to have fun with. A few examples:

I am a man above the crowd,
And with good reason am I proud;
Fate's own child, and destiny's man—
I stopped the beguine everyone began.
(Followed by music—"Begin the Beguine")

and

I gnash my teeth, I tear my hair,
In fact I lose all savoir faire—
When I to the movies for pleasure come,
And the guy next to me pops his gum.

After almost a decade of the sign–off system cue, "This is NBC, the National Broadcasting Company," now it had become "This is the Blue Network." One evening after *Omar* had been on a couple of weeks, I thought, in a lighthearted mood, that it might be fitting to alter the system cue ever so slightly so that it might sound more in keeping with the program. Something Omar Khayyam himself might have liked. So I changed it to "Thy Network Is Blue." The network executives liked it, and the restaurant diners liked it too, as did Jack Dempsey. So for the run of the show, we did it every night—"Thy Network Is Blue."

Before I get too far ahead into the 40s, let me not overlook an amusing incident which occurred in 1940. Fred Allen was a very funny man, a master of off-beat humor. His one hour radio show was broadcast from NBC's Studio 8H every Wednesday at 9 P.M. with a live repeat to the west coast at midnight. One night his guest was a Captain Knight, whose gimmick was a trained eagle named Mr. Ramshaw. During the performance Mr. Ramshaw, while flying high over 8H, to put it politely, misbehaved continuously, causing quite a mess as well as great hilarity. John F. Royal sent word to the producer not to allow Mr. Ramshaw to rise above the floor during the repeat show. But his orders were ignored, the eagle repeated his act, and later Fred sent the following letter to Mr. Royal. March 25th 1940

dear mr. royal...
    am in receipt of your letter commenting on l'affaire eagle as they are calling it around the young and rubicam office.
    i thought i had seen about everything in radio but the eagle had a trick up his feathered colon that was new to me. i thought for a minute i was back on the bill with lamont's cockatoos.

an acolyte from your quarters brought news to us, following the nine o'clock broadcast, that the eagle was to be grounded at the midnight show. it was quite obvious that mr. ramshaw, as the eagle is known around the falcon lounge at the autobon society rooms, resented your dictatorial order. when his cue came to fly, and he was still bound to captain knight's wrist, mr. ramshaw, deprived by nature of the organs essential in the voicing of an audible complaint, called upon his bowels to wreak upon us his reaction to your martinet ban.

toscanini, your house man, has foisted some movements on studio audiences in 8h, the bulova company has praised its movements over your network, but when radio city is being torn down to make way for another mcguiness restaurant in years to come, the one movement that will be recalled by the older radio fans will be the eagle's movement on wednesday last. if you have never seen a ghost's beret you might have viewed one on mr. rockefeller's carpet during our sterling performance.

i know you await with trepidation the announcement that i am going to interview sabu with his elephant some week.

yours for a wet broom in 8h on wednesday nights.

fred allen

For some silly reason, Fred never used capital letters in his self-typed correspondence. The Young and Rubicam he mentions was the advertising agency handling the program. Lamont's Cockatoos was a vaudeville act he had occasionally found himself on the same bill with in his early vaudeville days.

Another incident involving some of the gang in the "Blue Nework" ocurred in the English Grill.

"This will probably only take a minute" is what the new bartender probably thought one day during a slack few moments behind the bar in the English Grill. So he unzipped his fly and proceeded to pee on the ice cubes. But, unfortunately for him, he didn't know that at that very moment announcer Kelvin Keech was returning from a phone booth and was re-occupying his spot at the far end of the bar. Even though he was thirty feet away, Kelvin couldn't miss seeing what he was seeing and quietly tipped off Sam, the head bartender. Sam fired him on the

spot and banished the poor man from the premises almost before he had time to finish what he was doing and zip up his fly on the way out. End of story.

I should have said "end of that particular story." I know there were other memorable happenings which occurred in the English Grill in those days, two of which come to mind. First of all I mentioned earlier that the place was one of the favorite hangouts of the NBC crowd. And now with the Blue Network leasing NBC's studios and office space, many of that gang also enjoyed spending time there, myself included. What we all knew as the English Grill is presently known as the American Festival Cafe, and is located on the 50th Street side of Rockefeller Center's skating rink presided over by the statue of Prometheus arising from the fountain, which still appeals to the aesthetic tastes of countless visitors.

Prometheus and the fountain also attracted large numbers of pigeons. One day my friend Doug Browning, while standing alone at the bar in the English Grill, became fascinated watching pigeons gobbling up what was being tossed down to them from onlookers above on the street level. The mischievous side of good ol' Doug began to take over as he formulated a scenario in his mind. The huge sliding glass doors separating the interior and exterior of the English Grill were on a track. They might remain closed, which was most of the time, or open—however much the maître d' decreed. Doug's plan was very simple. Unostentatiously, he filled his pockets with peanuts from the bar. So armed, he wandered toward the doors which he had already observed were open slightly more than a crack. Unnoticed, he nonchalantly separated them enough to step between so that, outside, he could drop a peanut here and a peanut there and so wean the pigeons away from the largesse of the good people above. Undoubtedly Doug's peanuts were tastier than whatever it was those folks had been feeding his feathered friends because in no time at all he had become the pigeons' newest best friend. At least 25 or 30 of them became so attracted to him that when he walked back inside, still dropping peanuts, they followed him through the narrow opening.

Suddenly alerted to this wacky sight, the maître d' rushed over to try to open the doors wider so as to get rid of the fowl intruders. That's when the fun began. In rushing toward the doors, he had to plow through the pigeons, scaring them to such an extent that instantly they were everywhere—on tables, on the bar, in the air. It was utter chaos for a few minutes, bringing back memories of Fred Allen's guest, Mr. Ramshaw, the high-flying eagle. Decorum did not return to the English Grill until the maître d' had assuaged the diners. Especially those whose tables had suffered direct hits during the bombardment. In those cases the only assuagement that meant anything was when the maître d' tore up the check. Meanwhile, the one who caused all this commotion, Doug Browning, had quietly slipped out and down the hall to the bar at the Down Under which, he had known from countless previous visits, was out of bounds for pigeons.

One other well-remembered incident at the English Grill concerned Robert E. Kintner, who, you may remember, rose to the presidency of the Blue Network after Mark Woods lost that job shortly after he repeated the same speech within 20 minutes at an annual company outing. A while back I referred to Mr. Kintner, then the executive vice president, as a wanna-be president who was also well known for his boozing but had totally abstained that day. That good behavior eventually helped make his wanna-be dream a reality in that it gave the chairman, Edward J. Noble, who had been looking for a reason to give Kintner the job, a good excuse. In due time he kicked Woods upstairs to the vague job of vice chairman of the board. When that happened, Mark Woods couldn't help but get the message and he retired. Kintner became president.

One day President Kintner's secretary received a call from another executive urgently requesting her to come quickly down to the English Grill because her boss was behaving very badly at the bar. In a few minutes she arrived to find the reason he was behaving very badly was because he was very drunk. A pretty tough spot for a pretty young secretary to find herself in. Her brain reeling as to what to do, her first thought was to get him seated at a table before he fell on his face. With the help of the executive who alerted her, she succeeded. Figuring that more than likely he hadn't eaten anything all day, she made a quick decision to order spaghetti and meat sauce and, if necessary, spoon feed it to him. So that he wouldn't testily think she might be trying to deprive him of liquid refreshment, she included a glass of Chianti wine. A perfect combination, she thought. When the order arrived, however, he thought otherwise. No sooner had the waiter departed than the president of the Blue Network, the illustrious Robert E. Kintner, picked up the hot plate of spaghetti and meat sauce and dumped it over her head. Next he tossed the Chianti on top of that. He then rose from the table and stumbled out the door. The postscript to this is that Kintner's boss, Chairman Edward J. Noble, either was kept in the dark about it or heard and elected to do nothing in order to save face for putting him in the job in the first place. Bob Kintner remained until 1956, when he went to NBC to become president of the television network. He rose to chairman of NBC, which position he held until his retirement in 1966 despite his ill-tempered personality.

One day early in the war, word had come that the great French liner, the S.S. *Normandie*, was in flames at its dock, Pier 88 at 49th Street and the Hudson River. It was a usual working day for me, but every chance I got between assignments I hurried up to the observation deck of the RCA building utterly fascinated by the war drama, far from the scenes of actual battle, which was evolving before my eyes. I say war drama because it was always assumed but never definitely established that it was sabotage. If ever anyone had a front row seat, I did that day, along with many others. The scene was sadly spectacular. The magnificently beautiful *Normandie* was literally a huge ball of fire. While I was still watching, she rolled over on her side, all one thousand feet of her, completely knocked out, filling the air for miles around with acrid smoke. She remained there, causing constant rubbernecking slowdowns on the West Side Highway for the duration of the war.

I was saddened when Graham Mc-Namee passed away in the early 40s. Graham had been the first radio announcer to achieve great fame. He had been respected both by his peers and the listening audience. For a man of his professional stature, he couldn't have been kinder to me when I was starting out as the first junior announcer, so I wanted to pay my respects to him in death. He was reposing at Campbell's Funeral Home, a well-known mortuary on Madison Avenue. When I arrived at about 8 o'clock, I noticed the scarcity of people in the lobby. From my experience in attending wakes, especially on the last night before the funeral, I expected the lobby of a funeral establishment to be filling up with mourners going to different wakes. Not so here. Inquiring where Mr. McNamee was laid out, I was directed to take the elevator to the proper suite upstairs. Upon entering it I found it hard to believe that I was the only living person there. I was alone in the room with the remains of one of the most famous personages in America. Not even an attendant. Even when the deceased is a nobody, an employee/attendant is customarily close by. I knelt by the casket, studied his countenance, reflected on his remarkable life and prayed for him, all the while expecting to be joined by someone, anyone. For the best part of an hour I stayed, completely alone. An indescribable sadness came over me, as well as a creepy feeling. Still unable to understand it, I smiled for the last time at Graham McNamee and said good-bye. That night I tossed and turned an awful lot, wondering what exactly fame was all about.

Apartments I have lived in. A friend suggested that should be the title of my book, because in the 30s and 40s I certainly had my share. The last one I mentioned was when I lived with Radcliff Hall, where Doug Browning jumped from our second-floor balcony to go fetch a bottle of club soda. My next apartment came through a singer named Barry McKinley, who had a good deal waiting for him if he could move to Chicago, like yesterday. But he and his wife were encumbered by the remainder of a two-year lease which they couldn't get out of, so I agreed to take it over until it expired a year later. It was located at 413 East 58th Street, just off First Avenue, and it worked out fine because my rent was cut in half when a talent agent named Bob Coe joined me as a roommate. The thing I remember most about Bob was that he loved to bowl, frequently into the wee hours, at the Radio City Bowling Alleys in a building on Sixth Avenue which has long since been replaced by the Time-Life Building. One other thing that comes to mind about him—before our year together ended he had acquired a client by the name of Ed McMahon who did all right later on when he teamed up with a fellow by the name of Johnny Carson.

When that year ended, I found a reasonable studio apartment on 52d Street just east of Madison Avenue through an ad in the paper. It was around the corner from the CBS studios at 485 Madison. It was also five floors above one of New York's great restaurants at that time, Louis and Armand. Victor, the maître d', jokingly suggested I should install a hoist outside my window so I could phone my order and he could wrap it up, hook it onto the rope, and I could just hoist it up without ever having to step foot into the restaurant. But, I recall telling him, as ingenious as that sounded, it didn't appeal to me too much because I would miss the fun of actually being there and running into friends from the radio world. Because of its proximity to CBS, the likes of Edward R. Murrow and Bill Paley, the CBS chairman, frequently dined there.

Last but not least was the studio apartment I took which followed 50 East 52d Street. I really don't remember why I made the move, but it proved to be a good one, a happy one, my last as a bachelor. Like the other apartments, of course, it was furnished. Any furniture which I called my own was in the family house in Brooklyn. That apartment, too, I found through an ad, probably in the *New York Times*. It was on 61st Street just off Park Avenue, a wonderful location. The building had been built as a private mansion around the turn of the century and had been turned into apartments much later. Eventually, along with a few other such houses, it was torn down to make way for the Regency Hotel, which is there now. A two-flight walk-up, my digs consisted of one very large, beautiful room with floor-to-ceiling windows overlooking 61st Street, one bath, and a small but adequate kitchen—certainly enough for me, a noncook. The furniture was sufficient to my needs, including something I really didn't need because I had never continued the piano lessons I took for a while as a child. It was a mini–grand piano, with 66 keys instead of 88—interesting as well as handsome. I was glad it was there whenever any of my piano-playing friends dropped by. My rent was the going rate at the time— $75 per month with heat, gas, and electricity included.

Workwise, I had a pretty full plate approaching the mid–1940s. Although *Young Widder Brown* had seemingly become part of my life since its opening day in 1938, happily with no end in sight, some of the other programs and personalities which the Blue Network put on the air were added to my schedule. Cal Tinney, a humorist billed as "a present day Will Rogers," was one. For 15 minutes every morning I would put

him on and chat with him briefly; then he would fill up the time discussing whatever came to mind as long as it had a humorous twist to it. And even if the subject seemed dead serious when he started on it, the listener could always count on anything from a chuckle to a hearty laugh by the time he got through. As I recall, Tinney remained with us about two years.

The time slot from 1:30 to 2 every afternoon was given to another talented host, Galen Drake. Galen represented an organization called the Housewives' Protective League. Even though radio had advanced to the point where recorded commercials had increasingly come into vogue, it was a self-imposed rule by the Housewives' League that none were to be heard on any of its shows, whether it be Galen Drake addressing the New York audience of WJZ or its other spokesmen on other stations in other cities. The reasoning was that recorded commercial messages lacked the sound of sincerity, and therefore believability, which was to be gained by the very informal, low key, ad-lib approach of its hosts when talking about the sponsor's product. For instance, Galen didn't "deliver" a commercial. He would just quietly slip into it in his chatty fashion, give the salient points, and before you knew it he was on to another topic. My job on the show was to introduce him, chew the fat with him a bit about whatever, and if he made a funny be sure to show enjoyment of it by a giggle or, if it was a zinger, hearty laughter. Near the end of the half hour he would bring me back in and we would engage in a few more pleasantries as I signed him off. Galen Drake's real name was Foster Rucker. His wife Pauline was the sister of, in my opinion, one of the all-time great female pop singers, Jo Stafford. She and Frank Sinatra were part of the early singing group with Tommy Dorsey and his orchestra, when they made such memorable records as "I'll Never Smile Again." I liked Galen Drake. I liked what he did on the air and as a person. What he was as a person came through in his air performance, every day for five years.

The old saw about history repeating itself came true for me one day in late October 1995. At that time the two decades of the 40s and the 90s briefly came together in my life. I had been one of many special guests invited to the 20th Annual Convention of Friends of Old Time Radio at a Holiday Inn in Newark, New Jersey, and this year's get-together proved to be quite special for me. Talk about going down memory lane. I found myself announcing a re-creation of a program I had first put on the air a long, long time ago, *Ethel and Albert*. Yes, it pleases me to remember that I was involved in the debut of that wonderful show which ran for so many years. It was great to be reunited with Peg Lynch, whose fertile talent was responsible for such a new and different comic idea way back then. In truth, a very simple idea. But in writing those hundreds of *Ethel and Albert* scripts over a period of several years, she proved to be one of the outstanding comedy writers of her time. To say nothing of her gifted ability as an actress in portraying the role of Ethel.

With Peg Lynch, writer and star of Ethel and Albert, *at the Twentieth Annual Convention of Friends of Old Time Radio in Newark, New Jersey, in October of 1995. The actor who first played "Albert" was Richard Widmark, back in 1944. And I'm proud to have been there as the program's first announcer.*

The easiest way to describe an *Ethel and Albert* program is "funny, funny, funny." From their hysterical reaction, that's exactly how it affected those in Saturday's audience, too. Before starting the re-creation of the show, I thought the audience might get a kick out of knowing my history with it. So after greeting them, I said that this was indeed a nostalgic moment because "fifty-one and a half years ago, on Monday, April 17, 1944, as a staff announcer with the Blue Network, I went to Studio 8E to put a brand new program on the air. And you're going to have the pleasure of seeing it re-created now." I told them that that was the first time I had met Peg Lynch and that the actor who was playing Albert on that memorable day was Richard Widmark. Then I did the opening announcement: "The private life of Ethel and Albert, written by Peg Lynch, with Bob Dryden and Ron Lackman. It's the little things in life, familiar to all of us, that make up our everyday lives. Now let's see what's happening in Sandy Harbor at the home of Ethel and Albert..." Bob Dryden and Ron Lackman, both fine actors, have been on the New York scene a long time. Dryden's interpretation of the role of Albert was comically superb, while Ron Lackman, playing the part of Mike, a sewer worker trying to fix a gas line, had me in stitches. Besides *Ethel and Albert*, I took part in reenactments of five other old radio shows at that Friends of Old Time Radio convention. I had a real good time bathing in nostalgia.

Returning now to the 40s: one Monday morning in 1943 I was pleased to find that I was assigned to a new show starring Cliff Edwards that was to run five days a week at 8:15 A.M. Cliff's musical forte was the ukulele, for which he was also called Ukulele Ike. Arriving at the studio, I found him already in rehearsal with backup by Tony Mattola, one of the finest guitar accompanists in the business, and a male

quartet. We hit it off well right from the start when I told him how much I had liked his work in the movie *The Hollywood Revue of 1929* in which he introduced the song "Singin' in the Rain." There were lots of other movies I enjoyed seeing him in. Of course I was too young to have seen him onstage in his Broadway musical shows during the 1920s. But the motion picture which would prove to be a lasting monument to his talent as an actor, and especially as a singer, was Walt Disney's *Pinocchio*, in which the cartoon character Jiminy Cricket's voice was actually Cliff's. The beautiful Jiminy Cricket/Cliff Edwards rendition of "When You Wish Upon a Star" will long be remembered. Not long after Cliff's morning show was launched, the Harvel Watch Company evidently liked what they heard and sponsored Cliff Edwards, with me as announcer, on Sunday afternoons. The trade paper *Variety* had these kind words about the program sometime in 1943:

Cliff Edwards, a holdover from the flapper and coonskin coat era of the '20s, induces a heavy degree of nostalgia with his renditions of songs prevalent in that day. Revivals of such tunes as "June Night," "Paddlin' Madeline Home," "Fascinating Rhythm," make for pleasant listening for those who were around then.

Sunday afternoon program, highlighted by Edwards (Ukulele Ike), had him doing most of the work, everything to chiming in with the Harvel commercials with George Ansbro, the announcer, to introducing his own numbers and recalling moments with celebs with whom he hobnobbed in the '20s. To comparative oldtimers, it's surefire material and Edwards accomplishes his mission with a high degree of efficiency.

Cliff and I enjoyed each other's company. He also seemed to hit it off well with my friends and vice versa, so we spent a lot of time together around New York town. About which I will say more later.

29

WEDDING BELLS

Because of the scarcity of available young men during the war years, corporations all over America were pressed into hiring young women to fill their jobs. The two broadcasting companies in Rockefeller Center were no different. By 1944 the National Broadcasting Company and the Blue Network each had as many girls as boys on their page and guide staffs. They were called pagettes and guidettes. The girls hired in the mail room had no particular title. I guess if anyone were to ask one of them what she did she would probably reply "I'm in the mail room" or "I'm a mail girl." Not a particularly glamorous-sounding job. Not even an occupation you could attach "ette" onto giving it a lift, to make it seem a little more important than it was. I, for one, am happy to say I had arrived at the point in my life where titles, as such, didn't impress me. At any rate, one day in 1944 while I was lunching in the Kaufman-Bedrick Drugstore downstairs, someone introduced me to an attractive young lady who, it turned out, had fairly recently been added to the staff of the Blue Network mail room. Her name was Carol Dyer. We got along well not only that day at lunch but subsequently on a couple of dates. Shortly after I started to date Carol, I couldn't help but notice that the mail was being delivered to the announcers office by someone new. And if you had been there at the time, you would have been able to understand why I couldn't help but notice. To be truthful I had actually seen her first as she was waiting for an elevator on the third floor, the hangout for actors and actresses hoping to be discovered by a passing director, any

passing director. I remember thinking to myself I hope she can act because with her looks she should go far in the business, even though attractiveness was not necessarily a prerequisite for success in radio. The only thing she carried that day was a purse. But later, seeing her carrying a sack of mail into our office, I realized I was wrong when I had seen her on the third floor—she was not an aspiring actress but a new mail room girl, probably on her lunch hour. I also realized I had a desire to meet her. Fate took care of that. In a few days I was with Ray Diaz on our way to Hurley's for lunch when we ran right smack into Carol Dyer. We were getting off one elevator as she had just left another. Nor was she alone. She introduced us to her friend, Jo-Anne Chantal. And guess what? We all had lunch in Hurley's.

That afternoon, even though at lunch I had been quite aware she was considerably younger than I, I sought out Jo-Anne in the mail room to invite her for a drink after work. Her answer was yes but not for too long because she was expected home for dinner. So we met at the Down Under and had one drink. I walked her to the subway station beneath the building and watched her descend the stairs to the A train platform because she lived in Washington Heights. As I took the escalator back to the street level, I just knew my dates with Carol Dyer had ended because I was hoping something good and lasting would develop with Jo-Anne. I had experienced affairs of the heart before, however, as I had already broken two engagements.

So despite the admonishments from my friends and family about our age

Jo-Anne when we first met, age 17.

difference—she was 17 and I was 29—I continued to pursue her. It paid off because two years later we were married in St. Patrick's Cathedral and had our reception at the Waldorf-Astoria—both institutions still going strong, as is our marriage of 53 years. We have five wonderful children and six equally wonderful grandchildren.

There was one evening during our courtship when what I thought would be a nice gesture so embarrassed Jo-Anne that I almost lost her. We were in the Barberry Room of the Drake Hotel with Pauline and Galen Drake and Jo Stafford when we were joined by a New York character named Abe Bronson, who covered all the fancy clubs and restaurants while carrying an incredible inventory of jewelry. He was very good company as well as a walking jewelry store, and he had an impeccable reputation for his genuine gems and reasonable prices. He usually table-hopped among the rich and famous, which our three companions

were. I had never purchased from Abe but had been present when others did. Anyway, this night I was feeling expansive and in love so I quietly asked Abe to meet me in the men's room. He did and I purchased from him a gold snake chain necklace, price $100. I was so excited I just couldn't wait to give it to Jo-Anne at the table in front of the others. She was shocked and terribly embarrassed at what she felt was ostentation on my part. When I explained later that I was just excited and couldn't wait, she accepted the necklace with good grace. She is still wearing it today.

The afternoon before our wedding I was in the *Widder Brown* studio as usual. We had just finished dress rehearsal, so with about 20 minutes until broadcast I went down to get something from my locker in our lounge adjacent to the announcers' office. Somehow the back of my right hand scraped against a jagged piece of metal shelving which caused a nasty cut and a profuse flow of blood. This created a very difficult situation because I was due back upstairs shortly to put *Young Widder Brown* on the air. Thank God a card game was in progress in the lounge, and one of the players was Henry Dick. Henry, a Blue Network radio director, had lost a leg and suffered a few other wounds in World War II and had had lots of experience in doing what he was about to do for me—stanch the flow of blood from my hand. While he was doing this, one of the other card players called Studio 8B to alert Martha Atwell, the *Widder Brown* director, to try to find another announcer to substitute because I had been incapacitated and would have to get professional help ASAP. Martha, God love her, kept her cool and called the NBC announcers' lounge, where Ed Herlihy answered the phone, got Martha's urgent message, and miraculously arrived in 8B with no time to spare before the organ theme began on the air. Ed, true professional that he was, found himself sight-reading the show opening, the lengthy first commercial, and the lead-in to "today's episode." Meanwhile, Henry Dick and I went to the first aid room where the nurse inspected my hand, thought it needed stitches, and called Dr. So-and-So, who said I should come right over. The good doctor removed the tourniquet Henry had improvised, did the proper stitching, and wrapped my hand in a bandage, with instructions to try not to use it for a while. This was on a Friday afternoon so when I asked if I would be able to drive by Monday, he wanted to know what was so important about driving on Monday. I said: "because tomorrow I'm getting married. Sunday, as the Lord saith, I shall rest. And Monday I want to drive to Canada on our honeymoon, with both hands." His warm grin assured me that driving by Monday would be okay, and he concluded the visit with "Let me be the first to shake your left hand in congratulations."

The next day it wasn't easy at first, being right-handed, to remember to extend the wrong hand to well-wishers. But as the day wore on, it kind of became automatic. We were married during an 11 o'clock mass in the Lady Chapel of St. Patrick's Cathedral. My brother Jim, a member of the Passionist Order of Priests, married us. My other reverend brother, Jack, celebrated the mass. The age-old custom upon entering the Passionist Order was to assume a name other than the one bestowed at baptism, so when he was ordained he became Father Andrew. But to us family, he would always be Jim. Jack, however, was a parish priest in the Brooklyn diocese and, not being associated with any particular religious order, he was not required to take an alias.

Jo-Anne's matron of honor, Marge Phillips, was her closest friend. My best man was my dentist brother Ray, still a bachelor. Indeed the entire male contingent of the Ansbro siblings was fully accounted for at the altar on June 29, 1946.

Our wedding reception was held in the

Jansen Suite of the Waldorf-Astoria. It was a terrific, rousing, fun afternoon. So much so that none of the guests wanted it to end, so Jo-Anne's father engaged the musicians to play an extra hour. But after that, we really had to leave because the room was needed for another function that evening. However, a large group of diehards still wanted to party, so off to Hurley's they went. Many phone calls to us and our family, who were relaxing in our rooms at the Waldorf, finally persuaded us to join them in Hurley's. Shortly after we got there, Connie Hurley locked the doors in order to keep the public out. "Only good friends of the bride and groom allowed in. From here on there'll be no more paying customers. This is my private party," he yelled in his colorful Irish brogue above the din. Curious passersby glancing in would try the doors and couldn't figure out what was going on. A crowded saloon, with the doors locked? When someone had to leave, he would have to wait until Connie or one of his bartenders got a chance to hop over the bar to let him out. Connie made sure champagne flowed freely. Case after case of the bubbly kept appearing from out of thin air. Needless to say, the chef and his assistant were kept busy the whole time, as were Sol the waiter and his backup man. Cliff Edwards performed generously, as did many others. Earlier in the afternoon during the reception, Cliff had obliged with songs associated with his rise to fame, like "Paddlin' Madeline Home" and "Fascinating Rhythm." He had left a cherished memory singing "When You Wish Upon a Star." Now, at the Hurley's party, he again sang many of these songs. Everyone would join in when one of the revelers took off on wings of song, most frequently Irish songs, in deference to Connie the host, who hailed from County Galway in Ireland. It was one heluva night in Hurley's, a night that was discussed for years to come.

The following Monday after checking

Jo-Anne and I dancing at our wedding reception in the Jansen Suite of the Waldorf-Astoria, June 29, 1946. Seems like yesterday.

My friend Cliff Edwards singing "When You Wish Upon a Star" at our wedding reception. As the voice of the cartoon character "Jiminy Cricket," Cliff made the song famous in the movie Pinocchio.

out of the Waldorf we hit the road in my brother Ray's Chrysler convertible heading for Canada and the start of our three-week honeymoon. Actually the vacation I was embarking on was the first I had had in six years. As a staff announcer, I had a three-week paid vacation plus additional income from commercial programs like *Young Widder Brown*. When I started announcing *Widder Brown* in 1938, I was delighted to receive not only its fee from the Hummerts, but also fees for doing the twenty-second commercial cowcatchers and hitchhikes before and after *Stella Dallas*, another Hummert show. In 1939, when my NBC staff vacation came around, having heard that the Hummerts frowned on

vacations for announcers unless they had been doing their shows for a long time, I decided not to go away but to come in every day during my staff vacation for the Hummert stuff. In 1940, however, not knowing exactly how long was "a long time" in the Hummerts' mind, I got brave and took off from *Widder Brown* and the *Stella Dallas* commercials for one week to go on a Caribbean cruise during my staff vacation. Two substitute announcers filled in for me, one doing *Widder Brown* and another the *Stella Dallas* cowcatchers and hitchhikes. On the cruise ship, I pretty much forgot about my work and proceeded to do what you're supposed to do on a cruise—enjoy yourself. On the Monday after

The happy couple.

my trip, I went into the *Widder Brown* studio and was greeted by the cast and the director, and everything was hunky-dory. Not so in the *Stella Dallas* studio. Not until I walked in did I find out that my substitute during the previous week was to continue doing the cowcatchers and hitchhikes. It was shabby treatment, I thought, to say nothing of the embarrassment I felt in front of the cast members. My substitute, who now was to continue in my place, was every bit as embarrassed as I. He came over to me when he realized that I must be the guy he had been filling in for. He was as gracious as anybody could have been under the circumstances, especially since he didn't know me, nor I him when he said his name, Mark Goodson. He had just left the CBS announcing staff,

he told me, to freelance, and this was his first job since leaving CBS. Much as I wasn't happy to lose a nice piece of steady income because I had taken a quick cruise to Puerto Rico and Haiti, I at least felt a little better that it was being picked up by a fellow who had made a gutsy decision to leave the CBS staff and make a stab at the sometimes heartless freelance world. As I left the studio, I thought to myself, "Good luck to you Mark Goodson." Some years later he and a fellow named Bill Todman would become just about as big as you could get in the world of TV production with their company, Goodson-Todman.

As the time for my wedding was approaching, I found myself confiding to the *Widder Brown* director Martha Atwell, who had become my good friend, my worries about taking time off for a honeymoon because of what had happened six years earlier. She listened with both an understanding ear as well as an understanding woman's heart. She advised me to approach Mickey Scott, a vice president of Air Features, the so-called Hummert factory of soap operas. I met with him in his office and after a pleasant discussion he agreed that six years was indeed a long enough time to go without a vacation, and he said he felt quite sure Mrs. Hummert would agree with his decision that I could leave *Young Widder Brown* for three weeks, enjoy my honeymoon, and relax with the knowledge I would be welcomed back when it ended. Needless to say I left Mr. Scott's office much lighter than when I went in. He had lifted quite a weight off of me, which was reflected in the lighthearted manner I seemed to approach everything for some time after, most especially our wedding and honeymoon.

Peter Donald and I had been good friends since long before Fred Allen picked him to play the part of Ajax Cassidy, a glib-talking Irishman, on the *Fred Allen Show*. I first knew Peter in my boy soprano days on Milton Cross's *Children's Hour* along with the likes of Risë Stevens, Ann Blyth, Florence and Billy Halop, and other kids who later became adult stars. One of the programs that brought him to the attention of Fred Allen was *Can You Top This* where Peter gained great renown as a joke teller, either straight or in any dialect under the sun.

Sometime in the mid-40s, he starred in an audience participation show called *Talk Your Way Out of It* with me as his announcer doing the Aunt Jemima pancake flour commercials and helping him pick pairs of individuals from the audience. Peter would set them up by verbally putting the two contestants into a ridiculously silly situation and then tell them to "talk your way out of it." The prizes they received depended on how well the audience, by its

applause and laughter, liked their efforts. Fortunately, all the programs were recorded several hours in advance of broadcast time. I say "fortunately" because one day, for whatever reason, things just weren't going too well. Maybe it was that the people who were brought up from the audience laid an egg, or that the audience's reaction to the goings on was lukewarm. Whatever it was, it got under Peter's skin and caused him to completely lose his cool and drop all pretense of being funny as he bawled out his audience as if they were naughty children. It took a moment before they realized he was serious and some started to boo, while others yelled back at him. This of course incensed him even more, to the point where he really blew his top, and yelling like a nut, he ordered them out of the studio. Later, when he calmed down, he was quite mortified. But knowing the show must go on, he gathered himself together sufficiently to give a credible performance, live, on the air at the usual time. And with an audience which was made up of participants gathered from the studio tours who were only too eager to be part of a live broadcast. There was no publicity about his outburst that day. But, as might be expected, word got around. It saddens me to say it was the beginning of a long, tragic downward slide from wealth and fame to poverty and with lots of assistance from John Barleycorn, to an early death for my friend Peter Donald.

One of our guests at an at-home gathering shortly after we were married was Vladimir Brenner, a concert pianist on the musicians' staff at the Blue Network. When he arrived, Vladimir took an immediate interest in our mini–grand piano with its sixty-six keys. The only time he had ever seen one before, he said, was when he was a young man in his native Russia, and he asked if it would be all right if he refreshed his memory by sitting down at ours. And also would it be okay to refresh everybody with his homemade vodka which he always brought along to parties. Naturally my delighted answer was yes to both questions. So while I served the drinks, he made himself comfortable at the piano. Watching him play, however, I came to realize that in all likelihood there was such a scarcity of mini–grand pianos in existence because any good pianist couldn't be bothered with the restrictions they imposed. Even Vladimir's accomplished fingers seemed to be having a problem keeping within the narrower scope. On one particular reach with his left, hand his fingers came down hard onto keys that weren't there—beyond the lower end of the keyboard. After that he just didn't play anymore. Sensing his embarrassment, Jo-Anne came up with what I thought was a great idea. It seems our downstairs neighbors, the Robinsons, had gone off for the weekend and left their key with us so we could feed their cat. They had also left the phone number where they could be reached. Most important, for our purposes, Jo-Anne reminded me of the concert grand Steinway which graced their living room, and also the facilities of an additional powder room off their kitchen.

At first Louise Robinson was sure we had called because something had happened to their cat. Assuring her that was not the case, I explained what our predicament was and that one of our guests, a celebrated classical pianist, was embarrassed because he wasn't happy playing on our little mini with its sixty-six keys. And, just as I had hoped, she insisted we move our guests downstairs. "Above all tell your friend to play our piano to his heart's content. Remember, the more a piano is played the better it is for it." After I thanked her, everyone helped carry drinks and refreshments below. Once there Vladimir really came to life. As the evening wore on, he thrilled us with his piano magic. His homemade vodka made a big hit too, especially for the vodka drinkers. Later, while cleaning up, I decided that it was pretty nice to have such accommodating neighbors. And

that it was remarkable what 22 additional keys and an extra john in a borrowed apartment could do for a party.

Speaking of pianists brings to mind a couple of other interesting happenings. During that period there was a very famous pianist named Alec Templeton, who was in constant demand as a guest on radio shows. He played before packed houses on the concert stage. Without a doubt what added to his fame as a pianist was the fact that he was totally blind from birth. One day I was assigned to announce a program of classical music by an orchestra made up of house musicians. I don't remember which house conductor was on the podium, but I very much remember who the guest was—Alec Templeton. I had never had occasion to meet him, but I had seen him play. And I had heard that he was utterly charming, had a great personality. This I discovered to be true soon after I went into the studio. He and the orchestra had just finished rehearsing, so, as usual, before going on the air I was in conversation with the conductor, checking out the selections to be played. I became aware that standing nearby, waiting to speak to the conductor, was Mr. Templeton. I said something to the effect that I was through and "May I introduce myself?" But before I could go any further, he bowled me over by saying that while standing there he had recognized my voice. Explaining that he was a great fan of soap operas and that *Young Widder Brown* was one of his favorites, he very kindly said, "Sorry I stepped on your line but I knew you were George Ansbro before you got a chance to tell me. I'm happy to meet you and work with you." Wow! What a gentleman. He's happy to meet me and work with me? Immediately I knew my hat might never fit my head again.

For the couple of years after we were married that we continued to live on East 61st Street, we grew fond of a restaurant a block away on Madison Avenue called Cerutti's. Besides the good food and atmosphere of the place plus the celebrity watching which could always be expected—people like movie star Miriam Hopkins Sunday brunching with famed author John Gunther—we liked to relax and enjoy the pop music of another blind pianist, a black man whose name unfortunately I just can't remember. The first time I had occasion to speak to him was to request that he play some particular song, at the same time letting him know how very much my wife and I enjoyed his style. As I spoke he broke out into a broad smile and at the same time, shaking his head from left to right, he said, "I just can't believe it." Understandably, I asked "What can't you believe?" He said, "It's nice to have an old friend stop by to ask for a request." When I told him this was the first time I had ever spoken to him, he had a real good laugh and said: "Oh no, it's not. You speak to me every day on the radio, Mr. Ansbro. On *Young Widder Brown*. I've been hearing you on that and other programs for years. And I want you to know I'm happy to make your acquaintance." Our friendship continued a few more years until he no longer played there. I still can't help but marvel at how loaded with talent those blind musicians were. And their kind remarks stayed with me a very long time.

When Edward J. Noble decided to change the name of his radio network in the forties, no longer would its hue be blue, which was too reminiscent of NBC's former Red and Blue Networks. It was said he had in mind something which might connote patriotism. But he frowned at the sound of "the Red, White and Blue Network," which had been suggested by Bob Kintner, even though such a name would do the trick patriotically. Well, why not just quit with the colors and come right out with the word those colors stood for, American, the defining word for most of us then living in the 48 states. So that's how he settled on the name change. No more could I sign off with "Thy network is blue." Henceforth it would be "This is ABC, the American Broadcasting Company."

30

WORKING WITH ELEANOR AND ANNA ROOSEVELT

In the mid-forties the first stirrings of commercial television were then beginning to occur. Occasionally sample programs were put before the cameras. Studio 3H was no longer used as a radio studio but had been transformed to TV use, and the earliest programs out of there were strictly experimental, reaching less than a handful of viewers in or near New York City who owned sets. TV receivers have come a long, long way in the 50 some years since then. By the same token, the business of telecasting a program has also changed a lot. Several times I was sent to 3H to do experimental newscasts at six P.M. They were not on every night—this was long before anything was regularly scheduled. When I would get to the studio, I was greeted by a copy boy from the newsroom with reams of stuff that had come off the copy machine and had been laid out by an editor for me to read to the camera. The era I'm talking about predated filmed commercials on TV or even live commercials because there was practically no audience. The thing I remember most about those sample shows was the unbelievably intense heat coming from the klieg lights overhead, a situation which has long since been corrected. But I distinctly recall that when I had finished the newscast, my clothes could have been wrung out, the lights were that hot.

The lavish reception area of the third floor had always been a place where wanna-be actors spent a lot of time, with high hopes but rarely meeting with much success. The advent of television and the much publicized fact that 3H was an experimental TV studio brought a somewhat different breed of wanna-bes to that same third-floor lounge. So it was that one day as I was walking past the assortment of characters occupying the seats and lounge chairs, suddenly I was sure my eyes were deceiving me. Quietly seated in one of the larger easy chairs and seemingly minding his own business was a huge brown bear. He obviously was in the charge of a man seated next to him because that fellow was holding one end of a leash which extended around the neck of the remarkably relaxed yet massive mammal. As I stared, it occurred to me that this was undoubtedly the strangest, if not the wackiest sight I ever saw on the third floor, in spite of all the odd varieties known to have hung out there. Here was a ferocious looking but tame, you might say docile, brown bear actually sitting there as if he were waiting to keep an appointment for an interview, his hindquarters tightly encased within the confines of the chair. So by now I felt impelled to approach the chap holding the leash. And as I thought, he was the bear's keeper and also his trainer and owner. He, I felt sure, would have been happy to speak to anyone who might be helpful in finding future employment for his performing bear. Sensing this, I told him I was not an agent but an announcer. I said, however, that I was friendly with an executive, a vice president who, rumor had it, was slated to be switched from radio to TV and that if and when that happened he just might be interested. "As a matter of fact," I said, "would it be possible to go to his office now and surprise him?

Knowing him I'm sure he would get a big kick out of having a visitor like your friend drop in on him." As I expected, he thought that was a super idea. Then we got into introductions. Of my two new friends, the only one whose name I remember, will never forget, was the bear. His name, yes it was a he, was Burly, Burly the Bear!

What I had in mind was to pop in on Charles "Bud" Barry, a vice president in our program department and a guy with a great sense of humor. He was also known for his creativeness. It honestly had occurred to me that besides enjoying the fun of having such an unusual visitor to his office, he really might be able to do something for Burly and his boss in television. I gave a moment's thought to calling Bud first but dismissed the idea because it would spoil the element of surprise and the big laugh I felt sure the bear would get.

The next thing was to start the fairly long trek to Bud's office. Coaxing Burly out of his chair was something to watch. Mr. Keeper would give a command, and like magic, Burly instantly obeyed. Needless to say, by now there was quite an audience of third-floor regulars taking this in. l explained to the keeper that Mr. Barry's office was quite a walk through the corridor connecting the studio section, where we were, to the office section at the far end of the third floor. His reaction was, "No problem. Let's go." With that comment, he instructed his big, brown beauty to raise himself up from all fours to hind legs only. Then he asked me to hold on to Burly's left foreleg while he held the right one. But this in no way was meant to support Burly, which would have been impossible, only to guide him down the long hallway. Brown Beauty proved well able to support himself, thank you, as well as to walk on those two hind legs. So off we started, with several of the third-floor loungers bringing up the rear. As I look back in memory, it must have been quite a sight. Me and a man I had just met walking arm in arm with a real live bear I had also just met. And walking

as he was, on his hind legs, he towered over both of us. Was I scared? Did I have any second thoughts? In a word—no. The whole thing was so preposterous as well as so humorous that all I could think of was the look I would see on Bud Barry's face when we walked into his office. In a way I likened what we three must have looked like coming down that hall to the spectacle of another threesome, the Cowardly Lion accompanied by the Tin Man and the Scarecrow when they were on their way to see the "Wonderful Wizard of Oz."

Before we arrived at our destination, a couple of security men had persuaded our fun-loving followers to knock it off, leaving us unencumbered as we turned in from the corridor to the section where the program department brass had their offices. Programming v.p. #1 was Adrian Samish and v.p. #2 was my (and everybody's) friend Bud Barry. I guess their two secretaries were able to control the urge to scream when they saw that I was one of the guys escorting the freak visitor. My being part of this strange group calmed their nerves to the point that the two of them began to laugh. I told Mr. Barry's secretary I had brought Burly and his trainer in to meet with Bud if possible. She said he was out of town and added, "What a shame because I'm sure he would have enjoyed meeting your friend Burly very much." Of course I knew that, which was why I was there to begin with. But at that moment what went through my mind was how I could have been so stupid not to have called Bud's office in the first place. I felt like a child not knowing quite what to do when things didn't turn out the way he expected. I wanted to get out of there before Adrian Samish, a person I hardly knew, might open his door and catch the spectacle in his outer office. I had just told the bear's keeper "too bad we missed the boat" when Samish did come out. And this was the last thing in the world I needed. Samish was no Bud Barry. No sense of humor, I had heard. And he could be nasty, to boot. Well, to put it mildly, he was scared to death at the sight of Burly and wanted no part of explanations from me. Indeed he wasn't happy, saw nothing amusing in the situation and gave orders to "get that animal the hell out of here quick!" If ever there was a no-win situation, this was it. I didn't quibble, I just apologized quickly and left. With my newest best friends, Burly and his boss. We got on the freight elevator to the main floor on the 49th Street side of the building, where his keeper walked Burly across the street to the Rockefeller Center garage, put him into his cage on their truck which was parked inside, and with lots of onlookers, drove off and out of my life.

Sometime in 1948, Jo-Anne and I decided that, much as we liked our studio apartment, we would like more space. We found that even though the war had ended three years earlier there was still a scarcity of apartments. And so our search began, while at the same time we put the word out among friends. Before too long, we heard from one who knew a couple who had just bought a house in the suburbs and would be leaving their place soon. We looked at their apartment and liked it very much. The next step, they told us, was to put our name on the landlord's list and wait, hopefully not too long. They then gave us the name of the outfit that owned the building, Sailors Snug Harbor, which had been in existence a couple of hundred years. It was started with the intention of housing needy sailors in shelters the company maintained on or near the waterfront of New York Harbor. As time went on, the company expanded considerably, gradually accumulating properties further inland while moving uptown, so that by 1948 it had become one of New York's larger owners of valuable real estate.

The next day I ran into Bill Elliot, my friend from the Irving Trust Company. When he greeted me with "What's new?" I answered with what had been mostly on my mind since our visit to that nice apartment in Greenwich Village. When I finished telling him everything, especially the part about the necessity to get on a waiting list, he said that that was not unusual. And as for Sailors Snug Harbor, which I had never heard of myself, he was very familiar with the company. Next he surprised me by asking, "Do you know anybody at City Hall?" Just as I was about to shake my head no, I suddenly remembered something. "Yes, in a way I do. The mayor, Bill O'Dwyer. When he was with the Brooklyn district attorney's office he lived across the street from my family in Bay Ridge. We were friendly with him and his wife. He and my father were active members of the Mayomen's Association. They were both from County Mayo, Ireland, and Pop saw him a few times after he was elected."

When I asked him what my knowing somebody at City Hall might have to do with getting an apartment in Greenwich Village, his answer was very interesting. He told me that when Sailors Snug Harbor began those many years ago something very unusual was written into its charter, a clause stipulating that whoever was elected mayor of the city of New York automatically became honorary president of Sailors Snug Harbor during his tenure at City Hall. His advice was to get my Pop to contact Mayor O'Dwyer and first of all let him know about this honorary position he held because, more than likely with all the other far more important things on the mayor's plate, he wasn't even aware of it. Then have my father give the mayor the necessary information about the particular Sailors Snug Harbor building I was interested in, its address, and other relevant details. And, very important, ask him if he thought that in his position as honorary president of the company he might be able to do us a huge favor and help us get the unit in the building that we wanted.

My father did write to the mayor and promptly received a courteous reply in which he thanked Pop for informing him of his honorary position which "makes it possible to do a favor for you, my old friend. As soon as that unit becomes vacant your son George and his wife will be free to move in." That is exactly what happened. A postscript to this story is that the apartment has been in our family ever since. My son John and his family are living there now.

About the same time that we moved into our larger quarters in the Village, I was given the prestigious assignment of working with Eleanor Roosevelt and her daughter Anna. This was three years after President Roosevelt had died. They were on the air Monday through Friday at 11 o'clock each morning and did the broadcast from 8E, the living-room–like studio used by Lowell Thomas and other speakers. I must say that engaging in small talk with them before air time was a very pleasant experience. Every day for 15 minutes the program consisted of mother and daughter discussing topical subjects of their own choosing. No script. Just notes and clippings from the daily papers that they might occasionally refer to in a very informal manner. My role was to introduce Mrs. Roosevelt. Then, after acknowledging my intro with "Thank you, George Ansbro," she'd bring Anna on and they would go into whatever was on their minds for that day.

During one of our brief prebroadcast small-talk sessions, I told Mrs. R. that when I had reached the voting age of 21 in the year 1936 my first vote was for her husband when he was running for a second term. I was pleased with how graciously she received that less than earth-shattering bit of information. When 1940 rolled around, however, and Al Smith came out against his old friend FDR in his bid for a third term and the headlines read "Al Smith takes a walk," I voted against her husband, as I did in 1944 when President Roosevelt ran for a fourth term. Needless to say I skipped telling her that. When my mother heard about this, I got a kick out of her reaction—"What Mrs. Roosevelt doesn't know will never hurt her!"

Near the end of 1949 Mrs. Roosevelt decided, for whatever reasons, to discontinue her daily radio stint with her daughter. After doing the program for more than 18 months, I guess she wanted to move on to other things. So on a Saturday during the pre–Christmas season, she had invited the top brass, along with other executives of ABC, to her apartment for cocktails. It was probably her way of saying thank you, Merry Christmas, and good-bye. There was only one guest there who wasn't an executive—me. And when I arrived and found myself in the company of Edward J. Noble, Bob Kintner, Mark Woods, and the other execs, none of whom I was close to, I was sorry Bud Barry wasn't there. Bud's good-humored presence would have made me more relaxed in such exalted company. As a matter of fact, after a year and a half of announcing Eleanor and Anna R.'s program every day, I found it much easier socializing with them, the most exalted. Small talk flowed much more freely than, for instance, with Noble or Kintner—he of the spaghetti and Chianti on his secretary's head incident. The only thing I had in common with Noble was ABC. Sure I did. I worked there, and he owned it.

Eleanor Roosevelt's apartment was in a large building on the west side of Washington Square just below the southern end of Fifth Avenue in Greenwich Village, a few blocks from where Jo-Anne and I had moved. It was a sizable floor-through unit, the front of which faced Washington Square while the rear looked out at Sixth Avenue and directly down onto a large parking lot. The parking lot had become the object of much press and newsreel attention at the time because it had been transformed into a place to buy Christmas trees. But at this particular lot, unlike all other Christmas tree sites, the trees were being offered for sale by none other than Elliott Roosevelt, one of Eleanor's sons, and his beautiful wife Faye Emerson, the actress. Understandably, because of the tremendous publicity about who the sellers were, the

On the air around midnight in the Blue Network newsroom on April 12, 1945, the day of President Roosevelt's death.

place was always mobbed with buyers. Sometime during the party Mrs. Roosevelt took a few of us to see highlights of her apartment. While showing us the dining room, she seemed to get great enjoyment out of having us look down from the bay window while she proudly pointed out the lot below and told us that that was where "My Elliott and his Fayzee are doing a land-office business selling Christmas trees." An hour later Elliott and Fayzee came upstairs and added new life to the party, as well as a bit of glamour.

Somewhere along the line, when the maid had not served drinks for quite a while, I took it upon myself to check out the kitchen to see what was happening and quench my thirst. Upon opening the door, I was greeted with, "Mr. Ansbro, what are you doing here, at Mrs. Roosevelt's?" My immediate response was, "And by the same token, Sam, what are you doing here?" It was Sam, the head bartender at the English Grill, and my good friend. I told him of my association with Mrs. Roosevelt on her radio program, while he explained that on days off he occasionally hired himself out for private parties and that Mrs. R. used him from time to time. He said he sure enjoyed getting a call to do a party for her because of the important people who were her guests. "Yes" I said, "but I'll bet this is the first time one of them ever busted into her kitchen to cadge a drink."

Also in the 40s, around the same time I worked with Eleanor and Anna, I was assigned to announce a program starring Gypsy Rose Lee, a half-hour show one night a week. Gypsy had started out as a chorus girl. In the mid-1920s, she had switched to stripping, gaining more success as the years went on until eventually she had become the reigning queen of burlesque. By the 40s Gypsy Rose Lee had indeed become the most celebrated stripper of them all. She continued as the exemplar of the bump and grind trade for quite a while until, I suppose, she eventually got tuckered out. And bored. After all that bumping and grinding, wouldn't anybody? So, even though she offered a visual commodity, ABC decided to take advantage of her fame and put her on radio, and in an audience participation show. I must confess I don't remember what the gimmick of the show was except that I helped her pick people from the audience, some of whom would win prizes. That's more than I can say for the program. It won no prizes. Even way back then ratings were all. Poor ratings meant bye-bye program the same as today. In less than a year, the word went out that Gypsy would no longer be on the ABC schedule. Those of us involved pretty much expected it from the increasingly unenthusiastic reactions of her studio audiences.

Let's face it, there was a big difference between watching her tossing her tassels while removing yet another portion of her very scanty costume as a mostly male burlesque audience egged her on by hollering "take it off" and seeing the same lady innocuously attempting to interest a predominantly female studio audience in playing whatever the program's game was, thus leaving the radio audience at home yawning "so what" and turning the dial in the hopes of finding something better in spite of her fame.

Gypsy spread the word that she would like all of us involved in working the show—producer, director, engineer, about six house musicians and me, the

announcer—to gather at her house (a brownstone in the East 60s) for a farewell party after the final show. But when the last show was over, she was gone from the studio in an instant. The producer got to the rest of us quickly to say that Gypsy had asked him to steer us downstairs to Hurley's instead of to her house because the painters had made a mess of the place so she would meet us there instead. We were all disappointed that we would not get to see what her house was like, but we took her at her word and repaired to Hurley's. Upon arriving there, our disappointment became mixed with anger when Connie Hurley told us that Gypsy had slipped in the side door just a few minutes before and left money with him to buy us all a drink. He went on to say she had asked him to tell us how sorry she was she couldn't stay because something had come up and she had to leave. When one of the guys asked him how much money she had left, it turned out there was just about enough to cover one drink each, with a little left over for a tip.

This was some years before Ethel Merman starred in *Gypsy*, the hit Broadway musical which celebrated the life of Gypsy Rose Lee. Yes, Gypsy was a very famous lady. So was Eleanor Roosevelt. I worked on the air with both of them, but I'll give you one guess as to which one I have fonder memories of.

Before the 1940s decade ended, I found myself working with John Daly five nights a week at 10:30. He had been with CBS news for several years and had become quite respected as a newscaster. His mellifluous voice could be instantly recognized after you had heard him only once. Without a doubt John Charles Daly was a class act. On December 7, 1941, John was the first to announce to the world that the Japanese had bombed Pearl Harbor. His program, on the ABC Radio Network, was sponsored by Sterling Drugs, the same company that sponsored *Young Widder Brown*. *John Daly and the News* was produced by ABC News and was the only

Sterling Drugs radio program Frank and Anne Hummert's company had nothing to do with. If for no other reason than John Daly's reputation as a newsman and a gentleman, I was very pleased to work with him. During this period he had begun a TV show on CBS, *What's My Line?* which during its long run catapulted him to the heights of TV stardom. While that was still on the air, he took to the ABC-TV airwaves doing 15 minutes of news at 7 P.M.. Monday through Friday for Pontiac, and I was again privileged to be his announcer, this time before the TV camera. Besides introducing and signing him off, I pitched the product, Pontiac. After the first couple of months on the air, the Pontiac people offered me the opportunity to purchase a new 1949 Pontiac at cost, an offer I was quick to take advantage of. I interpreted their generous offer to mean they were satisfied with my nightly TV Pontiac spiel. I was also very pleased because the deal at long last made me a car owner. No longer need I borrow my brother's or, when his was unavailable, depend on Avis or Hertz.

During those days a singer named Lucy Monroe had become quite popular. The public really got to know her after Pearl Harbor. She, however, had been on the scene a long time prior to that. I had first known her in my page boy days at 711 Fifth Avenue when she was part of a vocal group called the "Sixteen Singers." She toiled through the thirties in one singing group or another, occasionally soloing. Not long after we were in the war, as fate would have it, a gentleman friend who was very well connected around New York town was instrumental in getting her a booking as

soloist at a huge patriotic rally in Madison Square Garden. Her friend was Jimmy Sauter, president of the Hummert radio factory, Air Features. Her appearance was quite successful, so much so that Mr. Sauter had no problem in booking her into other similar gatherings. At these affairs she had only to sing one song which always, as they say, brought down the house. Especially so because this was wartime, and her audiences were further imbued with patriotic fervor every time she rendered her song of songs, "The Star-Spangled Banner." And Lucy never sang anything else but "The Star-Spangled Banner," at least in public. She became the official soloist for the American Legion and the Veterans of Foreign Wars, singing, what else, the National Anthem. She sang it at New York Yankee baseball games and at every Yankee World Series between 1945 and 1960. She sang before Presidents Franklin Roosevelt, Harry Truman, Lyndon Johnson, and John Kennedy. She intoned the anthem at hundreds of patriotic and civic events. While all this was going on, she and Jimmy Sauter had become what Walter Winchell referred to in his column as an "item." It seemed that when she wasn't singing you-know-what somewhere, she could be spotted in all the best clubs and restaurants with, who else, Jimmy Sauter. So much so that a story went around about the dowager who kept seeing Lucy and her friend in those elegant establishments. One night when visiting the Stork Club, the old girl saw Lucy again. So she asked her escort, "Who is that man who's always with Lucy Monroe?" "My dear," he replied, "that's Francis Scott Key."

31

AMERICA'S BOYFRIEND AND AMERICA'S SWEETHEART

One evening in the late forties, I could hardly wait to get home to the apartment to tell Jo-Anne I had been selected to do a new half-hour show every day, Monday through Friday at 3 o'clock. I was especially keyed up because of who the star was, Buddy Rogers. When I blurted this out to her, the look on her face told me she had absolutely no idea who I was talking about. "Who's he?" she asked. It was at that moment I realized our age difference had everything to do with her not knowing who he was and my exuberance. "Now that I think about it," I said, "I can understand why you wouldn't know who he is."

I explained that he was the star of the first movie ever to receive an Academy Award, *Wings*, one of the last silent pictures. "I was twelve and a celebrity nut and you were just born. It was 1927. No way you could know who he was!" I then told Jo-Anne about the time *Wings* was showing at the Brooklyn Paramount, which was the showcase theatre of Brooklyn, and Charles Buddy Rogers was appearing in person. For the price of a quarter or thirty cents, I was lucky enough to get in before they closed the box office because of overcrowding on that beautiful Saturday afternoon in Brooklyn so very long ago. In the picture Buddy played an American flying ace during World War I. When it was over, the audience went wild. The next thing I knew, there smiling at us was the real live, flesh and blood Buddy Rogers. I don't think I had ever heard so much noise in my young life. For me it was a strange sensation. One minute Buddy was in an airplane shooting down other airplanes—German enemy airplanes—and the next minute he was standing there waving at us from the stage.

On the way out of the theater, word spread that he was going to appear on the fire escape outside his dressing room in a few minutes. By the time I got through the lobby and out onto the street, there was a near riot what with those hundreds of people rushing around the outside to the rear of the Paramount to be sure to get in a good position to see Buddy Rogers the second time that day, even if he was on such an unglamorous perch as a fire escape. He was in a dressing gown and seemed delighted with the warm reception from us Brooklynites. As he leaned over the railing, his attempts to be heard were lost in the noise made by the crowd below, so after about ten minutes he gave one final wave, blew a lot of kisses, and disappeared into his dressing room.

After listening to all this, Jo-Anne could understand my enthusiasm about the pleasant news I had brought home. When I asked her if the name Mary Pickford meant anything to her, she said "Wasn't she an old-time movie actress or something?" I told her her youth was showing again. I said Mary Pickford was not just "an old-time movie actress or something." She was the very first movie star and without a doubt the most important female star since the invention of motion pictures, who also happened to be Mrs. Buddy Rogers and had been since 1937. Before that, she had been the wife of Douglas Fairbanks, a tremendous star of early films, whose son, Doug

Jr., had followed in his father's footsteps to become a picture star in his own right. I went on to say that since his marriage to Mary Pickford, Buddy had lived with her in Pickfair, a magnificent estate in Beverly Hills. During the 19 years she had been married to Fairbanks, they of course had shared Pickfair. The name Pickfair was a combination of the first syllable of each of their names. I told Jo-Anne that when she divorced Fairbanks the name of her beautiful home remained the same because besides the worldwide fame of its occupants the name of the mansion itself was just as well known and she decided it should stay that way.

Mary had been crowned "America's Sweetheart" by her adoring fans. To them she could do no wrong. But when Fairbanks caused her so much emotional distress because of his open carryings on with a lady of the British aristocracy, Mary's legions of fans understood and supported her decision to end her travail by divorcing him. Sadly, after that event, his life went straight downhill. In 1939, two years after Mary married Buddy Rogers, Douglas Fairbanks passed away. He was only 56.

Buddy's program was called *Pick a Date with Buddy Rogers*. Since I had brought the news about my doing the show home to Jo-Anne, I had really been looking forward to beginning it. When I walked into Studio 6A for rehearsal on a Monday afternoon in mid-1949 and Charlie Powers, the ABC director, introduced me to Buddy, I liked the way Charlie handled it. "This is the first time I've ever had the pleasure of introducing the star of a new show to his second banana. Buddy Rogers say hello to George Ansbro." Buddy liked it too, which he showed by laughing heartily as we shook hands. It was a warm beginning, leaving me with a feeling of pleasant things to come in our relationship. At the top of my list of things to do at that moment was to pay attention to Charlie Powers as he explained to both Buddy and me what the gimmick of picking a date with Buddy R.

was all about. I honestly don't remember now what the gimmick was except to say that in the course of a half hour several ladies out of the studio audience competed onstage, with Buddy guiding them, for the prize of the day—a date with the man himself, B.R. How they competed is what I don't recall but, whatever it was, the lady who received the loudest volume of applause from the studio audience was declared the winner, which was standard procedure in those days for all game shows.

As it turned out, there was an unusual demand for tickets to get into the show, which showed that Buddy Rogers still had a lot of drawing power. Being in that studio with him day after day, I could easily understand his attraction, especially to the ladies. He was strikingly handsome to begin with, and his warm and outgoing personality captured their attention as he seemingly kept them mesmerized from the moment I would introduce him and bring him onstage. I guess the easiest way to explain it is to say they felt he was their friend. Each day's winner enjoyed her date with Buddy right after the show. Most often he took his winning date downstairs to the English Grill, where in addition to the thrill of being with Buddy she could sip cocktails or tea while checking out the skaters on the famous ice rink under the watchful eye of Prometheus, the mammoth statue signifying Rockefeller Center. During the first few weeks of the show, Buddy would ask me to join him if his date happened to have her child along or if she was accompanied by a friend. But that idea didn't work out because we would no sooner be seated in the English Grill than I would have to leave to be on time for my 4 o'clock *Young Widder Brown* rehearsal.

Buddy and Mary closed Pickfair and rented an apartment on Park Avenue, where they lived during the run of the show. Once in a while Mary would come along with Buddy to the studio and quietly sit in the rear to watch. Understandably, I was delighted the first time I met her, and I couldn't

Every afternoon in 1949 and 1950 I played second banana on Pick a Date with Buddy Rogers. *Above, Lorry Stone, on the left, who was a program assistant, watches while Buddy and I josh with a contestant. Buddy's wife was the famous star of silent pictures, Mary Pickford.*

have been more pleased when she confided that Buddy had told her how well he thought we worked together. She preferred not to appear on the show itself because she thought it was Buddy's showcase and she didn't want to seem to be butting in. Once, however, when the show was over, Buddy pointed her out to the audience, so I went to her seat in the rear of the studio and escorted her to the stage as they went wild at the very sight of her. She very graciously thanked them for their kind reception and let them know how happy she was to be there and how proud she was of her Buddy.

It so happened that on that same day Jo-Anne stopped by, which she had done once or twice before, so she had already met Buddy. Now, on this day, she met Mary too. That's when a friendship developed between the Rogers and the Ansbros. Mary graciously invited us to tea at their gorgeous apartment many times. Once we found ourselves sipping tea with another guest, Mary's oldest and closest friend from early in her movie career, Lillian Gish. Just we four—Mary Pickford, Lillian Gish, Jo-Anne and George Ansbro. No Buddy Rogers, because he was off for a weekend of golf, which he loved.

While walking by Hurley's one day after *Pick a Date with Buddy Rogers* had been on the air several months, I heard a knock on the window and instinctively turned to see if it was for me. In a jiffy the knocker was by the side door, with a wide grin ear-to-ear and his hand extended, which I grasped as I greeted him with, "Bert Capstaff, you old devil. What brings you to New York?" Bert had been an NBC studio engineer, an audio man, in the 30s. and I hadn't seen him since he had transferred to NBC in Hollywood about ten years earlier. He answered that he was in New York with Bob Hope while Hope was playing the Paramount. He then explained that when he first went to Hollywood, NBC assigned him to Bob Hope as his audio man, and they got along so well that Bob prevailed upon him to quit NBC engineering and become his general assistant, sort of a right arm. I then went back inside Hurley's with him to the bar, where an idea hit me which I thought might interest him. And it did. I told Bert I was doing a daily show with Buddy Rogers and that Buddy frequently had guest stars, most often picture people from Hollywood. I said, "A couple of days ago he had Rock Hudson. What I have in mind now is a swap. If I get Buddy Rogers to guest star at the Paramount for one performance, you could reciprocate with Bob Hope on Buddy's radio show one day. And the fact that they are good personal friends, especially golfing friends, should make it a snap. Just a clean, easy, simple deal, and no exchange of money involved."

During the next week, the swap came to pass. So from a knock on Hurley's window and a few minutes at the bar, two old friends got two other old friends together, professionally, on each other's turf. I went to the Paramount with Buddy one evening and backstage we met with Bert Capstaff, who was waiting for us with Bob Hope. There followed animated greetings between Rogers and Hope—"long time no see" stuff. When the picture ended and the curtain went up, Hope strolled onstage. After his opening monologue, he brought Buddy on to enthusiastic applause from the crowded theatre. Buddy was a fine musician, having had his own band for some

years before he started doing the *Pick a Date* show. Now at the Paramount he demonstrated his musical talents by jamming it up with the theater orchestra, beginning at the piano. Then as the medley progressed, he displayed his versatility by playing six other instruments borrowed from the musicians and knocking himself out with each. Before getting off the show, he calmed things down a bit by singing a romantic popular ballad of the day. He ended with some good-natured ad-lib banter with Hope, who seemed mighty pleased with Buddy's appearance. The next day it was reciprocity time. Capstaff brought Bob Hope over to Studio 6A, where they arrived with not too much time to spare before air time. That turned out to be a blessing in disguise. Hope had no idea what the rules of the *Pick a Date* game were and not enough time to find out, so when Buddy introduced him on the air he proceeded to turn the place into a hysterically merry madhouse. Lots of jokes, funny observations, picking people from the audience to kid around with, and proving once again for I guess the zillionth time why he was the world's most beloved comedian. Because Bob Hope was there, the *Pick a Date* rules were suspended for the day, and accordingly (and, I'm sure, happily), Buddy had a breather from having to sit and exude charm for an hour with yet another totally strange lady.

Shortly after Buddy's swap deal with Bob Hope, he did a week's engagement as the star of the show at the Latin Quarter, a big Broadway night spot which featured both Latin music and big-band, American-style music. It was a perfect setting for Buddy's musical virtuosity. One afternoon during that week he asked me to do him a favor. He said that since Mary had been back in New York she had been hoping to revisit Mama Leone's, a restaurant famed for its wonderful Italian food, and would I be good enough to escort her there? That evening when I picked her up at the apartment, I found that I was also escorting her personal assistant who had been with her for the previous 25 years. This was Tess Michaels, whose association with Mary began at the height of Mary's glory days with Douglas Fairbanks.

It was a really fun evening because Tess was a delightful person. In no time at all, I felt as though I had known not just Mary but Tess Michaels, too, for years. Early on, something I said caused Mary to make the observation that I was Irish. "Now what in the world ever made you think that?" said I, in the Irish brogue I always kept handy for any appropriate occasion that might arise. Instantly, now in her own Irish brogue, she rattled off several things about me that would indicate to "anybody but a blind man" that I was Irish. Then, good-naturedly, she said, "And that brogue, why it's almost as good as mine." And of course Tess got her licks in about her being Irish, too. So as dinner progressed, we three Irish-Americans washed it down with very good Chianti wine in a fine restaurant run by a non–Irish lady named Mama Leone.

After close to two years, *Pick a Date with Buddy Rogers* was going to leave the airwaves. So Jo-Anne and I planned a party and started inviting the folks who had been involved with its production as well as some other friends and family. I rented a piano for that night and hired a professional pianist, Charley Bourne, to keep things hopping. When I asked Buddy to come and of course to bring Mary with him, he said he wished we had checked things out with each other first because they were planning to have a party too, but unfortunately on the same night as ours and he hadn't gotten around to mentioning it to me yet. "But I'll tell you what," he said. "Ours is going to be a late party, so I'll drop in at your apartment first, but I'm quite sure Mary won't be able to come. Though I know you'll catch up with her at our place when your gang has left." His response didn't surprise me. After all, being the gentleman that he was, no way would he not come to a farewell gathering of the guys and gals who'd been working in his behalf all this time. I was sorry Mary wouldn't be able to come, but I understood why she couldn't, what with hosting her own party that same night.

On the evening of the final *Pick a Date* program, our guests began arriving around 6 o'clock. By 7:00, pretty much everyone was there except one guest, Buddy Rogers. By 7:30, Jo-Anne and I decided something had happened to make him a no-show. But a few minutes later our buzzer rang, and when I opened the door, what a pleasant surprise, Buddy and Mary. I remember asking Mary as I led them into the living room where the party was in full swing, "Do I introduce you as Mrs. Rogers or Mary Pickford?" She answered, "Mrs. Rogers, but I won't get angry if later they just call me Mary."

After they had been mingling with the others for a while and dancing to Charley Bourne's piano music, she asked me if I thought he could play an Irish jig. I told her Charley could play just about anything, but I suggested: "Why don't you ask him yourself? I'm sure if you did he would be thrilled." No sooner said than done, and in a jiffy our apartment was resounding with the strains of a lively jig. Mary had spotted one of our guests whose face gave away his ancestry. The map of Ireland was written all over it; he was an older gentleman, more in her age bracket, by the name of Jack McCormick. She approached him and in true ladylike fashion, affecting a touch of her fine brogue, asked if he would care to attempt a jig with her. Now Jack had been in the john when she and Buddy arrived, so he had absolutely no reason to feel anything unusual about this attractive stranger except, perhaps, to be flattered by her. And jigging, or for that matter any other kind of dancing, was not his forte. But good sport that he was, he joined forces with the lovely lady and in no time at all their performance was so outstanding that everyone else circled around happily clapping in time to the music while shouting unanimous approval. Without a doubt, it was the highlight of the evening. When it was over, I asked Jack if he knew the name of the lady with whom he had stopped the show. He said he didn't know, she just came up to him and suggested they dance and that was it. No, he didn't think she had said her name. "Why? Should I know her?" he asked. "Well," I said, "You know her but you've never met her before. Look at her and see if you don't think she looks familiar." From where we both stood across the room, he began to really scrutinize her as best he could and he slowly began to agree that, yes, she did seem familiar. I said, "She's, would you believe, Mary Pickford?" "By God, you're right! Sure it is! I can't believe it! Imagine me doing an Irish jig with Mary Pickford."

Mary took me aside and told me to bring as many of our guests as would care to come along with us up to their party when ours was over. I took it that this was her way of letting Jo-Anne and me know what a really good time they had had. Having been there for tea on occasion, I knew she meant it when she said to bring as many as might want to come. Their apartment was a duplex penthouse capable of comfortably handling who knows how many. When the festivities ended at our place, only a handful of our guests came with us; the others were just too tired to do anything but go home to bed. Those we brought, added to the bunch the Rogers already had, and the music of an eight-piece orchestra made for a never-to-be-forgotten evening. It was broad daylight when the party broke up.

During the 1950s we stayed in touch with Mary and Buddy and got together whenever they came to New York. They made it clear we had an open invitation to visit them whenever we could. But what with one thing and another, we just never seemed to have time to travel west of the Hudson River. In 1960, however, I called Buddy to tell him we were planning a first-time trip to Las Vegas and I suggested he and Mary join us there. He seemed quite

receptive to the idea and said he would call me back after discussing it with Mary, which he did, saying Mary agreed and they would be delighted to meet with us in Vegas, but on one condition. We must promise to return with them to Pickfair for our long-delayed visit. Now, who in the world could say no to that? Understandably we agreed.

We had a great time in Vegas seeing all the shows but most especially because of the VIP treatment that having reservations in the name of Mary Pickford and Buddy Rogers gave us. I was astounded that their names still had such importance. We also met and chatted with many Hollywood celebrities because Buddy was playing in the Pro-Am Golf Tournament being held while we were there.

During the flight from Las Vegas to Los Angeles, Jo-Anne sat with Buddy while Mary and I sat together. Something had put Mary in a reminiscent mood. More than likely it was seeing all those people in the casinos, as she said, "throwing all their hard-earned money away." She just found it difficult to understand. She then went on to tell me that when she was still very little her father had passed away, forcing her mother to seek stage careers for her and her younger sister and brother, Lottie and Jack. Her mother decided to pick up and leave Toronto, where they were born, and head for New York and the bright lights of Broadway to seek stage work for her brood. The family's name was Smith and she, the oldest, was Gladys Marie Smith. It was David Belasco, the great Broadway producer, who recognized what he sensed was unusual talent in Gladys Marie, and he successfully persuaded Mrs. Smith to change her little girl's name to Mary Pickford, which he considered more suited to a theatrical career. He then cast her in a featured role in *The Warrens of Virginia*. The play ran for two years, after which Mary was at liberty again. As a result, she told me, her family once more felt the familiar financial pinch. One day her mother said: "How about trying one of those picture companies? There's one called the Biograph Co. down on 14th Street." But when Mary appeared shocked at such a suggestion, fearful of what Mr. Belasco would say, her mother reminded her, "Mr. Belasco isn't paying the bills for the butcher and the grocer." So down to 14th Street they went, where the Biograph people saw her, liked what they saw, and hired her at $5 a day. Mary recalled that at the time she felt it was the greatest possible comedown in her very young life because the "galloping tintypes," as the early movies were known, were "disgusting." But those galloping tintypes, as disgusting as they seemed to her, proved to be the foundation of her sensational career.

After our flight from Las Vegas, we were met at the airport in Los Angeles by Fenton, the man in charge of just about everything at Pickfair. Fenton had been with Mary so many years I doubt he was sure exactly when he had started. He was responsible for the help, who at one time numbered 14 but, because the days of the big parties were over, had dwindled down to six.

Pickfair was situated atop Summit Drive on several acres overlooking the city of Beverly Hills. Fenton drove us in Buddy's Rolls Royce, a birthday gift from Mary, up the long, brick-paved driveway to the red-lacquered front door of the mansion. But instead of bringing us inside right away, our host and hostess thought we ought to first visit our quarters in the guest house, just a stone's throw away. Fenton carried our luggage, while Mary and Buddy showed us around the attractive one-story dwelling which was fronted by formal gardens, including some exquisite bronze statuary. It consisted of a very large, beautifully decorated sitting room between two bedrooms, each almost as large as the sitting room itself. "Make yourselves at home," said Mary. "When you're ready for breakfast, just dial 36 on the house phone for Tony, and he will be happy to serve

you. Or, for that matter if there's anything else you might want, Tony is the man to bring it to you. I want you to know he has been assigned to look after your every need as long as you're here. I think you'll like him." Later when we met him, we knew Mary was right. We did like him very much. Imagine, I thought, we have hardly been here ten minutes and we've been given our own private butler.

There was one more thing for us to see before going inside—the swimming pool. Buddy said it had been the first private pool in Beverly Hills. The first of hundreds of all different sizes and shapes which were to follow. Now, back up to the house itself. Twenty-two rooms beautifully decorated and filled with the finest and rarest of antiques. Pickfair had been for many years the center of Hollywood's social activity. I understand that in those days its parties were considered command performances. Charlie Chaplin, Rudolph Valentino, Clark Gable, and Joan Crawford were among dozens of famous stars who attended. Princes and politicians vied for invitations, and gossip columnists flashed the news from Pickfair as if sending bulletins from the White House.

For two people who were never able during the 1950s to travel west of the Hudson River, our initial trip to Pickfair in 1960, ten years after *Pick a Date with Buddy Rogers* went off the air, became the impetus for the continuation of many more such delightful visits. On one of those subsequent vacations, I happened to mention we had never been to San Francisco and were thinking of flying there for a look-see before returning east. Mary insisted we not fly but drive up to San Francisco along the coast highway in one of their cars. "It's one of the most scenic drives in the world," she said, "and well worth seeing." She went into great lengths about the beauty and unusual features of the Hearst Castle, which had been built and occupied by the fabled publisher William Randolph Hearst and was located about halfway to San Francisco at San Simeon on the Pacific Ocean. Of course we had both read about it, but it was something else to hear about the remarkable place from someone such as Mary who in days gone by had been there innumerable times as a guest of Mr. Hearst and to listen to her as she described it in her own amusing way. But then she put the icing on the cake. She picked up the phone and called one of Mr. Hearst's sons, George, who she knew was still in residence in a guest house on the vast property. After the usual amenities, she explained that we, her houseguests, would stop off on our way to San Francisco and how much she would appreciate it if he would see to it that we would have no problems when we got there, "what with those constant long lines of sightseers." She gave him our names and approximate time of arrival and thanked him. Before long we were on our way.

Some hours later we pulled up to the booth where the paying sightseers first stop before ascending the five-mile driveway to the castle. No sooner had I told the attendant my name than a gentleman stepped forward and pleasantly identified himself as Mr. George Hearst's butler and said he was "here at the behest of Miss Pickford" to show us "all that can be seen at the top of the hill." And he requested we follow him. The higher we drove, the more spectacular was the scenery, but the view from the top was absolutely breathtaking. I don't think we had ever seen such an awesome sight. The fabulous castle immediately behind us, the vast Hearst acreage all around us, and the Pacific Ocean just beyond. For the next couple of hours, the butler continued to show us just about everything one could possibly see inside the huge structure, with a delightful running commentary dwelling largely on the famous guests who had stayed there in its earlier days—royalty, presidents, movie stars, and theater personalities. Our visit to San Simeon, thanks to Mary, was really something special.

On one of our later visits to Pickfair,

that nice person Tony, whom Jo-Anne and I when in a silly mood privately referred to as "our" butler, felt friendly enough to let us in on a side business he conducted from the servants' quarters. Shocked as we were, our curiosity compelled us to lend an ear. Simply put, it consisted of his selling original oil paintings by contemporary European artists. We just couldn't say no when he asked if we would be interested in seeing the four paintings he had on hand if we wouldn't mind the short trip to his room. It turned out his room was directly below us in the lower quarters of the guest house. Arriving there, he suggested that "it would be appreciated if we didn't feel compelled to mention this to Mr. or Mrs. Rogers." We assured him "mum's the word." And that's how we became owners of four lovely works of art at lower than market-value prices. Tony told us, and we had no reason not to believe him, that similar paintings would bring at least double the amount we paid him for our fabulous four at the "snooty" galleries on Rodeo Drive. Before we left for home, we decided to check out a few of the "in" places and, sure enough, two of the artists whose works we had bought from Tony had others of their paintings currently being shown in one of those galleries, and at considerably higher prices. Tony even rolled and wrapped the paintings so that, when we left, Fenton had no idea of the pleasant secret we were carrying with us as he drove us to the airport.

In 1961 the last of our five children had arrived. On May 25 of that year, the good Lord was overgenerous when he blessed us with lovely twins, Karen and Katie. John had arrived two years earlier, in 1959, Mimi in 1952, and our first born, Drew, in 1950. I mention our children at this point because we are so glad they were lucky enough to have been guests in such a legendary home. Mary's fondness for children was shown when, during a visit to New York in 1963, she, Buddy and Tess Michaels drove to our home in New Canaan, Connecticut, to, as she put it, "see them all together at the same time to check up on how you two are bringing them up." After a pleasant afternoon, satisfied I guess that we weren't mistreating our offspring, they took to the road for the two-hour ride back to the big city.

Our visits to Pickfair were to continue into the 1970s. The last few times, about 1976 or 1977, Mary preferred to stay in her room because she "just wasn't up to seeing anyone but Buddy." She wanted, however, to keep up with who was there and what was happening. This she did by using her Buddy as a willing conduit, and by telephone.

On May 29, 1979, at the age of 86, Mary passed away. In 1970, Robert B. Cushman, of the American Film Institute, had this to say about her:

MARY PICKFORD

May 23, 1960

Dear Jo-Anne,

The red roses were perfectly beautiful. In fact, there is still a bowl of them in my bedroom.

It was such happiness for Buddy and me to have you and George here at Pickfair, and also at our little hideaway in Palm Springs.

Hope to see you both on our next trip to New York.

Buddy joins me in affectionate good wishes to you both.

As ever,

Mary Pickford

MP/s
Dictated but not signed.

Mrs. George Andrew Ansbro
New Cannen, Connecticut

Miss Pickford left town before I could get this signed.

Silvia Gray
Silvia Gray
Secretary

It is doubtful that any other figure in entertainment will ever achieve the level of popularity held by Mary Pickford, for hers was truly a universal medium, silent movies. The most similar recent phenomenon would be Beatlemania, which even at its height, pales in comparison with the world's affair with Mary. In 1925 a crowd of 300,000 turned out in Moscow, of all places, just to see Mary and Doug arrive at the train station. Similar throngs gathered in London, Rome, Paris, Stockholm, Berlin, and Tokyo. Perhaps only those who lived at the time and were witness to Mary Pickford's world-wide supremacy can ever really comprehend it. She was one of the most charismatic and truly legendary personages of the century.

In the early 1980s, Pickfair was sold,

MARY PICKFORD

April 2, 1962.

Dear George,

I have tossed your suggestion back and forth
for weeks now and have finally come to the
conclusion that, until and when I have taken
off the necessary weight, I should not and
must not appear on television. These crash
diets have done dreadful things, not alone
to the face, but to the entire system.

Quite confidentially, I cannot visualize
the same film including Douglas and Buddy.
Buddy is very sensitive about that part of
my life when we did not know each other.
However, I am sure that you could get around
this in some way, but the fact that Buddy and
I might not appear at our best; that is, in
competition with ourselves of twenty-five
or thirty years ago, is a very important
factor in my decision to wait until such
time as I feel that he and I can be
photographed to the best advantage.
I know you will understand.

In the meantime, George, be assured that
I will not discuss your idea of THE
SPECTACULAR with anyone.

With fond regards to you, Jo-Anne and the
children in which Buddy joins me, I am

                    Affectionately yours,

                    Mary

Mr. George Ansbro
American Broadcasting Company
7 West 66th Street
New York 23, N.Y.

I had proposed a TV special to be done at Pickfair as a celebration of the Rogers's 25th wedding anniversary.

and Buddy built a new home on a portion of the property for himself and his new wife.

Another incident involving Mary and Buddy was funny but could have been extremely embarrassing. On one of their visits to New York, after the four of us had had dinner, Buddy suggested a bit of further pub crawling, but Mary said no more carousing for her, so the three of us took off. We did a few of the jazz clubs on 52d Street and down in the Village, finally winding up in the wee hours at the Howdy Club. The Howdy was a well-known spot which featured a gay show, all the performers in drag, the "ladies" of the chorus typically in scanty costumes. As always when with Buddy, we were at a front table. And enjoying the evening because from the word go the show was aimed at the funny bone, and the audience that night responded accordingly. Lots of laughter. Especially when the pièce de résistance came on. But as the voice on the loudspeaker identified "her" as the "great and glorious star of the silent movies era, Mary Pickford," we three were thunderstruck. For a moment we could neither laugh nor cry. Many in the audience, and in the show, couldn't help but have observed that Buddy was there and have known who he was, his face was that familiar back then. No doubt those people felt great embarrassment for him, as did we. Especially when the drag queen proceeded to prance about and do whatever "she" did. Buddy, however, in the tradition of "the show must go on," saved the day so to speak. He stood up and said loudly "You

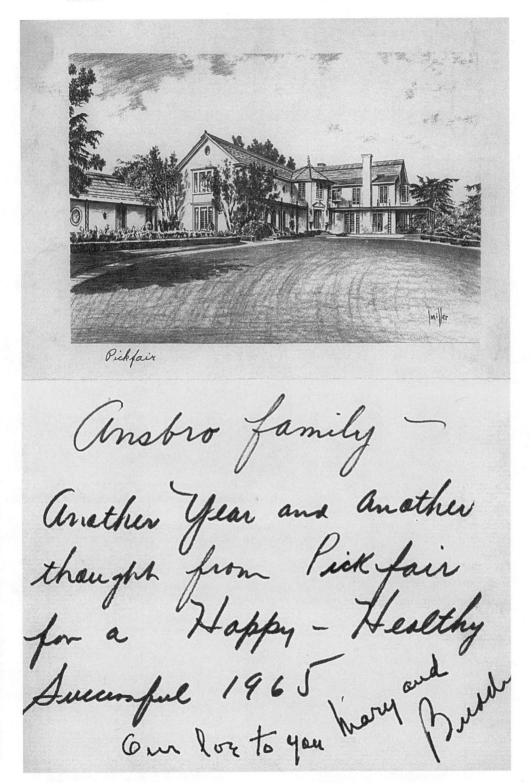

Pickfair

Ansbro family —

Another Year and Another thought from Pickfair for a Happy — Healthy Successful 1965

Our love to you Mary and Buddy

Christmas card from Mr. and Mrs. Rogers—also known as Buddy Rogers and Mary Pickford.

Mary and Buddy spend a day with us in New Canaan, Connecticut. From left: *Mimi, Buddy, Katie, Mary, John, Drew, George, Jo-Anne, Karen, and mother's helper is Mary Learned.*

forgot to introduce me, Mister Mary Pickford," and brought down the house. The applause was deafening. The tension was over. And, boy, were we relieved. Needless to say, thank God that Mary wasn't there with us.

32

UKELELE IKE
THROWS A PARTY

In 1951, Leonard Goldenson, president of United Paramount Theatres, met with Edward J. Noble to discuss a possible merger with ABC. Noble's asking price was $25 million, take it or leave it. At the time the figure was considered outrageous. But, it was said, the gambling instinct in Goldenson told him to take it, which he did. It took two years until February of 1953 before the government approved the merger and the new company became American Broadcasting/Paramount Theatres, Inc., AB/PT. For brevity's sake, however, it continued to be known as ABC. Little did Leonard Goldenson know then that some 30 years later a relatively unknown company, Capital Cities Broadcasting, would merge with his ABC. Nor could he, or anybody else for that matter, have even dreamed that in 1995, five years before the turn of the new century, the gigantic Walt Disney Company would fork over 19 billion dollars for the privilege of owning what had begun as the Blue Network of the National Broadcasting Company. In 1943, Ed Noble had paid only $8 million for the network, but I suppose there was considerable growth factor involved, as well as inflation. But 19 billion big ones! If old Ed Noble were still around, the mere thought of such a figure for a company he once owned and "gave away" for a measly $25 million would have driven him up the wall.

When the war ended in 1945, the U.S. government began unloading military surplus, getting rid of what equipment was no longer needed or usable. That's how, a couple of years later my friend Cliff Edwards came to purchase a surplus supply boat for very little money. I don't remember the exact price, but I do know he put more into renovating this very large floating plaything than what it cost him. He kept it moored at the dock at 79th Street and the Hudson River, just off Riverside Drive. After months of renovations, his new toy was finally ready, and Cliff invited lots of friends to the launching party. Included were Walter Winchell, the Stork Club owner, Sherman Billingsley, John Carradine and Robert Young, both big movie stars at the time. Mr. Young would later play the leading role for many seasons in the hit TV show *Father Knows Best*. We cruised up the Hudson as far as West Point, did a U-turn, and returning down the river, proceeded out into New York Harbor to the Statue of Liberty. Another U-turn and back up to the dock at 79th Street.

Needless to say, the bar was busy with plenty of hors d'oeuvres for soaking-up purposes. Cliff had hired Charlie Bourne to keep everybody happy with his great piano music. Two ABC execs who were close friends of mine and Jo-Anne's were also there, Wally Tepper and Al Nicol. It seems the more Wally drank, the more amused he became by John Carradine's very long hair. At the time such long hair on a male was unheard of, but he was growing it for a part he was going to play in a movie. For some reason, unbeknownst to me, Wally never did like Mr. Carradine. While browsing through the galley, Wally had picked up and pocketed a pair of kitchen shears, and several times during the trip he jokingly told us he was going to cut off Mr. Carradine's lengthy tresses. And, believe it or not, he did, very stealthily, making sure he wasn't observed by anyone else but us. He cut off a small portion in the back, but considerably more than a mere snippet. And when Cliff Edwards's party boat arrived back at the 79th Street dock, I won't ask you to guess who were the first four guests to debark.

About a decade ago, Pete Hamill wrote an article for *New York Magazine* about well-known saloons. It caught my fancy, but I thought it left one out that in my opinion ought to have been mentioned. With the best of intentions and in the spirit of filling this void, I took pen in hand to apprise the editor of Mr. Hamill's omission. Inasmuch as they chose not to print my effort, I would like to include it now among these recollections, in which I earlier recounted the celebratory events which took place in Hurley's on the evening of my wedding day on June 29, 1946. My letter follows:

December 22, 1987

To the Editor, New York Magazine:

Pete Hamill's excellent piece "The New York We've Lost" left this native New Yorker soaking in a sea of nostalgia. Having been around this town seemingly forever I share Mr. Hamill's great sense of loss. One legendary hangout he didn't include was the Radio City Bar and Grill, better known as Hurley's—or more formally, Hurley Brothers and Daly—on the corner of Sixth and 49th, where I had my first taste of booze in 1933 shortly after Prohibition ended and John and Connie Hurley and Paddy Daly were no longer running the place as a speakeasy.

Hurley's was a favorite watering hole for the thirsty and hungry of Rockefeller Center. And the gang from NBC, and later ABC, myself included, did their best to keep Hurley's in the black. Conviviality was the usual order of the day, and most of the night. But this pleasant pacificity was occasionally jarred by violent "disagreements" between John Hurley when he was on one of his frequent benders and Paddy Daly, his hated partner, who was rarely off one. On such occasions it took two bartenders, the cook and the waiter to prevent a possible homicide. After Daly died some of us were witness to John's newest peccadillo while in his cups. He'd come in the side door in pretty bad shape and try to put the arm on his own customers for their loose cash sitting on the bar so he could "buy them a drink." And when this proved unsuccessful he'd make quite a commotion while attempting to cadge drinks from others. This conduct invariably prompted his brother Connie and Sol the waiter to toss him bodily out onto Sixth Avenue.

One of the joys of being a Hurley's regular was the unpredictability of the place. The building is still there and so is the name Hurley's. But new ownership has understandably changed everything. The original Hurley Brothers, and probably most of their customers, except me, have long since departed this vale of tears.

George Ansbro

An afterthought that is both sad and funny just occurred to me. Several times when John Hurley reached the bottom of the barrel so to speak, Connie and Sol would pack him into a cab, "escort" him to Grand Central Station, and then pour him onto a train after pinning some cash into his pocket. His destination was intended to be someplace in Arizona where his older brothers, long since deceased, used to send him on such occasions to dry out. They, however, had had better results than Connie. He and Sol, having made sleeping car arrangements for John, would leave after generously tipping the conductor to keep an eye on him. But John, drunk as he was, was a wily one. The first stop after Grand Central was 125th Street, where John, escaping the busy conductor, would exit the Arizona Express, get into a cab, and arrive back at his bar less than two hours later.

33

A MAIDEN TRIP
ON A MAIDEN VOYAGE

Sometime in June 1952 I was notified that I would accompany Ed and Pegeen Fitzgerald on the maiden voyage of the SS *United States*, spend three days in Paris or London, and then return on the ship to New York. It was one of the most pleasant notifications of my career. The Fitzgeralds were the very first breakfast talk-show hosts and they invented the art of doing radio chitchat over morning coffee. I had come to know them very well and always enjoyed their company. The purpose of their presence on this round trip was to conduct a ship-to-shore broadcast every day, shortwaved back to ABC, recounting the happenings during the great liner's progress. I was to be their helper-outer, approaching passengers who were well known in whatever field—politics, entertainment, the arts, business, etc.—and invite them to accompany me to the Fitzgeralds' suite to be interviewed.

So on July 3, we were off. The United States Lines hoped that its new ship would break the existing record for crossing the Atlantic, which had been set by the HMS *Queen Mary* in 1938. On its initial crossing, the SS *United States* did just that and then beat that record by a few hours on its return to New York. The man taking the bows for both record-breaking trips was Commodore Harry Manning, the boss man of the ship.

Every day during both crossings I sought out prominent passengers to join me in a trip to Ed and Pegeen Fitzgerald's suite. And I must say that during both trips not one celebrity I approached said no to

being interviewed. There was so much going on all the time that there was no possibility of anyone being at a loss for something interesting to talk about. I guess my biggest catch was David Sarnoff, chairman of the board and founder of the Radio Corporation of America, RCA, but the vessel abounded with big fish, so to speak. President Truman's daughter Margaret was one. A few others that come to mind were Mrs. Vincent Astor and, on the return trip, Milton Berle with his fiancée, who were married not too long after they returned to Hollywood. The one thing all of these interviewees had in common was their desire to inform the world how utterly fabulous the voyage was. With Milton Berle, I had had a "hello how are ya" kind of relationship around the studios in Radio City during his rapid rise to becoming Mr. Television. But he made me very happy by the pleasant and gracious way he reacted when I first approached him about a Fitzgerald interview. He treated me like an old friend, and during the interview with the Fitzgeralds he got in a funny about "the classy gofer" they were using to "hornswoggle the likes of me" into their stateroom. Later, he invited me to join him and Ruth, his fiancée, after dinner in a private section of the main lounge, where they had a small gathering of friends they had met on board. His guests, including me, had such a good time he repeated it two nights later. Ever since that trip I think of Milton Berle as a genuinely nice person who reached out when he didn't have to.

Shortly before the day of the sailing I

With Margaret Truman aboard the maiden voyage of the SS United States *in July of 1952.*

charmed her with something brilliant like "Maggie Marnell? From ABC?" She replied, "Yes, I am and you must be the George Ansbro that Pegeen Fitzgerald told me I would likely be running into." It seems she too was a good friend of Pegeen's, which made it a lot easier for both of us conversationally, breaking the ice. My suggestion for cocktails that evening worked out just fine, especially when I got Ed and Pegeen to join us. The cocktail hour continued into dinner, all of us chattering nonstop. Of course with Ed and Pegeen, chatter was their stock in trade, what they had become celebrated for. Maggie Marnell didn't do badly either. And I guess I was no shrinking violet myself. As close as I had previously felt toward the Fitzgeralds, our warm get-together that second evening out on the briny deep proved to be so delightful we all agreed that we should at least dine together every night if possible, without necessarily nailing down the cocktail hour too. "After all," said Pegeen, "you know what they say about too much of a good thing." And I didn't dare come back with "No, what do they say?"

Ed and Pegeen, having known Maggie, were aware that she had been engaged for some months, with the wedding bells scheduled to ring not too long after the return voyage. As a matter of fact, Maggie had said, her fiancé and others of her family and friends had come to see her off at the sailing, as did my wife Jo-Anne with others of my family.

Among the friends who came to see me off was Marge Phillips, the gal who was Jo-Anne's matron of honor at our wedding and also her best friend. Marge was pregnant, quite pregnant; in fact she was overdue. It got so that friends were almost taking bets—would she or wouldn't she? And if she had given birth in the midst of all this bon voyage atmosphere just as the gangplanks were about to be raised, would the ship's sailing have been delayed from 12 noon, thus causing a monumental screw-up in the schedule of the most publicized

had heard that someone else from ABC was to do the round trip, the same as I. She was the head of some department or other, and why she was sent I frankly have long since forgotten. I'd been told her name was Maggie Marnell, but ABC, even then, was fast growing and I knew I had never met her. The second day out, however, as I stepped onto an elevator an attractive young lady was standing there who looked vaguely familiar, and I got the feeling from the expression on her face she thought the same thing as she looked at me. I guess I

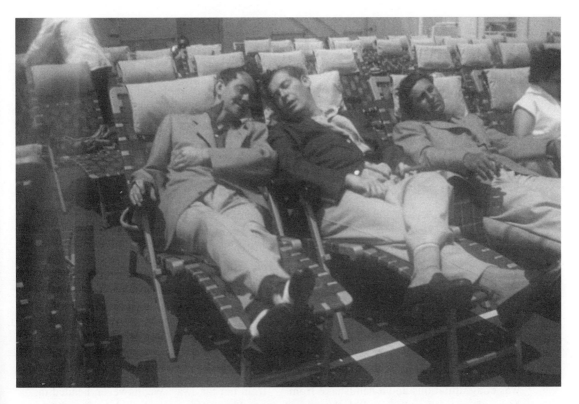

Relaxing on deck with Milton Berle.

maiden voyage ever? We will never know. Baby Bridget Phillips had evidently decided to wait another nine hours after the mighty SS *United States* had embarked on its maiden voyage before she made her maiden appearance on this earth. She arrived safe and sound around 9 o'clock that night, July 3, 1952.

As the trip progressed, various new friendships evolved. Two that come to mind were Jerome Zerbe and John Perona. Jerry was a very well-known photographer who first became noticed in the 1930s when he pioneered the type of photography adopted decades later by the paparazzi: candid shots of socialites and entertainers out-on-the-town. His pictures appeared in many national magazines and in books. He helped turn El Morocco into one of the world's best-known nightclubs. The owner of El Morocco, John Perona, for a man who ran such a successful enterprise as El Morocco, was a very down-to-earth kind of person,

extremely pleasant to be with. Someone else I hadn't seen since my boy soprano days on Milton Cross's *Children's Hour* was Walter Scott, the child violinist Milton used to jokingly call Sir Walter Scott. Here he was the first violinist with the ship's orchestra, not just any old ship's orchestra but the very prestigious Meyer Davis and his orchestra, for years the favored orchestra at White House functions. I first noticed him while dancing with Maggie Marnell early in the trip. When he didn't return my nod of recognition, it occurred to me, "Why should he? When he last saw me I was a kid only knee high to a grasshopper and now I'm taller and 37 years old." At any rate I sought him out between dance sets, and then he had no problem remembering. So on the rest of the trip as well as the return, we got together several times on deck for gab fests.

I was dancing with Pegeen that first night we four had dinner together when I was bowled over by her suggestion that I enter a dance contest to be held on the ship. It was not a Fox-trot contest or anything so mundane. It would be a Viennese waltz contest, my deah! She said that when she was dancing with me she thought I danced pretty well and when she was back sitting at the table observing others on the dance floor her attention was drawn to Maggie and me while Meyer Davis was leading the orchestra in a waltz. The thought struck her then that we waltz well enough to at least enter the contest and, hopefully, win. That's how it came about that, with much more pushing from both Pegeen and Ed Fitzgerald, we entered the Viennese waltz contest. And of course you must know by now that I wouldn't have even brought the subject up in these nostalgic meanderings if there had been any doubt of the result. Yes, we copped first prize, which, for Maggie, was a magnum-size bottle of French perfume. My prize was congratulations and a handshake from Meyer Davis. When I was a kid, there was a saying, "That and a nickel will get you a ride on the subway."

Let's talk prices, 1952 prices aboard ship. Not just any ship but the great and majestic SS *United States*, the Tiffany of ocean-going behemoths. As on all ships, food service was included in the price of passage. And as to be expected there was a charge for alcoholic beverages. As I frequented many cocktail lounges aboard ship or ordered something from the bar while having dinner, the prices, as I recall, seemed pleasantly moderate, what with no tax included. But again, that was then, in 1952. Today, however, as these words are being written in the late 1990s, looking back at mid-century booze and wine over-the-bar costs on that maiden voyage might make one hunger, or might I say, thirst for such prices again?

For many years John Perona had crossed the Atlantic to visit with his relations and his siblings in Italy. The one thing this annual visit had in common with all his other

visits was that down below in the hold of the SS *United States* was a brand new Cadillac which he would drive to his hometown. He said he liked to break in his new cars in Italy without worrying about being stopped for speeding every so often. He told us Italy had no speed limits. This conversation was a day before the ship was to dock at Le Havre. Earlier he had invited three of us to drive with him to Paris, we three being Maggie Marnell, Jerry Zerbe, and yours truly. He had been aware that we had chosen to get off at Le Havre and take the boat train to Paris for a three-day stay instead of continuing on to Southampton to spend the three days in London, as the Fitzgeralds were doing.

We disembarked at Le Havre amidst a tumultuous welcome, word having spread everywhere that our beautiful ship had created a new speed record for the Atlantic crossing. Those going to Paris or elsewhere in France were trudging over to the boat train not far away. We, however, headed in another direction to where John Perona's new Cadillac was being lowered from the vessel. Before long we were seated in it, John and Jerry Zerbe in front, Maggie Marnell and I in the rumble seat, it being a roadster. Wasting no time, John drove off and away from the pier. He knew which road to head for from his earlier trips, and pretty soon we were all convinced it wasn't just the SS *United States* that set a new speed record that day, what with the way our friend John Perona zipped along the road to Paris. When we got there, John dropped Jerry off first at wherever it was he was staying with friends. Maggie had booked a room at the Georges V, as had I, and after John left us off he continued on to somewhere in Italy which, based on the drive we had just experienced, shouldn't have taken him too long.

The view from my window was so exciting I had to call Jo-Anne right away to tell her about it, to tell her the Eiffel Tower seemed so close I felt I could reach out and touch it. And to tell her I wished she were

Winning the Viennese waltz contest with Maggie Marnell of ABC.

there with me. Fortunately, several years later we were able to make a European trip together so she too got to see the Eiffel Tower.

Three days in Paris can go by all too quickly, even though I realized how lucky I was to be there at all. I was grateful the Fitzgeralds had requested that I go along to help out. Sitting in my room, analyzing everything, I could come to only one conclusion—it was a great assignment.

Maggie and I did most of the usual sightseeing together. This very pleasant chore was tremendously simplified for me by the fact that she spoke French like a native, having been born and brought up in Montreal, Canada. For me it meant instant translation, which came in mighty handy. The one place I was on my own, however, was the Eiffel Tower. Although quite healthy, she had acrophobia (a fear of high places), and the famed Tower was 984¼' high, so that was a no-no for Maggie.

The next morning after I had seen the magnificent view of Paris from the top of the Tower, I got in touch with another lady who was pretty good with the French language, my wife's great aunt Lillian Harde. Jo-Anne's paternal grandmother, whom we were very close to, lived in New York, but two of her sisters had decided after many visits to take up residence in Paris. It was being done quite a bit at that time, the 20s. Although they remained very close to their two brothers and sister in the United States through frequent visits, air mail, and telegrams, they stayed in Paris all through World War II, a harrowing experience for two American maiden ladies. I had met them both on one of their visits to New York, but by 1952 only Lillian was alive. I spent a wonderful afternoon visiting with her and other neighbors in her flat. Later she took me to a favorite neighborhood restaurant for dinner, where it was fun being the only tourist in the place.

One could spend a month in the Louvre, much less a day. But for Maggie and me, three or four hours was the best we could do with our limited time. So much to see yet where to begin? Of the viewing we were able to cram in, what I best remember was the gooseflesh that came over me when I saw the Mona Lisa—*the* Mona Lisa. Not an imitation but the original painting done by Leonardo da Vinci over four hundred years ago. The whole afternoon we spent at the Louvre was a memorable experience. We couldn't let it be said we had visited Paris without taking in a nightclub. So we wound up our stay in Paris by checking out the Crazy Horse Saloon and its elaborate floor show, which was a lot of fun. The next morning was adieu to Paris. Back to

Le Havre, this time without the celebrated John Perona as our private chauffeur. We returned to the famous port city on the boat train. And who greeted us with open arms when we got there but our estimable friend, Jerry Zerbe.

Our return voyage was every bit as interesting and exciting as the trip over, new passengers returning to the United States replacing those who had left the ship to travel in Europe. When the ship stopped at Southampton, we were reunited with the Fitzgeralds who had spent their three days in London, as did many others of the press. (Those of us from the networks, or newspapers and magazines, all came under the general classification of *press*. The word *media* didn't come with general usage until much later.) Interestingly enough, on the return trip the great ship outdid itself in speed and beat its own record. The whole experience was something that will stay with me forever.

Maggie married her fiancé shortly after our return. During the following year, Jo-Anne and I got together with the newly-weds several times and were joined by Jerry Zerbe and John Perona whenever we stopped in at El Morocco. There's a sad ending to all this which I must include. Hardly more than a year later Maggie was diagnosed with cancer and before too long she became another of its victims.

34

MANHATTAN MAHARAJAH

Among the many, many radio programs I had done since I started as an NBC announcer, there was one that kept coming back. It was *Omar Herth, the Swingmaker*, Milt Herth's trio knocking themselves out with fabulous swing music and me reciting very silly stuff supposedly reminiscent of Omar Khayám, my tongue penetrating further into my cheek with each next line of foolishness. First we did it for two years in the late 40s. Next for a year out of Jack Dempsey's restaurant in Times Square, where I would sign off with "Thy network is blue." The third time we did it "Thy network" had undergone a name change to ABC. So also had the program. No more Milt Herth Trio, so without Mr. Herth it made sense to change its name. I dreamt up the singular title *Manhattan Maharajah*, conjuring up visions of Eastern potentates and all that sort of thing. In truth I, the Maharajah, had never been further East at that time than a dip in the ocean at Coney Island. Be that as it may, ABC supplied a live house orchestra of 15 pieces, and the program aired twice a week for a half-hour at 8:30 P.M., in prime time, for a couple of years to the full network. And I still loved doing it. Best of all, the audience response was warm and friendly, the obvious reason the powers that be continued to revive the program over many years.

This time the show was produced by Warren Somerville. Doris Gilbert, who had written it during the Milt Herth days, was not available, so Warren agreed to write it. With his wonderful sense of humor, he had fun composing the wacky poetry as much as I enjoyed reading it. After the ABC network dropped the program the local New

York ABC station, WJZ, presented *Manhattan Maharajah* in various time slots over several years with recorded pop music. And of course the Maharajah was, as always, yours truly.

With Warren Somerville now writing the script, the flavor of the East remained the same, but some of the four-liners grew to various lengths. I liked this because it allowed for much more latitude in my interpretation of what came out of Warren's typewriter. The many letters I received seemed to agree, as is illustrated by this one from a fan:

Feb. 22, 1950

Dear Mr. Ansbro,

This is the type of fan letter that is meant to blend in well with the morning coffee, and does not call for a reply.

On a number of occasions in the past several years, I thought of dropping you a line, but it wasn't until I read of your parents' golden wedding anniversary in Sunday's *Brooklyn Tablet* that I decided to put the idea into operation.

First, congratulations to your parents. May they have many more anniversaries.

Second, the real purpose of the letter, is to express the very belated appreciation of two fans concerning a program that by now you probably have completely forgotten. I refer to the morning show on WEAF, when, as announcer for the Milt Hearth Trio, you would punctuate their musical efforts with those clever poetic gems.

My wife and I still chuckle occasionally over the way we'd listen to the program. During the musical interludes (and believe me, I do mean "musical interludes," because to us, George Ansbro was the program), the usual morning routine, with its rush-rush-rush, would be followed. The end of a musical number was the signal to stop everything and listen.

Respectfully,
Frank and Marie Mooney

Doris Gilbert was the writer of all the shows I did originally in 1937, 1938, and 1939, when the show was called *Omar the Swingmaker*, with the Milt Herth Trio. It was on the Red Network of NBC Monday through Saturday at 8:00 A.M.

Doris wrote me to express her pleasure at the return of the show:

January 8th, 1951

Dear Mr. Ansbro,

Well, Manhattan Maharajah! Or you can't keep a good show down. I'm personally interested since Omar the Swingmaker first jumped out of my head more years ago than anyone would care to count. In any case, I came back to New York several weeks ago and heard NBC was looking for me. Flattering and startling. It seems they had a small five dollar check for the use of the opening and closing phrases of Omar the Swingmaker which I shifted around originally from Edward Fitzgerald. Small manna.

Am now listening to Manhattan Maharajah and was of course rocked that you're still the Bedouin Bard—and pleased. It sounds swell. Whoever is writing it is right in the tradition, if not an improvement. I, may Allah look kindly on me, am here doing television, God help us.

I was so tickled to hear it. Selah.

Best Regards,
Doris Gilbert

Variety also showed its enthusiasm in this review of May 9, 1951:

A new entry in the disk jockey sweepstakes, Manhattan Maharajah is a platter spinner with a twist. Prefacing each waxing with an adaptation of a poetry classic or an original ode, in a melodramatic recitation backed by oriental music, the Maharajah (George Ansbro) has come up with a diverting half-hour series. Despite corniness of the poetry's punch lines, this latter day Omar Khayyam should be able to grab off some late afternoon listening audience.

Ansbro has an expert tongue-in-cheek delivery for some of the lines. Show moves along at steady pace and the diversified selections help make the stanzas extremely listenable.

At this point I'm sure there's little doubt in the reader's mind of my affection for those shows. In the 30s and 40s NBC didn't make electrical transcriptions of *Omar* because it was not a commercial program. When it reemerged as *Manhattan Maharajah* later in the 50s on ABC, several shows were recorded on tape and I came into possession of them. I was crushed, however, when sometime in the 70s they were lost in a house move.

By now, having taken advantage of your good nature by delving into my fond thoughts of *Omar, the Swingmaker* and *Manhattan Maharajah*, it's time to move along to other memories that have withstood the erosion usually associated with the passage of time.

35

THE STORK CLUB

Happenings during the 40s seem to keep popping back into my head. One such, to say the least, was one of a kind. Gene Kirby was a fellow staff announcer, and Jim O'Hanlon was a news writer. On this particular day, as he had done innumerable times, Gene was on the air doing news. Also on this same day, as was not unusual, Jim had more than likely imbibed a bit too much at lunch. He walked into the studio across from the newsroom with an additional piece of copy to give to Gene, who was seated in front of the mike reading aloud. Incorrectly thinking Gene was only rehearsing, Jim in a playful mood leaned over Gene's shoulder and, affecting a conspiratorial tone of voice, said, "Up your ass, Kirby." Immediately Gene pushed the off button and said, "Jim, for God's sake I'm on the air—get out!" and continued reading the news. Jim O'Hanlon ducked back into the newsroom, put on his hat and coat, and never came back. There weren't any complaints, which was unbelievable in those days considering that his immortal line actually went out on the air.

When Jo-Anne and I were married, the ceremony took place in St. Patrick's Cathedral for sentimental reasons. We quite regularly attended the last Mass on Sundays, and we frequently ran into Mike Sweeney and his wife. Besides being a fellow parishioner, Mike was vice president of the Blue Network's sales department and a good friend. He had become one of five or six select members of the congregation who took up the collection when given a basket by the head usher to collect from however many pews the head

man designated. It was generally looked upon as something special, considering who a few of the other ushers were. People like the Honorable James A. Farley, who was credited with being the brains behind the political success of Franklin D. Roosevelt and who had been rewarded with the position of Postmaster General of the United States. One other I can still see in the block-long center aisle was Frank Fay, an actor who at the time was starring on Broadway in the comedy hit *Harvey*, that included a six foot rabbit.

If we happened to be seated in the section where Mike was collecting, we enjoyed watching him—that big good-natured smile never seemed to leave his face. While chatting outside after Mass, we would jokingly accuse him of using the smile as a ruse, the better to empty the pockets of the worshippers and thereby enhance his own chance of entering the Pearly Gates when his time came around.

Because we took off on a vacation for a while, we missed seeing the Sweeneys at Mass. After we returned, we still didn't see them and wondered about it. Some weeks later, however, we spotted them seated across the aisle. At collection time, Mr. Head Usher distributed collection baskets to Jim Farley, Frank Fay, et al., but ignored our friend Mike Sweeney in favor of somebody else. Outside, after Mass, we caught up with them. Mike told us this was the first time they had been back since it happened and he was still embarrassed. "Since what happened?" I asked. Assuming we had heard the story through the grapevine and then realizing we hadn't, he sheepishly explained. Routinely, as countless times before, Mike would give the collection basket to the first person inside the pew. After dropping a contribution into it, that person would pass it along to the next, and so on to the last person at the end of the ten-foot-long pew. Then that person would pass the basket to the person seated immediately behind, who then would send it on its way picking up its goodies until it reached the center aisle again and the trusting hands of Mike Sweeney. Sort of like a U-turn in church. As always, when Mike reached his last two pews, there was lots of moolah in the basket. But this time, trouble erupted at the center of the U-turn. Unfortunately for Mike, the person at the far end of his next-to-last pew was a little old lady who had great difficulty in lifting the very heavy basket over the back of her pew. As a result, crash. Coins and bills everywhere except where they were supposed to be. The noise momentarily echoed throughout the vast cathedral. But what shocked those devout souls within hearing was a very annoyed Mike Sweeney standing there in the center of St. Patrick's Cathedral loudly bellowing, "Oh, for Chrrist's sake!" By the time Jo-Anne and I stopped laughing at his tale of woe, Mike started to sing "Somebody Else Is Taking My Place," a song that was quite popular at the time. And very appropriate.

In 1953 I replaced Don Gardiner as the announcer on *When a Girl Marries*, which was first heard on CBS in May of 1939. It moved to NBC in 1941, where it stayed for ten years, and in 1951 the program went to ABC where after two years I took over from Gardiner. Mary Jane Higby was the star and Warren Somerville the director. For Warren, it was quite a change from *Manhattan Maharajah*. My opening announcement was the typical soap opera heart-tugger: "We bring you *When a Girl Marries*, the tender, human story of young married life, dedicated to everyone who has ever been in love." It was written by Elaine Sterne Carrington, whose credits also included *Rosemary* and *Pepper Young's Family*, both real biggies in the world of soaps.

Speaking of biggies in radio soapland, at the top of the list of organists was Rosa Rio. Rosa, as a matter of fact, had long held that distinction with me. In my beginning days on Pat Kelly's NBC announcing staff in 1934, Richard Leibert was head organist at the Radio City Music Hall, Lew White at the Center Theatre, and Jesse Crawford and Ann Leaf at the New York Paramount Theatre. I became acquainted with these giants of the organ during those early days when I was assigned to their radio programs. In some instances I worked with them at the theater, or depending on how things were set up, my end of the conversation would originate in the studio while they would do their gabbing from the theater. As time went on, I found myself working with many other organists, only a few of whose names come to mind—Bill Meeder, Abe Goldman, Milt Herth, Charley Paul, and Johnny Winters. Frankly, I can't recall exactly when or on what particular show it was that I first met and worked with Rosa. One thing I do remember, however, is that she was among the busiest of all the organists during those great days. So when *When a Girl Marries* moved to ABC in 1951 and acquired Rosa at the organ and, two years later, me at the announcer's mike, it became a three-a-day combo of Rio/Ansbro. The other two shows I did were *Between the Bookends* with Ted Malone and *Thy Neighbor's Voice*, which featured the wonderful bass baritone voice of Robert Mills. What made Rosa stand out head and shoulders above most of the others in her trade was that besides being proficient and talented, which the others were too, she brought great warmth and a remarkable sense of humor to whatever studio she might be working in. This period of my career was during the waning years of *Young Widder Brown*, so having done three shows with Rosa Rio, I would close out the afternoon with the *Widder Brown* cast and that show's organist, Johnny Winters. Invariably, Johnny would ask, "What Rosa Rioism do you bring with you today?"

This is a good time to sneak in a quote from James Thurber in the *New Yorker*: "A soap opera is a kind of sandwich, whose recipe is simple enough, although it took years to compound. Between thick slices of advertising, spread twelve minutes of dialogue. Add predicament, villainy, and female suffering in equal measure. Throw in a dash of nobility. Sprinkle with tears. Season with organ music. Cover with a rich announcer sauce, and serve five times a week."

After he had become settled in his position as chairman of ABC, Leonard Goldenson decided to go on a spending spree aimed at enhancing both the ratings and the reputation of his radio network. The overall concept was to be known as "ABC, the Live and Lively Radio Network," several full-hour shows beginning at 9 A.M. and continuing through 9 P.M. Monday through Friday. Everything was live, nothing taped. Each show had its own large orchestra, vocalists, announcer, and, of course, star. I was selected to be the announcer on *The Bill Kemp Show*, which aired 8 to 9 P.M., finishing off the "Live and Lively" day. Of the several programs on the schedule, the only one that was not new was *The Breakfast Club*, starring Don McNeil, which originated in Chicago, as it had for several years. And it aired in the same time period as it always had, 9 to 10 A.M. No doubt ABC decided to keep *The Breakfast Club* and use it as the lead-in to its lineup because of its proven track record. *The Herb Oscar Anderson Show* followed. Herb had been the star of his own early morning show on the local station in New York, WJZ, which had enjoyed high ratings locally. Of the other "Live and Lively" programs, two that stand out in my memory were *The Merv Griffin Show* and *The Jim Backus Show*. Not that I got to hear them much, unless the comedic talent of one or the other was borrowed, to replace the star of my show, Bill Kemp, when he neglected to show up because of "personal reasons." In truth, Bill had a drinking problem. On his non-appearance days, the director learned that instead of changing the format of the show at the last minute and have me make an apology for Kemp's absence because of "illness" and present the orchestra for an hour filling in with music, it was better to grab either Griffin or Backus and hopefully, if time allowed, get some rehearsing in rather than hit the air cold. Even though Merv Griffin and Jim Backus were well respected as professionals, there were several sketches in the course of the hour program involving the band leader Neil Hefti, the vocalist Betty Somebody, a guest star like Jonathan Winters, and me that made it almost imperative that they rehearse. In addition to announcing the program, I was written into all of the sketches, and I loved it. Those "Live and Lively" days lasted about eighteen months. This was quite a while before Merv made it real big in television with The *Merv Griffin Show*, one of the first successful TV talk shows, and it was very much before he became one of the top powers in Atlantic City when that town became a gambling mecca. As for Jim Backus, even then he had been around as a radio actor for a long time. He later attracted lots of attention as the voice of "Mr. Magoo," a cartoon character, and appeared in many movies. Those absences of the star of *The Bill Kemp Show* became a set pattern even though they were seldom longer than one day, and that was usually a Monday. Let's say the warning signs were up. But despite his absences, it is my feeling that ABC never fired him because he was an extremely talented guy who had great potential in the field of comedy. Despite his drinking, they had high hopes and thought he might have a future in TV. Once after Jonathan Winters had guested on the show, we three repaired to the Studio Steak House around the corner. It was one of those times I'll never forget. During the show that night, Jonathan had raised the decibel level of laughter to an all-time high. Once we had settled into the restaurant he never let up, making it difficult not only to eat the steak but even to get at it with knife and fork because with me when I laugh that hard I just shake all over. Bill Kemp was no slouch either. He got off some ridiculously funny cracks so that not only I but even Jonathan Winters found himself banging the table in raucous applause. Jonathan, himself a master of comedy, recognized Bill's potential in the comedy field. But when *The Bill Kemp Show* eventually left the airwaves, Bill went back to Toronto, his hometown and dropped out of sight—to my knowledge he was never heard from professionally again. How tragic—Bill Kemp—another alcoholic statistic.

Readers may be wondering at this point what the title of my book has to do with me or the things I've been telling about up until now. And you may have noticed that I've said nothing about my involvement with television other than John Daly's news show for Pontiac and those TV newscasts I did in the very early experimental days when I could have wrung out my suit after 15 minutes under the hot lights. We all know how much telecasting has improved since then. There was an ABC Radio Network show called *Dr. I.Q.* which traveled the country. It appeared weekly, originating in big cities before large audiences. When it came to New York, it broadcast from Madison Square Garden in front of a full house. A simple idea, *Dr. I.Q.* had a huge radio audience. After his opening greeting, Dr. I.Q., played by Lew Valentine, quickly got going by addressing one of several of us announcers scattered around the Garden, each with a hand microphone. His usual opening was, "Now let's get things mov-

ing as we go to Announcer X," who would then answer, "I have a lady (or gentleman), Doctor." The doctor would then ask that person a question. If he or she answered correctly, which happened more often than not because the questions were relatively simple (though not quite as simple as "Who is buried in Grant's Tomb?"), Dr. I.Q. would direct the announcer to "give that lady (or gentleman) ten, or whatever number the answer merited, silver dollars." The announcer would then, quite ostentatiously and with much clatter, dole out the silver dollars from a large sack hanging around his neck. If the contestant blew it, there was no consolation prize—just "Ooh, I'm so sorry. Better luck next time" from Dr. I.Q. Then he would give the correct answer.

As TV began to grow and network radio to diminish, it was inevitable that *Dr. I.Q.* would make the transition. When it did, it was no longer a traveling show but instead remained based in New York in one of the Broadway theaters ABC was using at the time, the Ritz on West 48th Street. Also, in the transition to TV, there was no longer the need for so many announcers because the Ritz was like a dollhouse compared to the vastness of Madison Square Garden. So the number of us announcers was cut to four. Art Fleming, Dirk Fredericks, Ed Michael, and I were chosen, with me stationed in the balcony while my colleagues held forth in other sections.

On television the show remained pretty much the same except that Dr. I.Q. was now played by Jimmy McClain. There was one slight difference in the opening, though. After Dr. I.Q. gave his introductory remarks from the stage, he would always get things going with "Let's first go upstairs to George Ansbro." To which I would always reply, "I have a lady in the balcony, Doctor." That opening never changed. After making sure I had a lady picked for the top of the show, later on I might have "a gentleman," "a young lady," or "a young lad in the balcony, Doctor." "I have a lady in the balcony" was a fun line. During the years we did the show, the line caught on with the public to the extent that whenever it was used, or quoted, everyone knew it was a good-natured ribbing of *Dr. I.Q.* These many years later, having decided to put my recollections down on paper, I thought I would resurrect the line I liked so well and make it the title of my book.

There were other early TV programs besides *Dr. I.Q.* I was part of at ABC, like the *Patti Page Show*, *The Early Movie Show*, *Press Conference with Martha Roundtree*, *The Paul Whiteman Revue*, *Life Begins at Eighty*, and *The Stork Club*. On all of the above programs, I was heard but not seen. But somewhere along the line a new program started. New, but with an old name. And you didn't have to be a wanna-be dancer to know the name. It was *The Arthur Murray Show*. On this one I was also on camera. I used to like to say that when Mr. Murray couldn't get Fred Astaire or Gene Kelly to dance with his wife Kathryn, he asked for me. But once, when I sprang that line on a couple of people at a party, I became uneasy when it dawned on me that they actually believed it. Here's what really happened. During rehearsal for the first show, Arthur approached me to ask how I considered myself as a dancer. As I recall, I answered I thought of myself as "fair to middling." Next thing I knew I was auditioning for the world-famous dancing school impresario traipsing around the stage with Kathryn, Mrs. Arthur Murray. After we had circled twice, he cut in on me and finished out the dance with Kathryn. Then he said "fine, we'll do it just like that." That's how it came about that on every show we did do it just like that. It became the show's standard opening. Incidentally, the music we danced to was a very sedate waltz. It definitely was not the then currently popular song with the line in it "Arthur Murray taught me dancing in a hurry."

The Patti Page Show featured Patti singing, and hosting such guest stars as Nat King Cole and Johnny Mathis. *The Early Movie Show* was just what you would expect it to be, movies shown early in the evening, beginning at 5:30. I was your friendly off-camera host offering a combination of pleasantries, movie talk, and commercials. *Press Conference with Martha Roundtree* was a discussion of the current political situation hosted by Miss Roundtree. *The Paul Whiteman Revue* was a Sunday afternoon hour. Mr. Whiteman had first become famous as the King of Jazz in the 1920s, and his fame continued so that several decades later he was both vice president of ABC in charge of music and conductor of his own program sponsored by Goodyear. I guess that is what might be called having your cake and eating it too. If a retrospective of important people in the music business is ever written, there would no doubt be unanimous agreement that one of the biggest of all was Pops Whiteman. Big in popularity and big in size. He must have eaten an awful lot of cake and other goodies to have amassed all that extra avoirdupois. In the 20s he was as famous for his massive size as for his great jazz. He was a tall man, well over six feet, and his more than three hundred pounds was largely concentrated around his middle. If his worth could have matched his girth, he would have been a zillionaire. Be that as it may, his TV program was top notch. On most Sundays, baritone Earl Wrightson was his star soloist, with someone of the stature of sentimental singer Jane Froman occasionally taking Mr. Wrightson's place. Besides the twenty-five-piece orchestra (which no longer featured only jazz), a mixed choral group and a chorus line à la the Rockettes completed the ensemble. Even though Mr. W. had lost considerable weight over the years, what he still retained occupied lots of space on the podium as he conducted the orchestra on *The Paul Whiteman Revue*.

I can't leave the subject of Paul "Pops"

Whiteman without relating an incident which is said to have occurred in 1925 when he was at his heaviest. He was on a road tour, giving a concert in a different town every night. Earlier in his career he had engaged a young man to stick close to him, to be at his beck and call, to be his gofer, valet, and whatever else Pops's needs of the moment might be. Harry was his name. Because Mr. W. was so portly, one of Harry's several tasks was to accompany his boss to the john whenever Pops felt the number one call of nature. Because of how difficult it had become for Pops himself to do, Harry was to unbutton Pops's fly, reach for his member, and aim it correctly so that Pops could then relieve himself without a problem. One night during the intermission Pops felt the number one urge creeping up on him only to discover that the archaic theater had no facilities, not even a sink, nothing except an outhouse behind the theater. So off to the privy he trudged, the King of Jazz with his faithful Harry beside him. But, horror of horrors, when they got there the outhouse was totally dark because of a burnt-out light bulb. By now with intermission time getting short, as was Mr. W's temper, he yelled "Harry, come on, let's go," which Harry proceeded to do. Mr. W. was aware of Harry's initial move, the unbuttoning. But the next, which normally took but a second, this time seemed interminable. Almost in desperation he shouted, "Harry, what in hell is taking so long?" "Mr. Pops, I can't find it," said Harry. "Well," thundered Paul Whiteman, "Goddammit, you had it last!"

Life Begins at Eighty was just as its title purported it to be—a panel of folks all 80 or older. And they were indeed, to use an old-fashioned expression, full of the devil. As I recall, Jack Barry was the emcee. Jack brought out the good humor and all-around fun in these seemingly youthful oldsters, two of whom were in their 90s. Another thing I remember about the show is that it was the first time I'd

ever heard of Arnold Bread, a new competitor in the field of baking products that was making its debut into television advertising on the show. I can now say that if *Life Begins at Eighty* was on the air today, I could still be on it, if they would have me, but not as the announcer. I could instead be a member of the panel because the age requirement would be no problem. I find this a very pleasing thought. It's especially pleasant just to pinch myself occasionally and know I'm still around.

On May 17, 1955, in his regular weekly column in *Motion Picture Daily* critiquing television programs, Pinky Herman had this to say: "Although the *Stork Club* show has never been our cup of tea we must admit the new version is an improvement. It has more entertainment value, more movement, and smooth direction by ABC-TV's Marshall Diskin. However for me the highlight of the show I caught the other night occurred when the announcer, George Ansbro, pointing out the Stork's elite customers, said in a deep pontifical tone, 'and there sits Mrs. Gloria Vanderbilt in a honey-bear *peau de soie*.'"

In a nutshell the above quote from Mr. Herman's column tells what my duties were as the announcer on the *Stork Club* show. I was sort of a nonversifying Manhattan Maharajah in a tuxedo. And pretty much always with tongue firmly implanted in cheek, though I'm sure the Stork Club's boss and owner, Sherman Billingsley, had no idea of such a thing, as sophisticated as he was thought to be. If it wasn't Mrs. Vanderbilt's height of fashion attire I was describing, it might very well have been what Mrs. John D. Rockefeller, Jr., was eating, who Joan Crawford's escort was that evening, who those other people with Humphrey Bogart and Lauren Bacall were, or how could it be possible that handsome Tyrone Power was dining alone? And on and on and on. There was no other night spot quite like the Stork Club. In the 30s, 40s and 50s and until its demise in 1965, it was without a doubt the

At the Stork Club with Jo-Anne and Martha Atwell in 1948. Martha directed Mrs. Wiggs of the Cabbage Patch, Young Widder Brown, Mr. Keen: Tracer of Lost Persons, *and many other programs. Working with her was a delightful experience.*

most famous club in the world. Nip and tuck with it, vying for the honor of first place, were El Morocco, the Colony Club, Toots Shor's, Rainbow Room and "21." But Mr. Billingsley's constant promotion of the Stork paid off spectacularly when you consider that as a young man, he started out as a bootlegger during Prohibition. Next he opened a speakeasy. When Prohibition was repealed, he went legit, christened his place the Stork Club, and in 1934 moved it to 53d Street just east of Fifth Avenue. It became a plush oasis, an institution in the lives of many people to whom it became like house and home. Parents brought their small children in. Those children grew up celebrating their

birthdays, Thanksgiving dinners, and Easter Sundays there. Debutantes' "coming out" parties ended up at the Stork Club in the early hours of the morning. Many young men had their first official hard drink sitting at the bar with their fathers in the Stork Club. It was an important place with an important clientele, and I was privileged to spend many memorable moments there. When ABC-TV decided to air the *Stork Club* program after CBS had dropped it, I was both pleased and flattered that Mr. B. chose me as his announcer from an audition. But I often wondered if he selected me because I had been a regular at the club since 1937 or because of my talents as an announcer. I never did find out. That the Stork Club eventually went out of business was largely attributable to Mr. B.'s stubborn seven-year refusal to negotiate with a union. Its doors closed for good in October of 1965. Two years later it was demolished to clear the site for a vest-pocket park that William S. Paley, chairman of CBS, bequeathed in honor of his father. The spot is now known as Paley Park. A year to the day after the club closed, Sherman Billingsley, who had been in poor health, died of a heart attack at 66.

UNWELCOME TENTH ANNIVERSARY GIFT

One of the loves of my life, workwise, was about to bite the dust. Toward the end of June 1956, there were notices in the entertainment sections of the press about the impending demise of *Young Widder Brown* from the airwaves. In his radio column in the *Long Island Star Journal* of Wednesday, June 27, 1956, William Ewald put it best:

Young Widder Brown, who for the past 18 years has battled bankruptcy, broken bones, blindness, and bubbleheaded boyfriends, becomes a dead widder this Friday.

NBC has decided to entomb the radio soap opera in the same chilly boneyard that houses such other departed epics as *Just Plain Bill*, *Portia Faces Life* and *Life Can Be Beautiful*.

Among the chief mourners of Ellen Brown, widder, will be George Ansbro, announcer. Ansbro, a veteran student of soaps who has worked with such moribund dramas as *Mrs. Wiggs of the Cabbage Patch* and *Amanda of Honeymoon Hill*, has announced for *Young Widder Brown* since it was launched on a sea of suds in 1938.

Ansbro, at present a staff announcer at ABC where he also toils for a new style soap, *When a Girl Marries*, feels *Young Widder Brown* will be missed.

He thinks people like to hear about other people's troubles. And Ellen Brown, a widow with two small children (they're still small after 18 years) seems to have had her share of them.

"You couldn't name the kind of trouble she hasn't had," said Ansbro nostalgically. "She opened a little tearoom when the show began, but I still don't think she has it paid off. She gets into financial trouble at the drop of a hat.

"She's broken every bone in her body—her legs, both of them I believe—her ankles and her arms. She's been shot at, her children have been lost and dozens of her friends have died. Once she had amnesia and another time a scoundrel turned up who claimed he was her dead husband. Well, you figure what complications that led to—we didn't clear it up for two years."

However, the high point of the long-running series, as Ansbro recalls it was when the widder went blind. "She ate some poisoned chocolate cake," said Ansbro, "and couldn't see at all. Only trouble was, the sponsor who followed our show sold flour and he complained. She regained her sight overnight and cake was never mentioned on the show again."

While I'm writing these recollections of the long ago, the Widder's finish is especially memorable to me and, of course, to Jo-Anne because the very last day of the program, June 29, 1956, fell on what normally would have been a festive occasion— our 10th wedding anniversary. Ending a pleasant daily habit, never mind the loss of income, which had, after 18 years, become part of my life did sadden both of us. But, as most sad moments have a habit of doing, thank God, our sadness soon disappeared as different interests, work and otherwise, replaced them. Looking back from my present vantage point in the late 1990s, it seems remarkable how quickly the intervening forty years, from our tenth to our golden anniversary, have passed. We capped our 50 years together by treating ourselves to a great vacation in the unbelievably beautiful state of Alaska which, in a word, is awesome.

I can't help but think how difficult it must be for younger people today as we near the 21st century to comprehend the unbelievable difference in the value of money compared to 50 years ago. I think this next recollection will bear me out.

SUING THE LANDLORD

In the summer of 1951, Jo-Anne was in Maine with our new first-born, Drew, visiting with her parents and showing off the greatest baby ever to come down the pike to her maternal aunts and cousins. Before she left New York, Dr. Perry Boynton had confirmed that she was, as they used to say, with child again. With such glad tidings, we then both decided it was time to look for larger quarters to shelter our growing family. Much as we enjoyed living in the apartment we had lucked into because of my father's friendship with fellow Irishman, Mayor Bill O'Dwyer, we thought we needed more than one bedroom. Of course with Jo-Anne in Maine, it was up to me to do the looking. This turned out to be anything but easy because I had to sandwich in my looking time between my work schedule. And in 1951 there was still a postwar apartment shortage, unless you were interested in something on Park or Fifth Avenues. Eventually I saw a place I liked very much in a fine building on Riverside Drive on the corner of 90th Street. The realtor who showed it to me scored a few points in its favor when she ever so casually just happened to mention that Babe Ruth had lived in the building on the opposite corner until his death just a few years earlier in 1948. Liking the apartment as I did, it was easy for me to conclude that if the neighborhood had been good enough for Babe Ruth, it clearly was good enough for us. And it was a lot closer to ABC than our apartment downtown. So, even though it had much more space than we needed or even wanted, what with the apartment situation in New York being what it was, I decided to get serious about

taking it. When I told the good lady about my serious intentions, she said something like, "I assume my office has told you that because of its location on the second floor, very desirable for a professional, it's the landlord's decision to rent Apartment 2A only to a professional." That shook me up a bit. Then I told her that I hadn't heard that interesting piece of information until this very minute and that no, I was not a doctor, lawyer, shrink or whatever of that variety, but yes I was a professional and my line of work, which I had been engaged in for quite a few years, was that of an announcer on radio and TV. Her level of interest went up immediately and prompted the questions I expected, like "When can I hear you?" and "What station?" She even took out her notebook to write down some of my answers. Next it was my turn to ask questions. The first was, "Do I qualify as a professional?" to which she answered: "The word professional embraces a wide range of endeavors other than just the medical or legal. I should be happy to recommend to the landlord that you are indeed a professional. Why yes, of course, yours is the radio-TV profession." My next question—"What rent is the landlord asking?" Answer—"$200 per month." "And if I were not a professional what would it be?" Answer—"Prior to its being designated as a professional unit, it brought $145 per month." Knowing I was being hornswoggled, I swallowed hard and took the apartment, 2A, at 180 Riverside Drive, with five double windows looking out over the Hudson River, eight rooms, and three and a half baths.

After we had been ensconced in our new

digs a couple of years and Jo-Anne's parents, who had been eager to leave Washington Heights, had succeeded us in our Village apartment, and well after Mimi, our second child, had arrived, I picked up a note that had been placed under our door saying a tenants' meeting would be held on the evening of such and such a date in an apartment on the 12th floor. It requested we be there, if possible, to join in a discussion of tenant affairs. From time to time since we had moved in we had received similar invitations but for one reason or another were never able to go. This time we resolved to attend, both to hear something about what went on in the building and to meet some of our neighbors.

While the meeting was in progress, we learned that shortly before I had rented our apartment the building's ownership had changed hands. The gist of the meeting centered on general unhappiness with the way the new landlord was running things. The other tenants complained about frequent problems with the elevators, which we hadn't found a problem in having to use the elevator even when Jo-Anne went out with the carriage. Other times we used the stairs. When the formal meeting ended, I was pleased to see the gentleman who chaired it approach Jo-Anne and me with hand extended to introduce himself. His name was Lyman Stansky, and he and his wife lived in the apartment where the meeting was being held. He was the head of the tenants' association, and during our conversation he asked what unit we lived in, how long we had been there, did we like it, etc., normal talk under the circumstances. Then he asked a question which changed the whole tenor of the conversation—"What rent do you pay?" I should say it was my answer that changed the course of thought. When I said $200, he stared at me in disbelief, while at the same time uttering the words, "I can't believe it, I simply can't believe it." "Excuse me, Mr. Stansky," I said, "I don't understand. What

can't you believe?" "No offense. But I find it hard to believe that living on the second floor you are paying the highest rent in this building," he replied. Now it was my turn to be amazed. He then noted that when he had introduced himself he had neglected to mention that he was an attorney but that because of the direction our conversation seemed to be going he thought, in fairness, we should know it. Then more questions, in lawyerly fashion eliciting from me as best I could remember the conversations I had had with the real estate agent or anyone else in the realty office, all the while jotting down notes as we talked. Eventually, the meeting long since over, we thought it time to descend to the most expensive apartment in the building, the spot we had called home for over two years—on the second floor yet. As we got up to go, Lyman Stansky said, "Mr. Ansbro, it is my professional opinion that you were snookered. And I would like very much to unsnooker you. So I'm offering you my services on a contingency basis to do just that. I would like us to face Mr. Landlord in court and rectify your situation. If we lose—no charge to you. If we win—I take half. Before you give me an answer go home and sleep on it, both of you, and let me know when you come to a decision."

Before the elevator had even reached our floor we had decided to accept Mr. Stansky's offer. How could we not? First thing next morning I called, told him we had full confidence in him and asked him to start the ball rolling.

Our case against the landlord was heard in a municipal court in lower Manhattan before a judge. There was no jury. I remember being on the witness stand 45 minutes. The landlord's only defense witness was the realtor who had rented the apartment to me. Lyman Stansky was just great and without much difficulty convinced the good judge that he should rule in our favor. In so doing he set our rent back to what it should have been, $145, plus a five-percent legitimate increase established sometime during our residency. The icing on the cake, however, was a monetary award of treble damages, which meant the payment of three times the amount of the difference we had been paying in rent as long as we had been living there. We had been paying $200 when it should have been only $145, a $55 difference. Times three equals $165. Times the 26 months we had been living in what the judge had, happily for us, just decreed, was no longer the most expensive unit at 180 Riverside Drive. The total amount was $4,290. So, as per our agreement, Lyman Stansky took half, $2,145, and we the other half. I guess the moral to all this is: Don't ever not reach for any piece of paper stuck under your door, especially if you live in a large apartment building.

38

SO LONG RADIO CITY, HELLO WEST 66TH

In February of 1952, ten years after the corporate separation of the Blue Network from NBC had become effective, its lease with NBC expired. Under its new name, the American Broadcasting Company, it was moving a mile or so uptown to West 66th Street between Central Park West and Columbus Avenue. The use of NBC's facilities, studios, master control room, office space, etc. was over. Actually, ABC had been using some of the new TV studios on 66th Street for a while before the move.

When the move was completed with everybody installed in the new quarters, for those who might become afflicted with a sudden thirst, or pangs of hunger, there was no longer the proximity of Hurley's to repair to. No more English Grill, no Down Under. Those establishments remained of course, they didn't go out of business, but we of ABC were gone. However, as might have been expected, the ABC clientele of those Radio City watering holes, now uptown, wasted little time finding replacements. For inveterate Hurleyites, there now was a choice of three places in the immediate vicinity and all of them run by natives of Ireland or their direct descendants. Healy's, owned, by Jerry Healy, was the closest, on the corner of 66th and Columbus. A few doors away, in the middle of the block between 66th and 67th was McGoldrick's, where Tim McGoldrick was the proprietor. Across Columbus Avenue, on the corner of 67th Street, Paddy McGlade also had the welcome mat out to attract the new ABC crowd into his place. In earlier years these three saloon keepers did cater to a clientele

from 7 West 66th. Strictly a horsey set because for very many years prior to ABC's purchase of the property, 7 West 66th had been a combination stable and riding academy. The upper crust of New York citizenry of those long ago days kept their horses there, very handy for the daily prance in Central Park just across the avenue. And for quite some time after the move, anyone with a sense of smell could tell immediately who the previous occupants had been.

Inasmuch as the big move occurred in February, by mid-spring 1952 all three of those spots were enjoying quite an upsurge in business. Another restaurant which attracted many of the newly installed ABC people was the Café des Artistes, across the street from the back door of ABC, on the ground floor of a large apartment building known as the Des Artistes at 1 West 67th Street. It is still enjoying great popularity in the late 1990s. I mentioned earlier my friend Ben Grauer, an NBC announcer, and the open invitation he had kindly extended to me to sleep on his couch whenever the need arose. That was in the mid-1930s and the couch I slept on was in his bachelor apartment in the Des Artistes Building.

I remember the first time I stepped foot into Café des Artistes. I was attending a birthday luncheon Ben gave for Pat Kelly, the supervisor of all us NBC announcers. Of course the entire staff couldn't attend because somebody had to stay behind to watch the store. But, looking back, I would say at least 15 of us were there, and a merry old time was had by all because

At the bar in Café des Artistes with former ABC radio director Telly Savalas and fellow ABC staff announcer Gilbert Hodges.

starting with Pat Kelly himself, there were some great storytellers around that table. Besides all the fun, food, and frivolity at that long ago birthday luncheon, something else caught our attention. Several lifelike wall paintings of beautiful young ladies frolicking in the altogether. No matter where one might be seated, at a table or at the bar, one or more of these elegant nudes were pleasantly visible. The artist was Howard Chandler Christy, who was noted both as an illustrator and for his expertise at painting nudes. He died the same year ABC moved into his neighborhood.

Sometime later Jo-Anne and I were introduced to his widow, Nancy, in the restaurant. I use the term "his neighbor-

hood" because Nancy told us how, as newlyweds, they were the first tenants in the building. The story, as she related it, was fascinating. Hoping to entice Mr. Christy, then a very famous artist, into the building in hopes that other artists would follow, thereby justifying the name "Des Artistes," the owners offered a quid pro quo the happy newlyweds just couldn't turn down. If Mr. Christy would paint a certain number of nudes on the walls of the Café des Artistes, the happy couple could reside in an apartment of their choice rent free as long as they would care to stay. It worked out perfectly for both parties. To this day the gorgeous Christy paintings help to keep the Café des Artistes busy, busy, busy. Even though Mr. Christy passed away at age 79, he and Nancy had been in residence there a long time, and she survived him for lots more happy years. After we had been introduced to her, Jo-Anne and I established a friendship with Nancy. On several occasions during that period, we visited with her in the apartment she had been living in since she was a bride. It was a beautifully decorated duplex. What stood out most, as one might expect, was the large number of Mr. Christy's works. It was breathtaking.

What now comes to my mind took place when ABC's presence was still very new on West 66th. It happened in the small control room of Studio 1A in the basement of the Radio Building at 39 West. I was there because I had been sent as a substitute for the staff announcer who regularly did the show; I have absolutely no memory of who he was or why he wasn't there. I also don't remember what time the program was on the air, late morning or early afternoon. Nor do I even remember the name of the show or its emcee. Of course all of the above details are unimportant. So let's talk about what I do recall.

Studio 1A was an unglamorous, rather small studio with a live audience capacity of 45 to 50 people, all of whom were already seated when I arrived and stepped into the control room to alert whoever happened to be in charge that I was there. Then I picked up a script to see what I was supposed to do, which turned out to be very little—just open the show and introduce the emcee. Looking through the control room window into the studio, I observed a person sitting on the platform—it wasn't really a stage. I recognized him as a British character actor, an older gentleman I had seen in movies and because of his so-so celebrity I deduced he was there to engage in a bit of on the air chitchat with the emcee and most likely the studio audience. His name was Wilfrid Hyde-White. And I do remember who the producer-director was—Art Henley. Because it was getting pretty close to air time, seven or eight minutes to go, Art told me he was quite concerned lest "he turns out to be a no-show." Not having the faintest idea who he was talking about, I said something like, "Oh! You're expecting someone in addition to Wilfrid Hyde-White?" He replied, "Yeah, but right now it doesn't look good." Almost before Art got those words out of his mouth, I learned who "he" was because suddenly the door opened and who stepped into the small control room but Henry Fonda, fury written all over his famous face.

With three of us in the room, he knew the fellow seated at the controls was an audio engineer so he ignored him and began to address himself to both Art and me. Art politely interrupted to clarify things, identifying himself as the producer and me as the announcer and saying how glad we were that he had made it on time. Mr. Fonda was so upset and excited he obviously didn't listen to Art, couldn't care less, and continued the tirade he had just begun, looking from one to the other of us. In traveling along life's road many, many things can slip one's mind. But Henry Fonda's brief tirade, even at this late date, I very much remember, won't easily forget: "They put me on a lousy daytime show that nobody ever heard of and match me with that old limey son of a bitch sitting in there. What's going on here? I am the best fucking actor in the world! But I want a good script. I don't want to sit in front of a bunch of fucking idiots not knowing what's coming next and stand a good chance of making a goddam fool of myself!"

With less than two minutes to go and not knowing whether the best you-know-what in the world would follow us into the studio or flee from the building, Art and I, of necessity, moved quickly to our proper places. When we did, it turned out that the "B.F.A. in the W." followed right behind us into the studio and as the bunch of F.I.'s spotted him the place went crazy. And continued as we took to the air, so much so that I doubt that the listening audience heard much of my opening announcement. The program progressed nicely. Mr. Fonda was quite credible in what he did. He was most gentlemanly with Wilfrid Hyde-White. A smile never left his face. When the show ended, I remarked to him how pleased and impressed I was with his change of attitude. He replied, "Christ! Everybody knows the show must go on."

39

HOWARD COSELL,
A RELATIONSHIP BEGINS

We enjoyed living in our spacious apartment a few years longer, but then Jo-Anne decided she would prefer to have the children raised in the country. The migration from the city to exurbia was a very hot topic of conversation at the time. I assume it was from the numerous articles, statistics, etc. that were constantly being written about in all types of publications. Exurbia is by definition "a residential area lying beyond the suburbs of a city." I suspect exurbia came into being because the suburbs were becoming not only very pricey, but crowded. We chose our move to exurbia for both reasons, our choice being New Canaan, Connecticut.

A friend put us in touch with a builder from nearby Wilton who was expanding his horizons a little by erecting three houses on the only remaining lots of a new residential street which had been started a year or so earlier in New Canaan. His efforts proved to be successful early on because by the time we had arrived at Overlook Drive to check out the houses, two of them had already been spoken for even though they were only about halfway completed. One more visit persuaded us that the still unfinished house on the acre at 3 Overlook Drive was going to become our future home. The agreed upon price was $29,000. This was in early 1954. Today, in late 1990s I've no doubt it would bring upward of $700,000. We moved in around mid-March, just after Mimi had arrived at her second birthday. We born and bred New Yorkers were now country folk. Gentle

people. As, of course, our children would become. My regular commute to New York was seven or eight times the 15-minute bus ride down Broadway from 90th Street to 66th where I hung my hat at ABC. But didn't some wise man once say that in order to live a better life you had to give something up, or some such profound remark as that? Now that we had made the big leap we were prepared to give our all and find out. To begin with, I occupied myself on those long rides on what was then called the New Haven Railroad doing something I had seldom given myself enough time to do, reading. And I found that this, in itself, was a pleasant plus. The passage of time, living in New Canaan, opened up new vistas to us—new friends, neighbors, places to visit, all of which we enjoyed tremendously.

Thinking back to that time when we were newcomers to New Canaan, I'm reminded of something I've always gotten a kick out of. One day shortly after our move, I was covering a broadcast honoring Grover Whalen, who, as I've mentioned earlier, had become famous as the official greeter of the city of New York during Mayor Jimmy Walker's regime and later as the head of the 1939 New York World's Fair. Mr. Whalen had written a book about his colorful life and was being lionized by the who's who of politics, business, the theater, and the press on the occasion of the book's publication. The gathering was held at the prestigious Metropolitan Club on Fifth Avenue at 60th Street. Among those attending from the world of business was the senior Thomas J. Watson, founder and chairman of IBM. Mr. Watson was undoubtedly the most distinguished tycoon at the gathering. He had been standing near the end of a slowly moving line of 15 or 20 other VIPs waiting patiently to offer the honoree their personal congratulations. The broadcast portion long since over, Mr. Watson happened to spot me off to the side of the huge room along with my audio engineer, who was busily packing up microphones and other equipment. Something prompted him to leave the line and walk over. Politely excusing himself for intruding, he confessed he had grown a bit weary while waiting and saw a big easy chair near me which happened to be empty and if I didn't mind he would appreciate it if he could take the weight off his feet for a few minutes before returning to his place on line. As I assured him I would be delighted, he thanked me and eased himself into the chair, at the same time initiating some small talk with "Great weather we're having," which of course I couldn't help but agree with. This was followed by a few more inconsequential, but pleasant, trivialities from both of us. Now, since I had become a New Canaan resident, I had been aware, as I'm sure was everyone else in town, that the Thomas J. Watsons were the town's most prominent family. They lived in a magnificent showplace, which I had driven by once or twice just to check it out. So continuing what I considered to be in the same polite small-talk vein, I decided to mention my recent move to New Canaan, "where I understand you've been in residence for many years." I guess it could be said he was a gentleman of the old school. He appeared to be genuinely interested that I had moved there, although he didn't know of Overlook Drive. He seemed to enjoy hearing about my young family. He wished us good luck and hoped we would be very happy there. Then as he left his chair to go back to the VIP line, he smilingly suggested, "Come ring my doorbell sometime and borrow a cup of sugar." But alas, being a gentleman of the new school, I sadly never did take up Thomas J. Watson, my fellow townsman, on his offer.

One day in the mid-50s, for whatever reason, I drove into the Big Apple instead of riding in on the New Haven Railroad. As I neared the city on the upper stretch of the West Side Highway in the vicinity of the George Washington Bridge, with lots of one-way heavy traffic, I was one of five poor unfortunates pulled over almost simultaneously. I later learned that the spot was a notorious police trap for alleged speeders. Five of us. All at once. One cop standing farther out toward the center of the road than any human being with a brain in his head should ever have ventured. Flagging us down all in a few seconds. "You, you, you, you, and you—follow me." Why such a stupid and frightfully dangerous situation didn't cause a massive accident I'll never know.

Reaching 66th Street, I parked the car in the garage, crossed the street to ABC's Radio Building, and ran into fellow announcer Dorian St. George just coming out of the announcers' office. Glad to meet a friend who might lend a sympathetic ear to the outpouring of fury which had built up within me about the speeding ticket, before I even opened my mouth he admonished me to "calm down before you blow a gasket." Accepting his advice as best I could, I proceeded to tell him my story, just letting it out made me feel better. When I showed him the ticket, his immediate reaction was, "Give it to Cosell." To which my instant response was "Who's he?" He then explained that Cosell, Howard Cosell, did a sports program on Saturday mornings aimed at kids. He thought it was called Little League Baseball.

Realizing I was off on Saturdays and unfamiliar with Saturday programming, he could understand why the name Howard Cosell meant nothing to me. "But," I said, "what does doing a kid show, or any other kind of show, have to do with taking care of a traffic ticket?" "Nothing," said Dorian. "However, I've heard he has connections in the right places. He once told me if I ever got a ticket to give it to him. But since that time I've been lucky, I guess. No tickets." With that, he took out his little black book and gave me Cosell's phone number, saying: "Here, call him. Let's see if he'll put his money where his mouth is for a friend of mine."

When I called, Mrs. Cosell answered. When she got to "Who shall I say is calling?" and I told her my name, she graciously said she had heard me on some soap operas over the years. Telling Howard who was calling, she gave him the phone. Having overheard her end of the conversation, he came on like he had known me all his life with "Hel—lo Georgie, what's happening?" which I assumed was his way of letting me know that he, too, had heard me doing whatever it was he had heard me doing. After I had explained about the ticket and the police trap and had mentioned that Dorian St. George thought he might be able to help, he very pleasantly suggested I "drop down to the apartment with the ticket and we'll talk about it." After agreeing on a date to visit, he gave me his address and added: "If you don't find it right away, don't give up. We're in Stuyvesant Town with a million other apartments." When I arrived at the appointed time, I learned he was quite right. Stuyvesant Town was a cluster of large apartment buildings. It was, and still is, spread over several blocks just east of First Avenue in lower midtown Manhattan. He answered the door when I buzzed, shook my hand, and was every bit as friendly as he had been on the phone. "Come on in and meet the family," he said. "This is my wife Emmy. And say hello to Jill and Hilary." He beamed with pride as each of his little girls stepped forward and shook hands with me. When we sat down and got on to the subject that brought me there in the first place, the ticket, both he and

Emmy agreed I had reason to be ticked off. Howard's feeling was that "it probably was an overzealous but not too bright cop. Let me have the ticket, Georgie. and I'll pass it along to my partner." I have to throw in here that throughout our many years following our first meeting, he continued to call me Georgie. Once when I asked him how come? he said it was because I was "a puddin' and pie kind of guy"—a silly tie-in with childhood's Georgie Porgie. Now back to Stuyvesant Town. "Your partner?" I said. He then explained that he and another chap, whose name I've forgotten, were partners. They both practiced law and shared the same office. Also, and without saying how, he indicated his partner was in a better position to handle favors such as "taking care of tickets." I have to admit I had a certain amount of skepticism after I left the Cosell apartment. But I had to accept what Howard said on good faith. After a few months, however, having heard nothing I relaxed. Whatever his partner's magic touch was, it worked.

I haven't mentioned my old friend Ray Diaz for some time. To recall, Ray had been Pat Kelly's assistant back in the NBC days, and when we of the Blue Network were split from NBC he became our announcing supervisor. That's when I and the others were happy to call him "boss." In time, however, it was decided by those above him that he should come up and join them in an executive capacity. Among other things in his new position, he was to be responsible for bringing in new programs, new ideas, and new talent in coordination with the news department, which also handled sports. A few days after my visit to Stuyvesant Town I happened to run into Ray in Healy's and joined him for lunch. I recounted the ticket episode, explaining that I had never heard of Howard Cosell until Dorian told me to call him and that when I did he cordially invited me down to talk about the ticket. Ray told me he had hired Howard a year or so earlier because Saturday morning air time was only for kids and when this guy walked in off the street, with a strong personality and what seemed like a sports program for kids which was both educational and entertaining he signed him up. And he was glad he did, he said, because as time went on Bob Kintner had indicated he was happy with it. "And everybody knows the only thing that makes Kintner happy is good ratings." Ray went on to say he thought Cosell came across on the show as someone who might offer possibilities if he were heard doing other sports stuff besides the kid show, and he was going to sit down and explore the idea with Kintner. No, he hadn't known he was a lawyer and he was fascinated with the thought that Cosell might quash my ticket through his law partner, which, in the long run, is what happened. That visit to Stuyvesant Town turned out to be the beginning of an off-and-on, hot-and-cold relationship between Cosell and me that continued for over three decades.

40

UNLOADING A SUPERVISOR

When Ray Diaz joined the executive elite of ABC, he of course had been replaced as our bossman. Our next supervisor of announcers was Jim Bixler. He came over to us from the Music Rights Department early in the 40s. I'm not sure exactly when, but I do remember that he and his wife were at our wedding in 1946 so my guess is he had come on board at least a couple of years before that. All of us on the announcing staff were fond of Bix. When he left, everyone was sorry to see him go. At the time I had heard that his departure came about because of a misunderstanding with an executive and that the executive was wrong but was too proud or stubborn to admit it. No, the executive wasn't Diaz. No way. But it was Diaz who was given the responsibility of replacing Jim Bixler. When she, yes, when she arrived for her first day on the job—of supervising us— there were some raised eyebrows in that office. Why their stuffy reaction? Well, back then the very thought of putting a female in charge of 20 or so males who weren't school children but fully grown men was hard to believe. Well, Ray Diaz believed it would work, and it did, beautifully. So much so that before too long the entire staff was delighted with Ray's selection. The reason I didn't share the others' attitude on her first day with us was that I had known her since I was 16, since my NBC days at 711 Fifth Avenue when I began as a page. Her name was Anne Kelly. She was divorced, with twin sons in high school. In 1931, when I started, she was secretary to the executive vice president of NBC, George McClelland, who had been credited with being the first to introduce commercials to the fledgling radio industry. He was known as the father of commercial programming. His office was close to that of Merlin H. Aylesworth, NBC's first president, usually referred to as Deak. As a page boy, part of my duties, when assigned to their floor was to run errands for the executives and their secretaries. And as secretaries went, she was tops. Never demanding, never cranky. Always seemed cheerful. So now, these many years later it made me feel good that she was going to run our office.

In 1955 after eight years under the stewardship of Anne Kelly, we were all sorry to hear of her decision to retire. But when we learned she was leaving to get married, we were indeed happy for her. Shortly before Anne's big announcement, a cloud of unpleasantness had appeared over our office. Five members of our staff had been summarily fired by an executive who had overextended his power while Ray was on vacation. This created a situation that upon his return was next to impossible to overturn. He did, however, try to salvage some good out of it. With Anne's imminent departure, he had to pick her replacement posthaste. It seems that of the five who had been let go, Ray thought he had a candidate who just might prove acceptable for the job and hopefully keep at least one of the unfortunate five from having to walk the streets in search of a job. The man he had in mind was Jim McConnochie. To help make his decision, Ray summoned Don Gardiner and me to pick our brains as to what we thought about McConnochie and the possibility of his being capable of taking Anne Kelly's place as our supervisor. We both immediately agreed it would be pretty tough to fill Anne's shoes. And neither of us had really known McConnochie well. But from what we had observed, he seemed like a pleasant enough chap. And certainly if our two cents worth might save him from being tossed out, we recommended to Ray that he hire him.

A bad recommendation. Very bad. The worst possible. This, unfortunately, turned out to be not just my opinion but the whole staff's. We found it hard to believe that this man who had been one of us for five years could change so overnight. Talk about a Jekyll–Hyde personality. Without spelling out the things he did in the running of the office which were so objectionable to all of us, let me just say that it became a very unhappy place. And this because of a person who only the previous week Don Gardiner and I had saved from joining the ranks of the unemployed.

The frustrating thing was that our complaints did no good. They reached deaf ears. Shortly after putting McConnochie into the job, Ray Diaz had been moved from his executive position in programming to an executive position in the Traffic Department. In traffic, understandably, he had no say over what went on in his old bailiwick regardless of how awful he felt for having hired the "SOB." His successor in the Program Department, Bill Hamilton, was the one who turned deaf ears. He was now Jim McConnochie's immediate boss. And it was Bill Hamilton who had overextended his executive power in the first place, while Diaz was away on vacation. Suddenly my happy life as an ABC staff announcer had been turned upside down.

In private discussions among ourselves as to why this great change in the man, the general consensus was that it had to be because of jealousy. When he had been a member of the staff, none of us could recall that he had ever done a show which paid a commercial fee. And as time went on, it must have rankled him and caused

him to resent us, individually and collectively. So that when the opportunity to lord it over us was dropped in his lap he didn't hesitate to take advantage of it.

We all had high hopes that our union, AFTRA, the American Federation of Television and Radio Artists, could do something. But it was a situation that was difficult to approach because disturbing as Jim McConnochie's conduct was and the unpleasantness which resulted from it, he was not breaking any union rules.

As time went on the atmosphere never seemed to improve. Weeks became months, and then 1956 was upon us. As I have earlier recounted, the program which had been a daily ritual during 18 years of my life, *Young Widder Brown* on NBC, finally succumbed to the devastating impact television was having upon network radio. Though its demise was inevitable, I missed seeing and working with the people connected with the show. And so my spirits sank even lower. I can remember during that dark period toying with the idea of resigning from ABC and trying my hand at freelancing. Or quitting the business entirely and taking a chance on getting into something else, anything else. At night after Jo-Anne put the two kids, Mimi and Drew, to bed, we would sit around and explore possible ideas for a complete change in our lives. One possibility was the brain child of Jo-Anne. And because of the reasons she gave, I thought it might be worth serious consideration. She thought that being part of an Irish Catholic family with two brothers who were priests, I might think about a line of work an many other Irish Catholic gentlemen were engaged in. Jo-Anne was convinced I would be good as a funeral director. She thought I would have no trouble learning the business. And possibly, she figured, Bishop Jim Griffiths, a close friend of my family, would be helpful with advice. "After all," she reminded me, "it was through his influence as a prelate of the Archdiocese of New York that we were privileged to be married in St. Patrick's Cathedral." She added, "Wasn't your mother's brother-in-law, John Timms, a successful undertaker in Brooklyn? And when he died, didn't his son, Joe, carry on the business? So it wouldn't be exactly new in the family, regardless of what raised eyebrows it might cause." And I myself could remember as a kid that when John Timms's name would come up at the dinner table my mother always had a good word for him—and his profession: "Don't ever forget, John Timms has done better than anyone else in the family. There's no such thing as a poor undertaker." Recalling this kind of talk gave rise to serious consideration of Jo-Anne's idea until, when looking further into it, I found that there were new rules guiding the mortuary business. Now, to get a license, the applicant had to demonstrate his ability to embalm personally any new "customer" brought into his establishment. So that was the end of that.

Whenever I reminisce, I prefer to dwell on pleasant happenings in my life. Following that thought, it's best I cut short the saga of Jim McConnochie. Briefly: it took five years before the ABC negotiators allowed themselves to be convinced by the AFTRA negotiators that the company would be better served if he were to leave. In February of 1961 we staff announcers were finally rid of him. A breath of fresh air then wafted into our office in the form of Ted Lyman. Ted remained as supervisor of announcers for the next 29 years until he passed away shortly after my retirement in 1990.

A year or so after our move to New Canaan I decided to quit commuting by train in favor of driving. Increasingly, during that first year I had found myself in the touchy situation of arriving late for program rehearsals because of late train arrivals at Grand Central Station. My solution was to purchase a Volkswagen Bug and drive. No longer did I have to worry about train schedules fitting in with my

work schedules—I just had to allow myself ample time for the trip, including extra time for possible delays in traffic. It worked out just fine, with no more embarrassing moments at ABC because of tardiness.

In time the good samaritan whose law partner had taken care of my traffic ticket, Howard Cosell, was doing better than when I first met him and that was because of the perception of Ray Diaz. In meetings with Bob Kintner, he had pushed the idea of more air time for Cosell. The immediate result of those discussions was a five-minute program on the ABC Radio Network, *Speaking of Sports with Howard Cosell* on Monday through Friday while he continued with the Saturday kid show. These daily programs were so well received by the radio audience as well as the network station managers that, before too long, Diaz again saw fit to speak to Bob Kintner about Cosell with the idea of an additional five-minute spot for *Speaking of Sports* every day. What with Cosell's good ratings which Kintner of course knew about, the Diaz pitch for another *Speaking of Sports* show became a reality. Howard Cosell was now well on his way in radio—"telling it like it is."

Around this same period, the people in charge of the local radio outlet in New York, WABC-AM, decided to use me to do the 6 o'clock news. The 15-minute program called *Newscope* featured happenings in the tri-state area of New York, New Jersey, and Connecticut. During those years when I did *Newscope*, Howard and I crossed paths frequently because we were both in the newsroom every day around the same time and the studio he generally used was right next to mine. So, understandably, the friendship which had begun earlier in his apartment in Stuyvesant Town was renewed because of this proximity as well as our mutual friendship with Ray Diaz. Every so often we three would lunch together. Seldom, if ever, was anything of great seriousness

Kidding around with Cosell at an ABC party at the Grand Ballroom, Plaza Hotel , 1981.

discussed. It was pretty much just the opposite—Cosell could be pretty funny when
the spirit moved him. Ray Diaz, too. I don't
remember what I may or may not have contributed, except I laughed a lot during those
lunch sessions, as did we all.

Howard Cosell was doing just great at
ABC. ABC radio, that is. The TV side of
ABC seemed not terribly interested in his
increasing success on radio. Occasionally,
but only occasionally, he would verbalize
his frustration about it. Then he would
catch himself and quickly drop the subject.
When the radio network gave him his third
five-minute exposure, a morning spot Monday through Friday, somebody of consequence in local television must have said to
somebody else of a bit higher consequence,
"Could we possibly be missing out on
something?" to which Mr. Higher Conse-

quence probably answered, "Yeah, we
could. We know what he sounds like, but
let's see how he comes across on camera. If
that's okay, which it probably will be, let's
start talking. Quick."

No, I was not a fly on the wall at that
meeting of the brass which of course I'm
only presuming took place. But from bits
and pieces I picked up at the time, this
imaginary dialogue comes close to explaining how the powers that be at the WABC-
TV local New York outlet of the American
Broadcasting Company opened up their
door just a crack to allow Howard Cosell's
big toe in. And once that toe got in, any
one of us who knew him could have predicted that before too long his whole foot
would follow. And that, metaphorically
speaking, is what happened. After they
were satisfied with his on-camera

With fellow ABC staff announcer Don Gardiner and Howard Cosell, during my bearded era, early 1970s.

appearance in a videotaped audition and the talks which quickly followed, they used him sporadically on the local WABC-TV 6 o'-clock news. So his big toe was indeed now into that crack in the door. And, sure enough, inside of a month his appearances were no longer sporadic but were every evening. Howard had become the regular sportscaster of the WABC-TV, Channel 7

Six O'Clock News. Now, as a few of us had expected, his whole foot was in on local TV. But who among us would have guessed it was to take as long as it did before the ABC-TV network brass were to recognize what was so visible right under their very noses? When might they open up their door to him and give him a shot at the really big time? Stay tuned.

41

"MONEYBAGS ANSBRO"

When Howard Cosell's radio appearances had spread from his doing only the Saturday kid show to include his first across-the-board *Speaking of Sports* shots, the additional income this provided was the impetus he needed to move out of Stuyvesant Town and join the exodus to exurbia. The place he and Emmy decided on was a lovely house in Pound Ridge, New York, across the Connecticut state line from where we lived in New Canaan. As I had done when we first moved out of the city, Howard became a railroad commuter.

I've neglected to mention that one of the first things our new announcing supervisor, Ted Lyman, did after he replaced McConnochie was to reinstate my weekends off. Thank God I no longer needed to go in on my days off to protect my commercial shows. So doing Monday through Friday shows worked out just fine once again. Not just the 6 o'clock *Newscope* on local WABC radio but cowcatchers and hitchhikes before and after *My True Story*, a half-hour tearjerker every morning at ten. Glenn Riggs, also on our ABC staff, announced the show itself, with talented Rosa Rio doing the honors at the organ keyboard. At 12 noon every day I was also on the air at the Little Theatre on 58th Street doing a TV show called *Across the Board*. Its emcee was a very affable chap named Ted Brown, who was quite successful on an independent New York radio station, WNEW, as their early morning man. For me it was an off-camera assignment—I was heard but not seen. And as with so many gimmick programs over those years on both radio and TV, I frankly don't re-member what the gimmick was on Ted Brown's *Across the Board*, nor exactly how long it continued on the air. My guess is about two years. But having been a fan of Ted's for a long time, it was a pleasure working with him during its run.

Back to Howard. Occasionally I thought I detected a note of grousing about his railroad commute. Never flat out saying he hated it—nothing like that. A little complaint here, a minor irritation there. But then in the next breath, upbeat excitement, like "Who do you think I met in the bar car last night?" And even if you couldn't care less about Sam Schmuck in the bar car, especially if you had never heard of him, politeness decreed that you feign interest. In a nutshell, he was a man of moods. One minute laughing and up on top of the world and in the next lower than a snake's belly.

As time went on I would know he was in a great mood when, always in front of other people, he would loudly blurt out: "Oh, that Ansbro. Just look at him. Boy! I'd give anything to have the kind of money he has." This outburst, or words similar to it, he enjoyed tossing out to anyone within earshot whenever the mood hit him, which was many times during his earlier years. I guess he got a kick out of embarrassing me, knowing there was no truth to the remark, while at the same time intending it as good-natured folderol. Did it embarrass me? It sure did, always leaving me standing there feeling like a fool. Nothing to say. Just a stupid grin on my face. Once I tried a comeback like "Oh, for God's sake Howard, quit repeating yourself," which made him laugh loudly as he struck back with "See, I've got Moneybags Ansbro's tongue tied." Thus he reduced me to the feeble reply, "I guess I just can't win." All the while I was cautioning myself not to fall prey to his goading and blurt something out I would probably wish I hadn't. So each time it would happen, I would just smile and come up with something as if it came out of the mouth of a kid in the eighth grade, a dull kid, "Wotsa matter, you nuts or sumpin?"

The last time he did it I went against my own advice. It had happened so often I could practically feel it coming by the "boy, am I gonna have fun" expression on his face. This umpteenth time and with him as usual playing to a small group, I quickly decided I had had it. Immediately after he finished his taunting line, I looked squarely at him and used Molly McGee's well-known put-down "It ain't funny, McGee." I then added, "And it's become quite tiresome." You know the look on a little boy's face when his lollypop has just been taken away? Exactly Howard's. At first, disbelief, followed by an expression of sadness. The little group taking this in, to cover their embarrassment, started babbling about who knows what. It was a nice thing to do because changing the subject enabled me to get involved conversationally, thus helping me to relieve my annoyance with myself for having disregarded my own advice. At that moment I genuinely felt sorry for Howard. He stayed, also in general conversation until the group broke up. But however mad at myself I was, it worked. He never did it again.

There were never any words between us about the little playlet I just described. He didn't show any animosity, which, I must confess, made me feel better—especially after the hurtful barb I had cut him with. Things between us went on as if that little scene had never happened. When he would see me, it was Georgie this and Georgie that. He rode the railroad to and from work every day while I commuted in

my little Volkswagen bug which I kept in the garage directly across 66th Street from the ABC-TV building and the studio he did his sportscast out of on the 6 o'clock news every night. His stint was always the last before sign off on the half-hour program. I had watched Howard do his radio broadcast Lord knows how many times. Now that he was on local TV I frequently saw him on the monitor in the radio newsroom. I wanted to see him do TV in the flesh. So once in a while before going into the garage to get into my VW for the drive home, I would stop in his studio just in time to catch him doing his sportscast. When it ended, there was very little time for small talk because he had to hustle to catch his train out of Grand Central.

One such night when I stopped by, instead of looking for a taxi he said: "Georgie, can I hitch a ride with you tonight so I can show you our house and you can see Emmy and the girls again? You know it's been quite a while since that day in Stuyvesant Town." Even though it took me by surprise, I thought it would be nice to see his wife and kids again and check out the house. I called Jo-Anne right away and told her that I would be home after dropping Howard Cosell off and that Pound Ridge wasn't too far from New Canaan, so she shouldn't worry.

About an hour and a half later, we drove up to the Cosell residence. Howard had called Emmy when I had agreed to give him a lift to tell her she had a night off from picking him up at the station, so when my headlights shone through her kitchen window, she hurried out to greet us and to welcome me to their new digs. Then she said, "Come on in, have a cocktail, and take the tour." Emmy had been preparing Jill and Hilary for bed, but that ritual was interrupted by our arrival, so they were allowed to linger and join their mother as she showed me around. They very politely said they remembered meeting me that time when I had been to the apartment in Stuyvesant Town, but I felt sure that they had been coached by Emmy, nice person that she was, before I got there. I must say that their beautiful house was a far cry from the small apartment they had lived in when I first met them. While touring their home with Emmy, he was in the kitchen preparing extra-dry martinis for two. None for her—the children must be put to bed. So after my cocktail and a very pleasant but short visit, I took off to New Canaan to join Jo-Anne and our gang of five.

In the radio newsroom the next afternoon, I made it a point to tell Howard my feelings about seeing Emmy and the girls again as well as the great choice they had made in selecting their house, a delightful place to bring up the kids. He, in turn, thanked me for the ride home, "a heluva lot better than the alternative." My reply was something to the effect that it was my pleasure and "maybe I can be of service again sometime." Without missing a beat, instantly he said, "Like tonight?" Quickly thinking to myself how pleasant last night's visit had been, no way could I say no. So I answered, "Why not?"

Little did I know what I was letting myself in for. I drove him home that night and countless other nights for the best part of two years. The fact that we both finished our day around the same time was why he asked to hitch a ride in the beginning. Very soon after that, however, no more asking. When I would get to the garage, there he would be, waiting for me. But a bigger surprise yet was when I walked in and he was sitting in my VW waiting for me. I found that hard to believe, but after a moment's

thought I realized the attendant had seen him leave with me on previous nights, so when he arrived ahead of me he asked the attendant to get my car down for me. I almost bit my tongue to keep from saying, "Gee, I'm sorry I'm late, Howard."

So the pattern had been established. Except when one of us for some reason had to cancel out, the routine was the same. The discussions we had were minimal, but friendly. During the trip we mostly listened to the radio, and because we both liked good jazz and pop stuff, Sinatra, Ella Fitzgerald, and such, we were tuned to WNEW all the way. Conversation-wise, one night he touched on something I can't help but remember. It seems that on an earlier occasion, just so he would know, I had mentioned that I was not a big sports fan, that actually I was not a sports fan at all but it didn't bother me when others who were got carried away when the subject came up. This particular night he said: "You know, Georgie, I kind of envy you for that. You just don't give a damn who wins, who loses, by how much, who scores a touchdown, who steals home, who strikes out—none of that stuff bothers you one way or the other. And for that I envy you." Coming from him that was very interesting. And quite a statement. Every once in a while he would say, with variations, "If I had my druthers, I druther be in something else, anything else, but this." I would say, "But you already are a lawyer and you gave up your law practice to get into this." He would reply, "Oh, forget it Georgie. I guess sometimes I just like to hear myself talk."

42

"AW, WHAT THE HELL, GEORGIE"

As the months passed, I began to notice a change in Howard. But it wasn't all that difficult for me to determine what it was that was bothering him. In a nutshell, he was becoming increasingly ticked off because of the nonactivity in his direction by the brass of ABC's TV network. As far as he was concerned, his local TV stuff was going just fine because the local TV brass kept telling him how happy they were. And on the radio side, his *Speaking of Sports* was gathering more audience all the time, so he knew he had no problems there. "But," he would say to me, "what do I have to do, drop a bomb on those dumb bastards in TV network?"

For three or four nights in a row, I found myself listening to the same stuff, the same griping about the people running the TV network. Completely exasperated, realizing I couldn't take any more, I finally let loose—"So they're making you wait longer than local TV did, because they're just not ready for you yet. Or, heaven forbid, maybe they don't even have you in their sights. Howard, for your own sake, why don't you just knock it off? When network wants you, if they want you, you'll know it. Remember when you had great fun needling me about being Moneybags Ansbro and the only way I could put a stop to it was to hurt you? Well, I'm afraid that time has arrived again, for a different reason. This constant prattle while driving you home every night has become quite tiresome. So please, for God's sake, let's either turn the music up or talk about other, more pleasant things. But, knock it off!"

Just as I had used the word tiresome to get him to quit the "Moneybags Ansbro" bit so, too, it worked here. My own reaction after each of my explosions was the same. I felt sorry for him for allowing himself to carry on to the point that he deserved what he got. And, by the same token, I was angry with myself for giving in to my urge to tell him off. That night, outside of the usual disc jockey pleasantries and good music emanating from WNEW, there was total silence the rest of the way to Pound Ridge. As we arrived in his driveway, he was the first to speak, "Ya coming in?" I replied, "I'm not so sure I should after that outburst." Howard then said: "Aw, what the hell, Georgie. So you let off a little steam. Maybe that was good for both of us. So come on in. If you don't, Emmy's gonna think something's wrong and I don't think we would want that. At a moment like this, a cocktail might do us both good." And so I succumbed. In retrospect I've come to realize that that night I had succumbed to Howard Cosell at his most gracious.

As time went on and Howard's appearance on WABC local TV every night increased his visual prominence, I had begun to observe, as did he, that people in other cars occasionally stared at him or pointed at him, or if they were stopped at a red light, they lowered the window to yell greetings to him. The first couple of times we noticed the people staring, Howard had fun with the situation by trying to insist they recognized me from the *Arthur Murray Show* when I danced with Kathryn

Murray and that they were my fans, not his. But I knew he was just joshing me because that show had been off the air at that point for quite a while. And I also knew they were looking at him, not me. Such light moments, however, I welcomed as a pleasant change. Especially when it dawned on him that he should at least acknowledge their attention with a return wave or a smile.

That night after we arrived at the house Emmy couldn't have been more pleased when I told her folks were beginning to sit up and take notice as we passed on the road. His reaction, when I brought the subject up, was like that of a kid muttering "Aw, shucks" to the slightest suggestion of flattery. This, to me, was a new and completely different side of him. Even at that early point in his career he had been referred to in many ways, but I'm sure "bashful" was never one of them. Yet, the thing about it that fascinated me most was that Emmy treated it as though it was normal, everyday, vintage Howie. To quote Yul Brynner as the king in *The King and I,* it was a "puzzlement!"

As I may already have indicated, those visits almost every night to Chez Cosell in Pound Ridge were, to say the least, always interesting. Which is not to say they were always pleasant. During that period of close to two years, I enjoyed meeting Howard's mother several times when she would spend a few days away from her home in Brooklyn. She was a very nice lady, as was her daughter-in-law, Emmy. During his mother's stay in his home, Howard was just not himself. For the half hour or so my nightly visits lasted, I couldn't help but feel sorry for the poor woman. Talk about having a case of the grumps. From the moment Howard and I would walk in the door, he seemed to have a chip on his shoulder. His unpleasantness was only directed at her. If he and Emmy and I happened to be talking about whatever, and she would say something to join in our conversation, he would bark at her

to please not interrupt because she didn't know anything about what we were discussing. That type of thing. He seemed to go out of his way to pick on her. If in his mind she appeared to dote on Jill and Hillary longer than necessary before they went to bed, he would come out with something like "what are you trying to do, Mom, spoil your only grandkids?" At any rate after the first few times, I made sure I would not be present for such scenes when I knew she was visiting by making up some excuse not to come in and then asking him to tell his mother hello for me. It would later occur to me that in taking the tack of declining to go in with him, I gave him a means to humiliate his mother further by saying something like: "Now, mom, you've scared Ansbro away. When I told him you were here, he changed his mind about coming in. But he asked me to say hello to you anyway."

I never did learn why he treated his mother like a housemaid he didn't like having around. I had hoped Emmy might touch on the subject sometime, possibly even apologize for his unmannerly behavior towards his mom. But Emmy never did. She probably knew how he might carry on if such were to happen. And she didn't want to jeopardize their good life together. I truly believe she loved him very much. And, to all appearances, so too did Howard love her.

One night I asked Howard why he didn't get himself another, smaller car so Emmy wouldn't have to drive him to the railroad station every morning. I said it would give her more time for herself and the girls while he drove himself to the train. I added that like most other commuters, as I had done when I commuted by train, you park the car at the station so that when you return in the evening you simply jump into it and drive yourself home, making it a lot easier morning and night for both of you. Without intending to I had hit a raw nerve or opened up an old wound. Into the immediate quiet that permeated that little VW, hardly above a whisper he said, "You through?" I was, so I said, "Yes." He continued, "Look, you don't have to draw pictures for me!" Then in a slightly louder voice, his words evenly measured: "Don't patronize me! When I want your advice about what to buy or not to buy, I'll ask for it. Especially if it's about a car. Let me tell you here and now—I do not drive! I don't ever want to have to tell you again. Nor do I need you or anyone else insinuating how I might better take care of the needs of my wife and children." Then back to his almost whispered voice, "End of discussion, Georgie."

Indeed, I went along with his dictum. Actually the more I thought about it, the more I was pleased that he decreed the discussion to be over. It simplified things for me. The way he had just twisted out of all proportion my suggestion to buy a second car was pretty tough to swallow, so rather than argue I kept my mouth shut all the way to his doorstep, where I muttered a brief "good night," turned around, and headed for home.

During that half-hour run from his house to mine, my mind was working overtime after the scene I'd just been through. "I do not drive" he had said, followed by words indicating I should never bring the subject up again. And then for him to turn my suggestion upside down about Emmy having more time for herself and the girls was absolutely incredible. He did not drive, indeed. No, but he was happy to accept the nightly favor of being driven by a jerk like me, a jerk who had allowed himself to be pushed into doing him the favor of chauffeuring him the first time under what, looking back, was the excuse of inspecting his new home and seeing his family again. Then, smart cookie that he was, showing up in the garage the following few nights knowing he had found a real, live sucker. After that it was simple. Just get the attendant to have my car there so he could smilingly

greet me from the passenger seat when I would shortly arrive. He had me figured out well enough to know that never in a thousand years would I have ordered him out. No more searching for a taxi to take him to Grand Central to join the hoi polloi running for their trains to wherever. No more being bored by the Sam Schmucks in the bar car. Boy, what a patsy I had been. Within a few minutes after his local TV stint ended every night, he was headed north to Pound Ridge. And with his own private unsalaried chauffeur. Except for a nightly cocktail which he more than likely considered a bribe, a very inexpensive bribe for the kind of service he was getting.

These and other thoughts were very busy inside my head as I neared my house. During this long period of time I had been denying myself the paternal pleasure of being with my kids before bedtime, of helping Jo-Anne tuck them in. And why? Because I should have been attending to such normal, everyday, family obligations in my own house by getting home on time every night instead of stupidly allowing myself to be used as Cosell's chauffeur. Well, no more.

One look at me as I walked in the door and Jo-Anne knew something was up. She didn't know what, of course, but she could see I was seething. I filled her in on what had happened between Howard and me. Her reaction: "I was wondering when you were finally going to wake up. I'm just sorry it took you so long. As you know the one time I rode home with the two of you was enough for me. The traffic was unusually heavy, and he carried on like a lunatic, as though the traffic was your fault. He showed absolutely no restraint or respect for my presence. And I told you then I thought you were a fool. Anyway better late than never, so give him a call tonight."

I did, and when Howard answered the phone I thought I detected a note of surprise when he heard my voice. Without beating around the bush, I told him our discussion while driving home had caused me to do much soul searching. I said his outburst after what I had sincerely intended as a helpful suggestion was ridiculous and decidedly uncalled for. And that he had closed out the possibility of our having a fair and equal exchange of words on the subject that seemed to upset him so, about his not driving, by insulting me with his imperious decree "End of discussion, Georgie." I finished by informing him: "This is to let you know not only is this end of discussion time, it's resignation time. Your chauffeur is resigning. I hope you can get along without him. Effective immediately. And before I sign off, please know I'm just sorry this had to happen."

The next afternoon in the radio newsroom when I saw him I nodded and simply said "Hi." No response from him except an empty stare. I was reminded of the old bromide "Boy, if looks could kill." When I finished *Newscope* at 6:15, I wasted no time getting to the garage. I was heading north— alone—at about the time his sportscast was closing out the 6 o'clock local WABC-TV news. I must confess it was refreshing to find myself driving with an empty passenger seat and able to enjoy the DJ and the music on WNEW. No doubt about it, tonight's cocktail would be in my house—maybe two.

43

LATE LUNCH AT TOOTS SHOR'S

During the many years of my employment in broadcasting, I had seen many changes. But seldom did they involve me unless a program I did on a regular basis was dropped, for whatever reason. Well, a week after l'affaire Cosell a young man was brought in from somewhere out of town by the manager of WABC radio to head up the WABC radio newsroom and he followed the old dictum "A new broom sweeps clean." Accordingly among some changes he made in what had been the regular program schedule was replacing me on *Newscope* with a friend of his he had brought along. l was informed of the change not by him but by Ted Lyman, our announcing supervisor, who was embarrassed to have to tell me that the new news director had installed his friend in my place because he "was just too good to leave behind in a small town" and that "besides being a good news reader he would also write *Newscope*." This was a slam at me, I suppose, but nobody had ever asked me to write it. No, I did not write *Newscope* nor had I ever written any newscast I had aired going all the way back to the mid-30s when I was the first daytime *Esso News* reporter. During all those years newsrooms were run in such a way that news writers were hired to write news which was read on the air by staff announcers.

The loss of *Newscope* brought with it the loss of the fee I had received for doing it which, understandably, was a further cause of annoyance. But there was a bright side. Now that I was finished with *Newscope* I no longer had reason to go near the newsroom. And the timing couldn't have been better. Having signed off as Cosell's nightly chauffeur, I felt sure he didn't want to run into me any more than I did him. So, in a strange way, the new news director did us both a favor on that score. Plus, this change in schedule enabled me to hit the road for home much earlier and see a lot more of Jo-Anne and the children.

The friendship we two had enjoyed, having come apart at the seams, did not preclude our ability to act as gentlemen when we found ourselves unexpectedly face to face while in the company of others, for instance, at ABC parties. On such occasions Howard acted pretty much as his old self toward me, even throwing in a "Georgie" once in a while. In a spirit of reciprocity as well as hoping to keep our differences from being observed, I did my best to do likewise. After all, I thought it was our business and nobody else's.

After we had met in these friendly gatherings a few times and nobody was the wiser, I had gotten the feeling he would just as soon keep it this way without facing up to a discussion of our problem. What was actually, in my opinion, not our problem but his.

Sure enough, before too long, he opened the door to TV-5 one day when I was alone on standby duty and pleasantly suggested he thought it would be a good idea if we let bygones be bygones because, he said, it seemed we had already made a good stab in that direction. With that, he extended his hand, which I accepted, saying: "It's fine with me but no more driving. As things turned out my change in schedule would have ended that anyway." Friends again. But to repeat what I said much earlier in these reminiscences, stay tuned.

The years moved on. Howard's career was moving upward and onward. Nor did he have to "drop a bomb on those dumb bastards in network TV" as he had once whined to me. Fortunately for him, as anyone recognizing his professional talent could have predicted, those dumb bastards eventually opened their door to him, as a result of which sports lovers everywhere, not just locally, became familiar with him when the network TV brass finally adopted an open door policy toward Howard Cosell, it put him well on his way to becoming an American household name.

Ray Diaz and I, for no particular reason, hadn't been in touch for quite a while, so when I received a message one morning that he had called, I got right back to him. After the "long time no see" stuff he suggested we make up for it, if I could fit it into my schedule, by having lunch together at Toots Shor's shortly after 2:00. And it so happened that the time was indeed good for me.

If I haven't already mentioned the fact, Toots Shor's restaurant was a large establishment catering to showbiz types, including radio and TV people, the Broadway and movie set, newspaper columnists, and the sports crowd. As well as Mr. and Mrs. Average Citizen, who liked to gawk at all of the above.

After we met, the maître d' led us to a table in the rear. Even though it was now after 2:30 the tables were mostly occupied by folks who were still dawdling over their coffee.

During lunch, after we had covered lots of other things, I decided to fill Ray in on the ups and downs of my association with Cosell. Inasmuch as it was Ray who had first brought him into ABC, I thought he would find my story interesting, to say the least. And, outside of Jo-Anne, nobody else knew it, and that was the way I had planned to keep it. But Ray Diaz, my oldest friend, was different. Him I just had to tell.

He had known about my beginnings with Howard, about my first visit to his apartment in Stuyvesant Town, and the squashing of the traffic ticket by his law partner. And I guess somewhere along the line I had told Ray how I had allowed myself to become a patsy by driving him home every night. So what I really had to tell him was about the way he treated his mother and what led up to my "resigning" as his chauffeur. I filled Ray in on our ups and downs and mentioned that ever since his "let bygones be bygones" visit to TV-5, we had been playing friends again.

As I was speaking, a glance around the restaurant told me the dawdlers were pretty much all gone and the bar considerably thinned out. I had just about finished my story when I heard myself say: "My God, speaking of the devil, there he is now. He just came in and he's casing the bar." Ray by now had seen Cosell himself and muttered, "Well, I'll be a son of a bitch." Then Cosell spotted us, which was very easy because, outside of a few waiters, we were practically alone back there.

All smiles and with a jaunty swagger, his way of indicating his pleasure at seeing us, he approached our table. I got up and shook hands. But Ray neither stood nor offered his hand. Wasting not a moment, looking up at him from where he sat, he launched into a verbal attack on our unexpected visitor with such vehemence I found it hard to believe this was my even-tempered, mild-mannered friend and mentor, Ray Diaz. I had seen him blow off a little steam in the past but nothing to compare with this. When he had finished what was on his mind, it was over. I wish I could remember what all he said in that very short few minutes, but I knew it was over when I heard him say: "Please leave. And don't come sucking up to me with an apology if your conscience ever bothers you. What am I talking about, you don't have a conscience."

It was probably the only time in his life Howard Cosell found himself completely speechless. He who in a few short years would reach the pinnacle of fame and fortune because of his mastery of the spoken word briefly glanced at me with a look of silent supplication. To which I could only shrug my shoulders in reply, meaning I would remain neutral—this was not my fight. So not really knowing what the exact problem was because Ray hadn't even had time to tell me, I relied on the old maxim "silence is golden," and watched as Howard turned around and, slowly shaking his head in disbelief, walked toward the revolving door and out.

Some weeks after the Toots Shor incident I was waiting for an ABC elevator as were several others when I saw Howard push the down button. He must have spotted me first because simultaneously with his pushing of the button he, in a fairly loud voice, began to address nobody in particular but obviously intending to be heard by all within earshot. His topic was me, George Ansbro, and what an ingrate I was. How "after considering Ansbro a good friend for years for no reason he turned against me, probably because of lies he had heard about me," and so on in that vein. I couldn't believe this was actually happening. And when he continued with the same sort of thing into the crowded elevator all the way to the ground floor, like the carryings on of a real nut, I wanted to pinch myself to be sure this wasn't a dream. I was at least relieved that I didn't see a familiar face so that nobody in his audience knew that the "ingrate" he was referring to was me. Nor was I going to take the bait from

him and make a reply. I just kept swallowing hard and got off the elevator with the others who, I'm sure, were wondering what that was all about. And those who knew who he was were probably thinking Cosell was cracking up. As for me, without even a glance at him, I hit the sidewalk quick.

In searching my mind as to why he would, or even could, lower himself to engage in such an exhibition, it wasn't easy to come up with an answer. After all, we had been on a friendly basis since he had dropped in on me in TV-5 with his request to let bygones be bygones. And nothing had happened between then and now to breach that agreement. So I had assumed that the more he thought about my not coming to his rescue during the Diaz diatribe in Toots Shor's, the more it bothered him. No doubt he had misinterpreted my choosing to be neutral that day as my way of writing off our friendship. And the elevator episode was his way of getting even. Some might call it revenge.

In my opinion that conclusion proved quite correct when a month or so later, hard as it is to believe, Howard repeated the elevator routine, lock, stock, and barrel. Same speech, "Ansbro the ingrate, etc." to a very surprised group while waiting on the floor and then continuing it for the benefit of new ears in the descending elevator. I don't know which consumed me more, anger or embarrassment. But regardless of his avenging schoolboy tactics, I didn't bite. Again, I kept my mouth shut. And, knowing him, I'm sure he would have preferred otherwise, for the opportunity to make mincemeat out of me.

44

"GEORGIE, I'M GLAD YOU CAME"

During the next decade Howard became far better known than he could ever have dreamed. His fame as a sportscaster far surpassed other biggies of earlier years, such greats of my youthful acquaintance as Graham McNamee, Ted Husing, Clem McCarthy, Bill Slater, et al. Howard Cosell outshone them all. He had reached the pinnacle.

For a long time I never saw him except on the tube when I would occasionally switch on *Monday Night Football* just to see how he looked, or on a night when he would do a Muhammad Ali fight. Correction. I did see him twice. One night at the Waldorf he was one of many ABC celebrities, along with Leonard Goldenson, ABC's chairman, Roone Arledge, and other executives. I had been assigned to do an opening and closing announcement. When the affair ended, Emmy spotted me and made it a point to come and plant a kiss on my cheek together with a few warm words of greeting. Howard was mixed up in the crowd and whether he saw me, especially receiving Emmy's kiss, I will never know.

The other time was when Jo-Anne and I were vacationing in Las Vegas at the then new and fabulous Caesar's Palace. While walking through the wild, crazy, and crowded lobby taking it all in, I was astounded to hear my name being shouted out. "Hey, Georgie—over here, over here—come on over." Finally I spotted Howard and Emmy with several others sitting in what I believe was called Cleopatra's Barge. We waved cordially but kept going to our own destination.

Some years later, in November of 1990, I read that Emmy had passed away, a victim of cancer. The notice said the funeral was to be private and that in a few weeks a memorial service would be held. When I saw the notice, I was indeed quite saddened because of the loss of such a nice person, who for all of Howard's success, I feel sure did not have an easy life with him. And, notwithstanding any differences he and I had had, I knew what a shattering blow this must have been. I must confess my heart went out to him, and I determined to attend the memorial service.

It was held in a church uptown on Lexington Avenue, which overflowed with famous TV faces, athletes, industry executives, and Cosell fans who came to pay their respects. There were numerous dignitaries in attendance, the highest ranking of whom was Cardinal John O'Connor of New York City, whose appropriately thoughtful words from the altar were, I'm sure, much appreciated by Howard and Jill and Hilary seated in the front pew.

The ceremony over, the church emptied onto the sidewalk, where many of the mourners gathered in groups in quiet conversation. Others, I noticed, formed a line which slowly moved toward the grieving widower to offer condolences. I took a place at the end, with others joining behind me, and the long procession edged along at a snail's pace as, one by one, Howard accepted each expression of sorrow. By the time I came to within four or five persons away, I could see that he was not the same person the entire country had known.

His appearance had changed markedly. The Parkinson's disease I had heard he suffered from was clearly visible—he had no control over his shaky hands or head. His voice was quite subdued. When the person I was behind ended a short visit with him and I was next, Howard seemed not only surprised but unbelieving as he stared at me for a couple of seconds, then wrapped his arms around me. At the same time, I heard him say: "Georgie, I'm glad you came. It means a lot to Emmy up there, and a great deal to me. Thank you, thank you."

During his last years I heard he saw no one other than his family. He was battling cancer, as well as heart and kidney problems, and the Parkinson's disease that was so evident at our final meeting. Less than five years later, on April 23, 1995, Howard joined Emmy, hopefully "up there."

45

THE CURSE OF ALCOHOLISM

Earlier in Chapter 25 I mentioned that of all the staff announcers I had worked with through almost six decades relatively few became alcoholics. Being a staff announcer during those early years was considered not only a glamorous career but a prestigious one as well. Every one of us enjoyed our work, along with the social aspect, which was considerable. That was so because, in spite of the fact that we may have had a long schedule to fill, there was frequently a lot of time to kill between rehearsals and shows. That time, if not spent schmoozing, reading, or whatever, was often spent in any of the nearby hangouts of the actors, musicians, directors, announcers, ad agency people, and the management crowd. Places like Hurley's, the Down Under, the English Grill and Toots Shor's. Unfortunately this did prove to be a breeding ground for potential alcoholics such as fellow ABC staff announcers Doug Browning and Bill O'Toole.

I bring the subject up again because I've saved a letter I received from Doug in March of 1989. It was his response to me about a newspaper clipping I had sent him regarding John Wingate, an excellent announcer, who had been around New York for many years doing mostly news on WOR. At this late date I don't recall exactly what it was the item spoke of but as soon as you read Doug's letter, which follows, you can deduce that the piece had either hinted, or actually said, that Wingate was a homosexual with a drinking problem. He died in April of 1994.

I had sent it to Doug because he

had been a friend of Wingate's, as had I. I felt sure it would interest him, which, as his letter will certainly attest, it did. You see, Doug had successfully overcome his own alcoholic affliction several years earlier.

The Bill O'Toole whom Doug tells about joined our staff when Bishop Fulton J. Sheen, after a highly successful series of TV programs on the old Dumont Network came over to ABC-TV. O'Toole had been the bishop's announcer at Dumont. Through the good graces of Bishop Sheen, ABC miraculously discovered there was room for another announcer on the staff. So, wonder of wonders, not only was O'Toole part of the Bishop Sheen package on ABC-TV but he became an ABC staff announcer as well.

Bishop Sheen had become one of the most prominent American clerics in the Roman Catholic church, largely because of his remarkable gift of oratory mixed with humor and his genius at public relations. Shortly after their move to ABC, Bishop Sheen officiated at Bill O'Toole's wedding. When Bishop Sheen eventually departed from ABC-TV, it was the general feeling among O'Toole's peers that he, no longer having the good bishop to lean on, began to accelerate his plunge into the depths, beginning with the disintegration of his marriage, which had started on such a high plane. So very, very sad.

I must mention before you read Doug's letter that both he and Bill O'Toole were fired from ABC because their alcoholism could no longer be tolerated.

Doug Browning died in August of 1992. Here is his letter.

Big Apple
March 22, 1989

George:

Thanks for the item. It really shakes a person up when the reading gets that touchy. Except for the fag-albatross I could easily say "there, but for the grace etc. etc." Wingate, with his problem of booze was also confounded by his sexual wants, the troublesome nagging of hiding it, and his attempts to keep it all hidden. All this while attempting to maintain some sort of social balance between uptown and downtown.

I suppose his irascible behavior could be accounted for in the fact that his secret was leaking out, and nothing could stem it. Just drink a little more, and it'll go away.

I don't wish to try and top his story; but I'll put up a friend's fight against his, any day in the week. If the true story of Bill O'Toole were ever written it would be dismissed as being contrived. A movie of the same story would never be allowed out of the can, and I know the story. And if I ever wanted to cash in on hard luck, there would be the place to start. But as I say, it wouldn't be believed. For one man to beat his body into complete submission with alcohol and sex, the latter was a twenty-four hour challenge to him and the alcohol kept him rolling. In between times he was consumed with the duties of getting money to sustain both habits. The women he used up, in the process, were beyond numbers....and unusually attractive gals. Unbelievable! The top hotels he succeeded in cheating, his countless incarcerations in the Tombs and Riker's Island, the many people he borrowed from, his being barred from the local race tracks as a result of attempting to change numbers on tickets. The times he called me to his place in the Dauphin in the middle of the night because he was seeing "things".... Therein lies

the story of a life down the tubes, and just one of many we can recall.

There was a guy named Brokenshire, remember? Charles O'Connor? Bill Farren? Fidgie McGrath, the great jazz pianist? You could probably, with your prodigious memory, recall a dozen others.

O'Toole's last visit to me was unforgettable. It was the same year he died, alone and broke, in a Newark, N.J. rooming house. When I worked at WPIX he used to call me from different bars every night. He even called me from a bar he had just held up, bought drinks for everybody in the joint, even while the owner was out getting the cops!

Anyhow, it was in February, bitter cold, and I was living at the Lincoln Towers. The doorman called me to report a very bedraggled guy was in the lobby and wanted to see me... his name O'Toole. He rang my bell, and I looked into the holes that held his eyes, black, despairing and hopeless. His meager clothes hung about his body as though it had no meat and they were as thin and ragged as his face. His pants were held up by a piece of rope, no toes in his shoes and he was hatless. I almost fainted.

I had no booze in my place and I knew he was very close to going into DT's. I threw his old junk into the incinerator and shoved him into the shower, as he had accrued about a quarter inch of coal dust on his hide. After the shower I gave him clothes that were fit for winter, good clothes. But I knew he would sell them at first chance. All I had was twenty bucks so I gave him that, at least it would get him a few drinks until....?

I closed the door and cried. Experience told me there was nothing more I could have done. His uncle called me a couple months later and told me of his death in Newark. He was alone but his uncle said he asked for me in the final moments. Did you know about Bill?

Regards,
Doug

46

TWENTY-FOUR YEARS WITH THE FBI

In 1965, Warren Somerville asked me if I would like to join him in a show he described as considerably more uplifting than all that mediocre stuff I had spent most of my life doing.

With an approach like that it's easy to understand that he certainly got my attention. And knowing him, I felt sure that whatever it was he was about to spring on me, the approach was strictly tongue-in-cheek Warren.

As indeed it was. I guess I hadn't even been aware that for the previous year he had been involved in directing a weekly program for the ABC Radio Network titled *FBI Washington*. Fellow staff announcer Fred Foy was assigned to the show which was done in Washington at FBI headquarters. Warren and Fred would go overnight to Washington every month or so and tape four or five programs. But now Fred would no longer be available to leave New York because, happily for him, he had been selected to announce a new TV show starring an up-and-coming personality, Dick Cavett, every morning at 11:30.

And happily for me, Warren was requesting that I replace Fred on *FBI Washington*. Inasmuch as I wasn't doing any shows which required my live presence Monday through Friday at the time, there was no problem. Announcements like the mid-break on *One Life to Live* which I had been doing for many years and continued up to my retirement were taped once a week in a session which lasted hardly a half hour. When I stepped into Fred Foy's FBI shoes, I had no idea my

newest assignment would last for 24 years. Twenty-four years, 1965 through December 1989. A month later in January 1990, I retired.

FBI Washington was prepared by the Public Affairs Office of the FBI and produced and directed by Warren. It was intended to provide a look at the activities of the FBI and its people. It afforded the listener insights into the FBI's approach to a diversity of topics, such as organized crime, white collar crime, foreign counterintelligence and, over those 24 years, a host of other topics.

After a few opening words, I would bring in a senior official of the FBI, who would then get onto the subject of that particular show, with me throwing in some appropriate questions as well as reacting to his remarks. Even though the programs were only five minutes long, they were obviously well received by the listeners in the 125 cities in 40 states that carried them. Otherwise I doubt very much the ABC Radio Network would have continued them for so long. Actually for 25 years, considering that first year Fred Foy did the show.

I felt especially privileged, as did Warren, that every FBI director beginning with J. Edgar Hoover saw fit to appear with us and to be photographed with us on *FBI Washington* at least once. After Hoover died, the director's office was occupied by Patrick Gray, who had been appointed by President Nixon. His tenure was short lived because he became involved in the Watergate scandal. At any rate, he did visit and exchange pleasantries with me on the show.

With the FBI's first director, J. Edgar Hoover, who was appointed by President Calvin Coolidge. His directorship extended over 47 years, December 10, 1924, to May 2, 1972. He served under eight presidents.

Mr. Gray was succeeded by Clarence Kelley. Director Kelley was kind enough to invite Warren to bring his son Rob to Washington when he learned of Rob's interest in the possibility of working in law enforcement. Rob, who had seen action in Vietnam, joined us on our next month's trip to Washington. While there, Director Kelley generously gave more than an hour of his time in discussion with Rob while Warren and I were interested bystanders in his office. Rob did indeed go into law enforcement and was the youth officer in his hometown of Rye, New York, until he burned out

With Patrick Gray, March 9, 1973. When J. Edgar Hoover died, President Richard M. Nixon appointed Patrick Gray as director of the FBI. Gray held the office from May 3, 1972, to April 26, 1973.

With Clarence M. Kelley on April 17, 1974. After Patrick Gray's relatively brief tenure, President Nixon appointed Clarence M. Kelley as FBI director in June of 1973. He continued until February 1978.

in that particular job. He is still there as a detective and frequently works closely with the FBI.

When Clarence Kelley retired from the director's position, his successor was Judge William Webster. Director Webster had invited Warren and me to lunch in his private dining room a couple of times and on one occasion pulled a very thoughtful surprise on us. After dessert he nodded to an atten-

dant, who brought to the table two plaques, one for each of us, featuring the official insignia of the Federal Bureau of Investigation with appropriate inscriptions and dated September 1982. This handsome piece, which I like to think of as my unofficial FBI badge, has adorned the wall of my den ever since.

When Judge Webster left the FBI, he didn't exactly leave town. And he was still

With William Webster in September of 1982. Appointed by President Jimmy Carter, Webster headed the FBI from February 23, 1978, to May 25, 1987.

With William S. Sessions who was appointed director of the FBI by President Ronald Reagan. He began as director on November 2, 1987, and continued to July 18, 1993. As his letter to me attests, he was a very thoughtful person.

a director because President Reagan had moved him to the CIA, where he was now director of the Central Intelligence Agency. Of course there was no void left at the FBI because Ronald Reagan made, in my opinion, another excellent choice as his replacement, Judge William S. Sessions.

Warren and I were invited to Washington to attend the official swearing-in ceremonies. President Reagan spoke, as did Ed Meese, the attorney general. Mr. Meese then introduced the newly appointed FBI director, William Sessions, whose remarks were well received by the audience, which included many members of Congress. After the ceremony, we joined the reception line to meet and offer congratulations to both Director Sessions and Mrs. Sessions.

During his tenure as FBI director, on occasion Mr. Sessions would get together with Warren and me during a taping session to lend a few pearls of wisdom.

Eventually, in December of 1989, it was announced that *FBI Washington* would be dropped from the ABC Radio Network schedule. Director Sessions ordered that a large room which was traditionally used for official receptions be opened and put into use to celebrate the windup of 25 years of program cooperation between ABC Radio and the FBI. ABC executives were invited down from New York. They joined with FBI brass to look on as we taped the last four shows. Mr. Sessions took time out from hosting the party to sit down and appear with me on the final show, which, after 25 years of one each week, was the 1300th show. But leaving out the 52 weeks of the program's first year, when Fred Foy started the series, it means I only did 1248 of those 1300.

Wait a minute, I still don't have that right. I just remembered the time Warren and I had just boarded a bus to La Guardia Airport to catch the shuttle to Washington when I suddenly got a sneezing attack.

U.S. Department of Justice

Federal Bureau of Investigation

Office of the Director

Washington, D.C. 20535

August 14, 1990

Mr. George Ansbro
Apartment 10-B
50 East 10th Street
New York, New York 10003

Dear George:

      I hope this finds you in good health and that you have
recovered from your operation. I would like to thank you for
working with the FBI for the past 23 years. Your professionalism,
marvelous style and voice helped make the "FBI, Washington" series
such a tremendous success.

      When entering the "broadcast booth" with you, as I did on
two occasions, which was a delight, you have a special way of
making a guest feel comfortable because of your terrific
personality and humor.

      Best of luck in the future, keep well, and again, thanks
for your tremendous help over the years.

                      Sincerely,

                      William S. Sessions
                      Director

Once in a blue moon an attack like this will be triggered by an allergy, and when it hits me there's just nothing I can do about it but let it run its course even though it scares the daylights out of anybody within earshot. By the time the bus started, my sneezing was already in full gear, and it got much, much louder and just wouldn't stop. Quite worried, Warren had the driver stop the bus, and good friend that he was, he insisted I get off, catch a cab, and return home. Need I tell you, I survived. But that attack caused me to miss doing five *FBI Washington* shows that were taped that day. Scott Nelson, section chief of the Public Affairs Office, was recruited to fill in for me. So that brings the total number of *FBI Washington* shows I did do down to a measly 1243.

47

RETIREMENT

About a year earlier, Jo-Anne and I had made the big decision that I would retire when I hit my 75th birthday on January 14, 1990. I wanted to give ABC a month's notice so I told Ted Lyman in mid-December.

On Monday of the second week after New Year's, my final week, I kept an annual appointment with my urologist, Dr. Gerald Zelikowski, where I was x-rayed to double check on my plumbing. The good doctor, after studying the x-ray, wasted little time in calling me to say he say no problem with my urinary tract but something else showed which concerned him very much, an aneurysm on my aorta. He explained how serious and dangerous an aneurysm is. He then called Dr. Giuseppe Rossi, an outstanding vascular surgeon, to make an appointment for me the next day. My visit with Dr. Rossi confirmed the x-ray, in spite of the fact I had none of the symptoms sometimes associated with an aneurysm, which, if not caught before it bursts, is invariably fatal. He booked me into Cabrini Medical Center for further tests on the following Monday, the day after my birthday, with surgery scheduled for Tuesday.

Dr. Zelikowski's sharp eye in reading my x-ray was actually the first step in saving my life. Dr. Rossi's expertise in performing the operation was the perfect follow-up.

After the surgery was over, I was in intensive care for the better part of two weeks. Dr. Rossi's associate, Dr. Robert Grossi, frequently came to check on me when Dr. Rossi was occupied elsewhere. Once, when both showed up together, I couldn't help but laugh. When they wanted to know what was so funny, I told them that their names, when spoken together, Rossi and Grossi, sounded like the name of a vaudeville act that might have played the Palace in the long, long ago. They were amused and declared that my laughing was a sure sign I was well on my way to recovery. As it turned out, they couldn't have been more right. Now that I've been retired some years, when someone asks, "How long did you work in broadcasting?" I throw in the words "and twelve days" to finish my answer. The full answer of course, as you've probably seen early in this book is fifty-eight years, three months, and twelve days—October 1, 1931, through January 12, 1990.

Because my birthday fell on Sunday, my last day of work was Friday. My final on air announcement was a 30-second promo at the end of *General Hospital.* My production and engineering coworker in the control room had introduced a pleasantly festive air for my final day in the form of cake and champagne.

Moments before I was to do the promo, one of them pushed the talkback button and said, "Why don't you give your name after the promo?" Because it was strictly forbidden, I automatically answered, "You want to get me fired?" But when I realized how silly that was, I went along with it. Now on the air, having finished the promo, I offered in my most pseudo-grandiose style to millions of listeners to *General Hospital* my less-than-earth-shattering last utterance on national TV, "This is your announcer, George Ansbro."

EPILOGUE

Soon after I retired, I got to thinking that because of all my years with essentially the same company the *Guinness Book of World Records* could very possibly be interested in my work history if, in fact, it was a record. The next day I called the Sterling Publishing Company, which handles what goes into the famous book. I asked a pleasant-sounding lady, "What is the eligibility criterion to get into the *Guinness Book*?" She asked for more specifics. I told her I had worked for my company and its predecessors for over 58 years and was wondering if that could possibly be a record. She replied that I didn't even come close, that the record was held "by an old duffer in London who had been with the same outfit for 90 years."

The thought of it struck me as pretty funny. And when I laughed, she did too and said, "So call me back in 30 years!"

INDEX

Numbers in **boldface** refer to photographs.

231